RALPH STORER is an experienced hillwalker who has hiked extensively around the world. Despite being a Sassenach by birth, he has lived in Scotland since studying Psych... ... ...a great affinity for the Highland... ... ...ills for a regular fix of nature, he ... ...nd produces darkwave music on

D1388590

His books are exceptional... S... ... *completely.* THE ANGRY CORRIE

Praise for *The Ultimate Guide to the Munros* series

Picks up where others – including my own – leave off
CAMERON MCNEISH

Fabulously illustrated...Entertaining as well as informative... One of the definitive guides to the Munros. PRESS & JOURNAL

Irresistibly funny and useful; an innovatively thought-through guide-book that makes an appetising broth of its wit, experience and visual and literary tools. Brilliant. OUTDOOR WRITERS & PHOTOGRAPHERS GUILD

The ideal hillwalking companion. SCOTS MAGAZINE

Praise for his complementary *Baffies Easy Munro Guide* series

   Packed to bursting with concise information and route descriptions. There should be room for this guide in every couch potato's rucksack. OUTDOOR WRITERS & PHOTOGRAPHERS GUILD

A truly outstanding guidebook. UNDISCOVERED SCOTLAND

It is perfect for anyone exploring Scotland's beautiful mountains, whatever his or her level of experience. GUIDEPOST

50 CLASSIC ROUTES ON SCOTTISH MOUNTAINS

The book begs to be picked up and thumbed through. It will stimulate walkers to head for the hills.
TIMES EDUCATIONAL SUPPLEMENT

50 BEST ROUTES ON SKYE AND RAASAY

What an excellent book. As comprehensive a guide to walking and scrambling on Skye as you could wish for.
HIGH

THE JOY OF HILLWALKING

A treat for all hillwalkers active or chairbound.
SCOTS INDEPENDENT

50 SHADES OF HILLWALKING

A fantastic celebration of this addictive pastime.
SCOTLAND OUTDOORS

SEE YOU ON THE HILL

If you read one book about hillwalking this year, read this one... a classic in the making.
UNDISCOVERED SCOTLAND

THE ULTIMATE MOUNTAIN TRIVIA QUIZ CHALLENGE

A thoroughly fascinating way to kill time – every bothy should be furnished with one.
THE SCOTSMAN

100 BEST ROUTES ON SCOTTISH MOUNTAINS
BAFFIES' GREAT OUTDOORS INAPPROPRIATE GLOSSARY
BAFFIES' GREAT OUTDOORS INAPPROPRIATE ADVICE COLUMN

The Ultimate Guide to the Munros

Volume 1: Southern Highlands

RALPH STORER

Boot-tested and compiled by
The Go-Take-a-Hike Mountaineering Club

Luath Press Limited

EDINBURGH

www.luath.co.uk

For Christine

Hillwalking and mountaineering are not risk-free activities and may prove injurious to users of this book. While every care and effort has been taken in its preparation, readers should note that information contained within may not be accurate and can change following publication. Neither the publisher nor the author accept any liability for injury or damage of any kind arising directly or indirectly from the book's contents.

First published 2008
Reprinted with minor updates 2009, 2010
Revised and updated 2014
Reprinted 2019

ISBN: 978-1-910021-58-3

The paper used in this book is recyclable. It is made from low-chlorine pulps produced in a low-energy, low-emission manner from renewable forests.

Printed and bound by CPI Antony Rowe, Chippenham

Typeset in Tahoma by Ralph Storer

All maps reproduced by permission of Ordnance Survey on behalf of HMSO. © Crown copyright 2014. All rights reserved. Ordnance Survey Licence number 100016659.

Front cover artwork by Sinéad Bracken

All photographs by the author, including front cover (Stuchd an Lochain), except those on pages 79, 84, 115, 130, 157, 164, 168, 213 & 219 by Allan Leighton

The author's right to be identified as author of this book under the Copyright, Designs and Patents Act 1988 has been asserted.

An iPhone app, containing route maps and descriptions derived from the contents of this book, is also available through the Outdoors app on iTunes.

© Ralph Storer

CONTENTS

6 Munros

8 Munros

INTRODUCTION

Route 22a

The Go-Take-a-Hike Mountaineering Club

Ralph Storer President

Compiler of routes, penner of words, stopper of bucks, all-round good egg. His packed lunch of choice: Marjorie's Seedling plum jam sannies.

GiGi Custodian of the Common Sense

Farer (fairer?) of the Ways, arbiter of disputes, friend to all. Named after the two embarrassing grooves occasioned by too much fence-sitting. Her packed lunch of choice: it depends.

F-Stop Controller of the Camera

Advisor of the Aperture. Recorder of the Ridiculous. So-named because he's always f***ing stopping to take photographs. His packed lunch of choice: ginger snaps.

Needlepoint Companion of the Compass

Wary Watcher of the Weather. Finds featureless plateaus intimidating, doesn't understand GPS, barely understands a compass. Her packed lunch of choice: fettuccini swirls.

Committee Members

Chilly Willy Keeper of the Cool

AKA Snowballs. Peely-wally, estivates during summer, has never seen a midge, likes his toast crisp and even. His packed lunch of choice: freeze-dried ice-cream.

Torpedo Expender of the Energy

Bald and streamlined. Loather of laziness. Scorch marks on boots. Ascends as fast as a falling Munro bagger descends. His packed lunch of choice: hi-energy nutrition bars.

Terminator Raveller of the Rope

Grizzled, monosyllabic, self-taught suicide commando. Hater of the horizontal. Measures his life in scars. His packed lunch of choice: doesn't need lunch, lives on air.

Baffies Entertainments Convenor

Allergic to exertion, prone to lassitude, suffers from altitude sickness above 600m, blisters easily, bleeds readily. His packed lunch of choice: triple chocolate layer cake.

Route Quality Ratings

***** **Outstanding**

The best. Outstanding routes in every respect. The reason we climb mountains. The stuff of memories.

**** **Excellent**

Still great, but just lacking that extra something that would make them outstanding.

*** **Very Good**

Maybe not the best, but still commendable, perhaps outstanding or excellent in parts.

** **Good**

Nothing to prise the uninitiated off the couch, yet still good enough to provide a satisfying hillwalk that brings a smile to the visage.

* **Fair**

Could be better, but all Munros are worth booting up for, aren't they?

Route Rage Alert

Flagged on routes where 'challenging' terrain makes a beach holiday seem not such a bad idea after all.

Route Difficulty Grades

G1 **Mostly good going**

Mainly on good paths or good terrain. There may be occasional steep or rough sections, but not for long.

G2 **Appreciable awkward going**

Notably rough or steep terrain, perhaps prolonged, but not involving handwork on rock.

G3 **Minor handwork required**

Use of hands required on rock, e.g. for balance or a step-up, but not difficult or prolonged enough to constitute scrambling.

G4 **Easy scramble**

Includes one or more sections that require movement on rock with good holds.

G5 **Hard scramble**

One grade below a rock climb for which a rope would normally be required. Compared to G4, holds are often smaller and exposure is often greater.

OF MOUNTAINS AND MUNROS

It's a big place, the Scottish Highlands. It contains so many mountains that even resident hillwalkers struggle to climb them all in a lifetime. How many mountains? That depends...

If two summits 100m apart are separated by a shallow dip, do they constitute two mountains or one mountain with two tops? If the latter, then exactly how far apart do they have to be, and how deep does the intervening dip have to be, before they become two separate mountains?

Sir Hugh Munro (1856–1919), the third President of the Scottish Mountaineering Club, tackled this problem when he published his 'Tables of Heights over 3000 Feet' in the 1891 edition of the SMC Journal. Choosing the criterion of 3000ft in the imperial system of measurement as his cut-off point, he counted 283 separate Mountains and a further 255 Tops that were over 3000ft but not sufficiently separated from a Mountain to be considered separate Mountains themselves.

In a country with a highpoint of 4409ft (1344m) at the summit of Ben Nevis, the choice of 3000ft as a cut-off point is aesthetically justifiable and gives a satisfying number of Mountains. A metric cut-off point of 1000m (3280ft), giving a more humble 137 Mountains, has never captured the hillgoing public's imagination.

Unfortunately Sir Hugh omitted to leave to posterity the criteria he used to distinguish Mountains from Tops, and Tops from other highpoints over 3000ft. In his notes to the Tables he even broached the impossibility of ever making definitive distinctions. Consider, for example, the problem of differentiating between Mountains, Tops and other highpoints on the Cairngorm plateaus, where every knoll

The old sign at Achallader Farm, which issued an irresistible invitation, has sadly not been moved to the new car park.

Sir Hugh Munro himself never became a Munroist (someone who has climbed all the Munros). Of the Tables of the day, he climbed all but three: the Inaccessible Pinnacle (although that did not become a Munro until 1921), Carn an Fhidhleir and Carn Cloich-mhuilinn. The latter, which he was saving until last because it was close to his home, was ironically demoted to Top status in 1981.

surpasses 3000ft.

The Tables were a substantial achievement in an age when mapping of the Highlands was still rudimentary, but no sooner did they appear than their definitiveness become the subject of debate. In subsequent years Munro continued to fine-tune them, using new sources such as the Revised Six-inch Survey of the late 1890s. His notes formed the basis of a new edition of the Tables, published posthumously in 1921, which listed 276 separate Mountains (now known as Munros) and 267 Tops.

The 1921 edition also included J. Rooke Corbett's list of mountains with heights between 2500ft and 3000ft ('Corbetts'), and Percy Donald's list of hills in the Scottish Lowlands of 2000ft or over ('Donalds'). Corbett's test for a separate mountain was that it needed a re-ascent of 500ft (c150m) on all sides. Donald's test was more mathematical. A 'Donald' had to be 17 units from another one, where a unit was one twelfth of a mile (approx. one seventh of a kilometre) or one 50ft (approx. 15m) contour. Munro may well have used some similar formula concerning distance and height differential.

Over the years, various developments have conspired to prompt further amendments to the Tables, including metrication, improved surveying methods (most recently by satellite), and a desire on the part of each succeeding generation of editors to reduce what they have regarded as 'anomalies.' For example, the 'mountain range in miniature' of Beinn Eighe was awarded a second Munro in 1997 to redress the balance with similar but over-endowed multi-topped ridges such as the seven-Munro South Glen Shiel Ridge. Changes and the reasons for change are detailed individually in the main text (see Peak Fitness for details).

The first metric edition of the Tables in 1974 listed 279 Munros and 262 Tops. The 1981 edition listed 276 Munros and 240 Tops. The 1990 edition added an extra Munro. The 1997 edition listed 284 Munros and 227 Tops. Since then, following GPS satellite re-measurement , Sgurr nan Ceannaichean (2009), Beinn a' Chlaidheimh (2012) and Knight's Peak (2013) have been demoted, leaving 282 Munros and 226 Tops.

Watch this space.

The first person to bag all the Munros may have been the Rev Archibald Robertson in 1901, although his notebooks bear no mention of him having climbed the Inaccessible Pinnacle and note that he gave up on Ben Wyvis to avoid a wetting.

The second Munroist was the Rev Ronald Burn, who additionally bagged all the Tops, in 1923, thus becoming the first 'Compleat Munroist' or Compleater. The third was James Parker, who additionally bagged all the Tops and Furths (the 3000ft summits of England, Wales and Ireland), in 1929. The latest edition of the Tables lists 1745 known Munroists.

BEN LOMOND

THE SCOTTISH HIGHLANDS

The Scottish Highlands are characterised by a patchwork of mountains separated by deep glens, the result of glacial erosion in the distant past. On a global scale the mountains reach an insignificant height, topping out at 1344m/4409ft on Ben Nevis. But in form they hold their own against any range in the world, many rising bold and beautiful from sea-level. For hillwalkers they have distinct advantages over higher mountain ranges: their height is ideal for day walks and glens give easy road access.

Moreover, the variety of mountain forms and landscapes is arguably greater than in any mountainous area of equivalent size. This is due to many factors, notably differing regional geology and the influence of the sea.

In an attempt to give some order to this complexity, the Highlands are traditionally divided into six regions, as detailed below. The potted overviews mislead in that they mask the variety within each region, ignore numerous exceptions to the rule and reflect road access as much as discernible regional boundaries, but they serve as introductory descriptions.

On Beinn Achaladair

The Southern Highlands 46 Munros	Gentle, green and accessible, with scope for a great variety of mountain walks.
The Central Highlands 73 Munros	A combination of all the other regions, with some of the greatest rock faces in the country.
The Cairngorms 50 Munros	Great rolling plateaus, vast corries, remote mountain sanctuaries, sub-arctic ambience.
The Western Highlands 62 Munros	Dramatic landscapes, endless seascapes, narrow ridges, arrowhead peaks, rugged terrain.
The Northern Highlands 38 Munros	Massive, monolithic mountains rising out of a desolate, watery wilderness.
The Islands 13 Munros	Exquisite mountainscapes, knife-edge ridges, sky-high scrambling, maritime ambience.

THE SOUTHERN HIGHLANDS

The region covered by this guidebook, as its name implies, is the most southerly region in the Scottish Highlands. It is bounded on the west by the sea, on the east by the Tay Valley (the A9 Perth – Pitlochry road) and on the north by a line that runs along the A85 from Oban to Tyndrum, up the A82 to Rannoch Moor, then eastwards along Loch Rannoch and Loch Tummel to Pitlochry. In the south it is bounded by the central belt of Scotland between Glasgow and Edinburgh, below which the Southern Uplands continue to the English border.

The region itself is divided into two distinct halves by a geological zone of fracture known as the Highland Boundary Fault, which runs in a straight line across the breadth of Scotland from south-west to north-east. From the west coast it crosses Loch Lomond at Balmaha, passes through the Trossachs at Aberfoyle and heads north-east through Glen Artney to the Tay Valley and beyond, eventually to reach the east coast at Stonehaven.

Although the fault is hundreds of millions of years old, tremors are still felt along it as the rocks continue to settle, making the town of Crieff the earthquake capital of the British Isles.

South of the Highland Boundary Fault lie green rounded hills, while north of it lie rougher mountains, including all the region's 46 Munros and accompanying 21 Tops, to say nothing of 36 Corbetts. The rocks are mostly sedimentary but they have been greatly metamorphosed, uplifted and folded over time. Rolling folds parallel to the Highland Boundary Fault have rippled the land into Munro-height mountains separated by deep depressions, of which the largest is the great strath that runs from Crianlarich through Glen Dochart to Killin, then along Loch Tay to Aberfeldy and Pitlochry.

Although the ground to the north of the fault is rougher than that to the south, it is nowhere near as rugged as further north and west in the Highlands, while the igneous Cairngorm plateaus to the east are different again. The Southern Highland landscape is more gentle, more rounded and more verdant, though with enough geological variation and Ice Age sculpting to include an occasional rock playground for climbers and scramblers. Examples include the overhanging rock faces of The Cobbler, the great Prow of Stuc a' Chroin and the craggy corries of the Bridge of Orchy mountains.

Apart from some notable exceptions, the Munros cluster in groups separated by lochs and deep glens, which carry an extensive road system that eases access. Within each group the Munros are often close enough together to make multi-bagging trips practicable. The region therefore has the best of both worlds. Its Munros are easily accessible

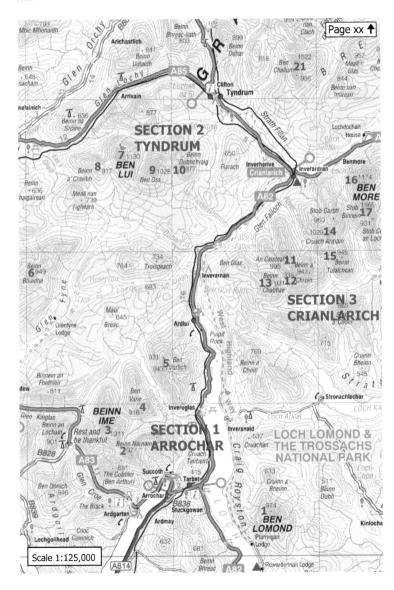

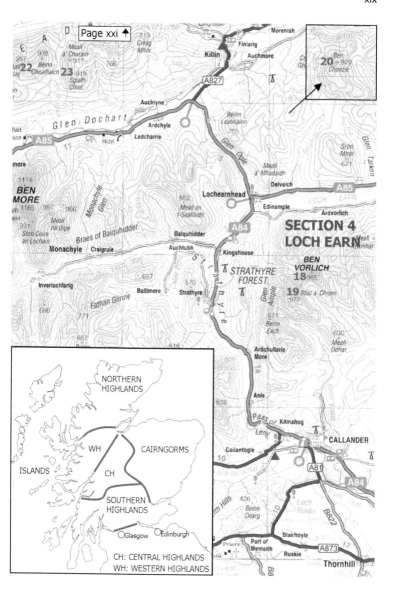

Page xxi ↑

SECTION 4
LOCH EARN

CH: CENTRAL HIGHLANDS
WH: WESTERN HIGHLANDS

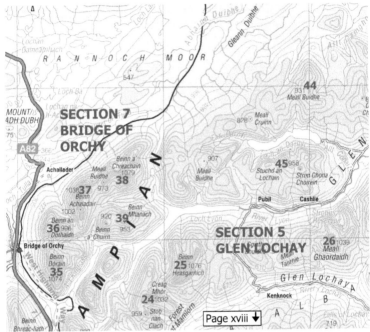

individually, while their clustering facilitates combined ascents.

The shortest route in this book bags a Munro for a mere 520m/1700ft of ascent (Meall Buidhe – Route 44a). Ben Lawers is unique in that the shortest way to its summit goes *over* a neighbouring Munro (Route 27a). By contrast, the longest route in this book would have you tripping the light fantastic over all seven Munros of the Lawers Range (Route 31d). You won't find in the Southern Highlands any remote expeditions of the kind possible in the Western Highlands or Cairngorms, but Lawers' Magnificent Seven and others will be more than

challenge enough for most.

The Munros fall naturally into eight groups, which form the eight sections of this book, presented in roughly left-to-right (west-to-east) and bottom-to-top (south-to-north) order. Each group is named after the glen, loch or village on which it is centred: 1 The Arrochar Alps, 2 Tyndrum, 3 Crianlarich, 4 Loch Earn, 5 Glen Lochay, 6 Loch Tay, 7 Bridge of Orchy, 8 Glen Lyon.

The three most westerly groups of Arrochar, Tyndrum and Bridge of Orchy contain the most bare rock, the shapeliest mountains and the toughest ascents. The Crianlarich, Loch Earn and Loch Tay groups are characterised

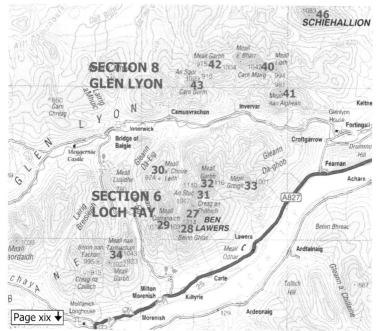

Page xix ↓

by distinctive summits linked by undulating ridges that give great ridge walking. The Glen Lochay and Glen Lyon groups are greener and gentler still, with less well-defined summits atop broad, rolling ridges that make great tramping country. Of course, these generalities mask some important exceptions.

As the nearest region to the most populated parts of Scotland, the Southern Highlands contain many of the country's most popular Munros. Only the Central Highlands' Ben Nevis, the highest in the land, is climbed more times than Ben Lomond, the nearest Munro to Glasgow and the centrepiece of Scotland's first National Park, created in 2002. Other popular mountains include Loch Earn's Ben Vorlich (one of the nearest to Edinburgh), the spectacular Cobbler (only a Corbett, but what a Corbett!), historic Schiehallion and Ben Lawers & Meall nan Tarmachan (reached by a road that climbs to a height of 550m/1800ft between them).

If you're new to the Scottish Highlands, the Southern Highlands are a good place to start: easy access, a variety of mountains, a whole host of different routes, extensive views over deep glens and ribbon lochs... and no less than 46 Munros to bag.

SEASONS AND WEATHER

From a hillwalking perspective, the Highland year has two seasons: the snow season and the no-snow season. The length of these seasons varies from year to year and from place to place.

From May to September, snow is rarely a problem. Historically, May and June have the greatest number of sunny days, with the air at its clearest. July and August are the hottest months but are also more prone to rain and haze, not to mention that blight on the landscape, the Highland midge. The biting season begins in mid to late June and lasts until the first chills of late September. By October it is colder, the hills get their first dusting of winter snow and good days are few and far between.

The months from November to April, though sometimes earlier and later, are characterised by short days, cold and snow. March and April are transition months, with little or lots of snow. In some years, snow can last into early summer and be a nuisance on some routes. If you are unequipped for it, turn back. Snow is more treacherous to descend than ascend, and spring snow often has a crystalline quality that makes it behave like ball-bearings.

In a normal winter (whatever that is, these days), conditions vary from British to Alpine to Arctic. An easy summer route can be made life-threatening by icy conditions and severe winter weather. When paths are obliterated by snow, hillsides become treacherous and walking becomes difficult and tiring.

On a clear winter's day the Scottish mountains have an Alpine quality that makes for unforgettable days out, but no-one should attempt a Munro in winter without adequate clothing and equipment (including ice-axe and crampons), and experience (or the company of an experienced person). The number of accidents, some of them fatal, that occur in the Highlands every winter should leave no doubt as to the need for caution.

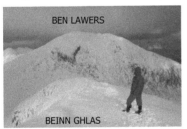

BEN LAWERS

BEINN GHLAS

Sample weather forecasts:
www.mwis.org.uk
www.mountain-forecast.com
www.metoffice.gov.uk (use menu to find specialist forecast – mountain)
www.metcheck.com/V40/UK/HOBBIES/mountain.asp   www.sais.gov.uk

Webcams may be available for specific Southern Highlands areas. Try a search. Here are three at the time of writing:
Ben Lawers: http://webcam.firbush.org
Ben More: www.benmorewebcam.co.uk
Ben Lomond:
https://lochlomondshores.com/webcam

USING THIS BOOK

Position in Munro's Tables (1 = highest)

OS 1:50,000 map number

Grid reference

▲ 1 Ben Lomond 179 974m/3195ft (OS 56, NN 367028)
Beacon Mountain, from the Gaelic *laom*

Many Munro names are Gaelic in origin. We give approximate pronunciations but make no claim to definitiveness. For example, the correct pronunciation of Ben is akin to *Pyne*, with a soft *n* as in the first syllable of *onion*, but it would be pedantic to enforce a purist pronunciation on a non-Gaelic speaker. The name Bealach, meaning Pass, is pronounced *byalach*, but many find it hard not to call it a *beelach*. And if you're one of those unfortunates who appear congenitally incapable of pronouncing *loch* as anything other than *lock*, you're in trouble.

In connection with the phonetic pronunciations given, note that Y before a vowel is pronounced as in *you*, OW is pronounced as in *town* and CH is pronounced as in Scottish *loch* or German *noch*.

Route 44a Meall Buidhe from Loch an Daimh
G1 *** NN 512464, 5½ml/9km, 520m/1700ft M212 —————— Page number of map

The maps used in this book are reproductions of OS 1:50,000 maps at 75% full size (i.e. 1:37,500 or 1.5cm per 1km).

Route distances are specified in miles (to the nearest half-mile) and kilometres (to the nearest kilometre). Short distances are specified in metres (an approximate imperial measurement as yards). Total amount of ascent for a route is specified to the nearest 10m (50ft) and should be regarded as an approximation only.

To calculate how long a route will take, many begin with Naismith's Rule (one hour per 3ml/5km + half-hour per 1000ft/300m). This can be adjusted by an appropriate factor to suit your own pace and to cater for stoppages, foul weather, technical difficulty, rough terrain, tiredness and decrepitude. (Bill Naismith, 1856–1935, was the 'father' of the SMC.)

River directions, left bank and right bank, refer to the downstream direction. When referring to the direction of travel, we specify left-hand and right-hand.

The symbols ▲ and Δ indicate Munros and Tops. An ATV track is an All-Terrain Vehicle track, rougher than a Land Rover track.

ACCESS

Land access was revolutionised by The Land Reform (Scotland) Act 2003 and the accompanying Scottish Outdoor Access Code (2005), which created a statutory right of responsible access for outdoor recreation. It is recommended that anyone walking in the Scottish countryside familiarise himself/herself with the Code, which explains rights and responsibilities in detail. Further information: www.outdooraccess-scotland.com.

Deer stalking considerations: Most of the Scottish Highlands are privately owned and non-compliance with stalking restrictions is likely to be counter-productive and cause aggravation for all concerned. If revenue is lost because of interference with stalking activities, estates may be forced to turn to afforestation or worse, thereby increasing access problems.

The red stag stalking season runs from July 1 to October 20 but actual dates vary from locality to locality. Access notices dot the roadside and information on stalking activities can be obtained from estate offices and head stalkers.

An increasing number of estates contribute to the Hillphones service, which provides daily recorded messages of where stalking is taking place. Further information can be found on the Outdoor Access website: www.outdooraccess-scotland.com/hftsh. Alternatively, obtain a leaflet from The Mountaineering Council of Scotland, The Old Granary, Perth PH1 5QP.

It is worth noting that there is no stalking on a Sunday and that land belonging to public bodies such as the National Trust for Scotland and the John Muir Trust is normally not subject to stalking restrictions. See main text for specific access considerations.

TERRAIN

Most of the standard Munro ascent routes have been boot-worn into paths and in some cases beyond that into ribbons of bog. In general, they have little in common with the kind of manicured paths found in the Alps or the Furth of Scotland (England and Wales).

Path restoration programmes began some years ago and continue apace, such that many popular routes now boast excellent renovated paths. At the other extreme some paths have degenerated into quagmires. Be prepared always for rough, rugged terrain and wear appropriate footwear.

The path from Beinn Dubhchraig to Ben Oss

1 THE ARROCHAR ALPS

The Arrochar Alps are a small group of rugged mountains, including four Munros, that tower over the village of Arrochar at the head of Loch Long, just west of Loch Lomond. As the nearest mountains to Glasgow, they are popular mountains that offer **great hillwalking in scenic surroundings**. They also sport formidable rock faces that have played a major role in the development of mountaineering in Scotland.

Their grandiose title owes more to alliterative endeavour than topographical reality, but they deserve the accolade if only for their *pièce de résistance*: The Cobbler. This **remarkable rock peak** is perhaps the most eye-catching mountain in Scotland, even though at 884m/2901ft it is ironically not a Munro.

Of the four Munros, Beinn Narnain and Beinn Ime have the most exciting scenery (Routes 2a – 2d), Ben Vane has the most distinctive shape (Route 4a) and Ben Vorlich has the best views (Route 5a). Two nearby Munros are also described here: prominent Ben Lomond, one of the most famous of all Munros (Route 1a), and retiring Beinn Bhuidhe, one of the least known (Route 6a).

And that's not all... There used to be a fifth Munro (see Page 19).

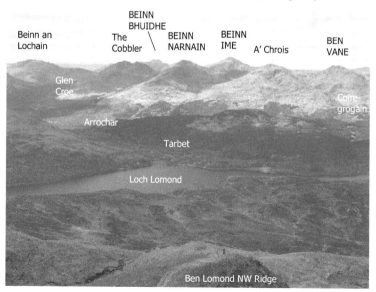

BEINN BHUIDHE

Beinn an Lochain · The Cobbler · BEINN NARNAIN · BEINN IME · A' Chrois · BEN VANE

Glen Croe

Arrochar

Coire grogain

Tarbet

Loch Lomond

Ben Lomond NW Ridge

▲1 Ben Lomond 179 974m/3195ft (OS 56, NN 367028)
Beacon Mountain, from the Gaelic *laom*

Ptarmigan　　NW Ridge　　　BEN LOMOND　　　　　　S Ridge

Loch Lomond

Peak Fitness: No change since 1891 Tables.

S econd only to Ben Nevis in popularity, this most southerly of all Munros is nowhere near as great a mountain, yet it has **undeniable presence**. Standing in splendid isolation, it shows up as a shapely cone from some angles, and it certainly occupies **a prime site** above its famously picturesque loch. The Tourist Path to the summit was renovated in the 1990s at a cost of £340,000 and now offers both a perfect ascent route for plodmeisters and an unrivalled opportunity to assess at first hand the merits (or otherwise) of modern path maintenance schemes.

GiGi: In olden times, the complex geography of the Highlands and the closed nature of clan society meant that even people living in neighbouring glens had little contact. When it was necessary to gather people together, e.g. to summon men to arms or warn of approaching danger (from the Romans or Vikings, perhaps, or even the English!), fires were raised on prominent hills such as Ben Lomond, hence its name.

Baffies: The roads and villages around Loch Lomond and the foot of the Arrochar Alps boast one of the best tea-shop crawls in the Scottish Highlands.

Route 1a Ben Lomond from Rowardennan:
The Tourist Path
G1 ***** NS 360986, 8ml/12km, 1000m/3300ft

This route merits five stars if only for the ease and viewsomeness of the ascent, although some traditionalists may find the mountain today a tad too browbeaten for their tastes. The path begins inauspiciously behind the toilet block at Rowardennan car park, at the end of the road along the east side of Loch Lomond. Once you've found the toilet block, directions are superfluous. Just follow the person in front of you! Even if you find yourself in the newsworthy position of having the mountain to yourself, the path is unmistakable.

It climbs through a forestry plantation onto open hillside and continues up grassy slopes to Sron Aonaich (*Strawn Ernich*, Nose of the Ridge, 577m/1893ft), where the angle eases at the start of Ben Lomond's broad south ridge. The summit looks disappointingly dull from here, like a great flattened pudding, but appearances are deceptive. The skyline is the lip of Coire a' Bhathaich (*Corra Vah-ich*, Corrie of the Byre), a craggy corrie hidden on the north side of the mountain (and whose name is misleadingly placed on the OS map).

The path rises gently up the south ridge before climbing more steeply to the corrie lip. The craggy corrie walls are too vegetated to offer much rock-climbing but, as they suddenly drop away beneath your feet, they certainly seem dramatic enough after the mountain's gentle southern slopes. The path continues along the corrie rim to the cliff-top ▲summit.

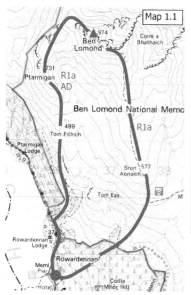

Map 1.1

GiGi: For a novel approach, reach Rowardennan, on the east side of Loch Lomond, from Inverbeg, on the A82 along the west side. A ferry runs from Easter to October. It leaves Inverbeg at 10.30, 14.30 and 18.30, and Rowardennan at 10.00, 14.00 and 17.30. Enquiries: Rowardennan Hotel (tel: 01360-870273).

F-Stop: The isolated summit affords **tremendous views** in all directions, especially north into the Southern Highlands and south over Loch Lomond.

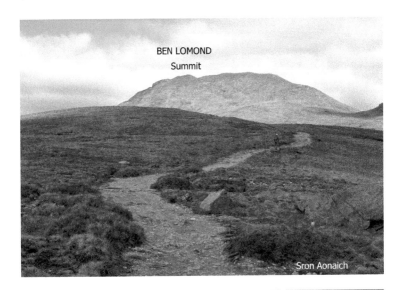

BEN LOMOND
Summit

Sron Aonaich

Torpedo: With judicious timing, Ben Lomond can be climbed between refreshment stops at one of east Loch Lomondside's numerous watering holes. And if you're feeling energetic... the Ben Lomond Race record (up and down from Rowardennan Hotel) stands at just over one hour.

Needlepoint: Thanks to excellent paths, neither the Tourist Path up Ben Lomond's south ridge nor the Alternative Descent via Ptarmigan should cause problems in cloud.

Chilly Willy: Ben Lomond's popularity makes it a tempting winter objective but, when the Tourist Path is obliterated by snow, the mountain's steep upper slopes demand care. As always in winter, ice axe and crampons are *de rigueur*. In addition, beware cornices overhanging Coire a' Bhathaich. The Alternative Descent is a more serious winter proposition, owing to its steep start.

Summit

Coire a'
Bhathaich

Route 1a Alternative Descent:
Ben Lomond North-west Ridge and Ptarmigan
G3 ***** Add-on: negligible mileage, negligible ascent M3

To make a round trip that gives close-up views of Loch Lomond, we recommend a return over the subsidiary peak of Ptarmigan (731m/2398ft). The route is both more intricate and more fun than the Tourist Path, with an excellent path that has been less conspicuously renovated than the normal route. Be advised, though, that it is by no means the 'leisurely afternoon stroll' of the Tourist Path.

BEN LOMOND

NW Ridge

Ptarmigan

Loch Lomond

First you must descend Ben Lomond's steep north-west ridge. The stony path makes light of it, but there are two short rocky sections that require a spot of easy handwork. If you can manage the first, immediately below the summit, you should have no problems further down. Below the second rocky section, which is hidden from sight just below the first, the path winds its way invitingly down to and along Ptarmigan's undulating summit ridge.

After passing a hidden lochan, the **scenic descent** from the end of the ridge, with Loch Lomond and its mosaic of islands spread out before you, is the equal of any in the Highlands. The path reaches the lochside at a forest track that is part of the West Highland Way and which will take you back to Rowardennan.

Loch Lomond

Ptarmigan

Descending Ben
Lomond's NW Ridge

Tourist Path

Rowardennan

Loch
Lomond

Ptarmigan

▲**2 Beinn Narnain** 259 926m/3038ft (OS 56, NN 271066)
Meaning obscure. Perhaps Mountain of the Notches (*Ben Vyarnan*, from aspirated Gaelic *bearn*) or Mountain of the Alders (*Ben Yarnan*, from aspirated Gaelic *fearn*)

▲**3 Beinn Ime** 118 1011m/3316ft (OS 56, NN 255084)
Ben Eema, Butter Mountain (butter was once made at shielings in its corries)

The Cobbler   BEINN NARNAIN

Loch Long

Peak Fitness: No change since original 1891 Tables, although nearby Beinn an Lochain across the Rest and Be Thankful pass on the A83 was also a Munro from 1891 to 1981 (see Page 19 for further details).

Despite encircling roads, these Munros conceal their best features from roadside rubberneckers behind convex slopes, such that they are more interesting to climb than their initial inconsequential appearance would suggest. Beinn Narnain especially sports some sizeable summit crags that fringe **a plateau-in-the-sky summit**. The two mountains are separated by the 637m/2090ft Bealach a' Mhaim (*Byalach a Vaa-im*, Pass of the Moor), which can be approached from a number of starting points to

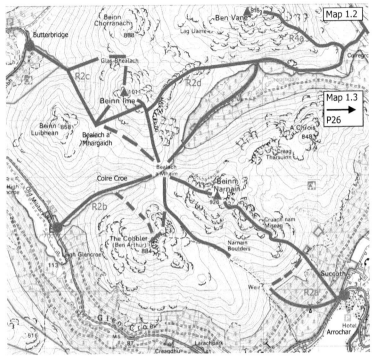

enable the two Munros to be bagged together by a variety of routes.

For a dual ascent, by far the most rewarding approach begins in the south-east near Arrochar (Route 2a). If you wish to avoid steep ground and the touch of rock, or are determined to set a new personal best, a shorter approach begins in Glen Croe to the south-west (Route 2b).

To climb Beinn Ime alone, an even shorter approach begins in Glen Kinglas to the north-west (Route 2c), while Beinn Narnain alone can be climbed by a truncated version of

Route 2a or 2b (although most will choose to extend the day to Beinn Ime). Note that Routes 2b and 2c, although shorter than Route 2a, ascend more tiresome terrain in duller country and in the event may seem not so short after all.

Ben Ime's main feature of interest is its rousing north-east ridge, situated at the heart of the Arrochar Alps and hidden from sight on most approaches. Intrepid scramblers may wish to consider it as **an adventurous wildside approach** to the two summits (Route 2d).

Route 2a Beinn Narnain and Beinn Ime
from Loch Long (Arrochar)
G3 **** NN 294049, 8ml/13km, 1300m/4250ft M8

When viewed from the shores of Loch Long, Beinn Ime is hidden behind Beinn Narnain, whose uninspiring lower slopes are overshadowed by the compelling rock faces of The Cobbler. But sulk ye not. Above the hillside in view, a broad, craggy ridge leads to Narnain's **scenic cliff-top summit**, with Beinn Ime readily accessible beyond.

The route begins just beyond the turn-off to Succoth on the A83 at the head of Loch Long, just outside Arrochar. Opposite the car park (small parking fee payable at machine), the new Cobbler Path begins a convoluted climb up the hillside, trending left into the glen of the Allt a' Bhalachain (*Owlt a Valachin*, Buttermilk Burn), between The Cobbler and Beinn Narnain. The path's first objective is the low point seen on the skyline at NN 280051, where the stream is dammed.

From the dam (marked as weir on OS map), a side path leaves the Cobbler Path to traverse right, back across the hillside, to the top of an old railtrack, where the Narnain path begins at a height of 330m/1100ft.

This point can be reached much

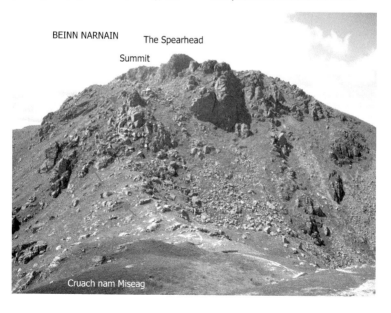

BEINN NARNAIN   The Spearhead

Summit

Cruach nam Miseag

The Spearhead

Spearhead Gully

Scramblers Route (see Page 13)

more quickly, and many would say much more enjoyably, by a direct ascent of the old railtrack. All that remains of the track, built during construction of the Loch Sloy hydro-electric scheme, is a line of intermittent concrete blocks, now linked by a rugged path. This path leaves the Cobbler Path c.70m from the roadside and climbs straight up the hillside. It is steep and rough but gains height fast and, unlike the Cobbler Path, makes you feel as though you're getting somewhere.

Above the railtrack, the Narnain path continues straight up the hillside. At first it is boggy in parts, it is indistinct in parts and it even crosses bare rock in parts, such that a spot of handwork may be required, but it improves with height and soon gives a straightforward ascent. At a height of

around 600m/2000ft it emerges onto Narnain's south-east ridge to open up views along Loch Lomond and over the Allt a' Bhalachain to the rock faces of The Cobbler.

As you continue up the ridge on grass among outcrops, one rocky knoll after another comes underfoot until you reach the 813m/2667ft highpoint of Cruach nam Miseag (*Croo-ach nam Mishak*, Mound of the Kid, i.e. Goat). A 30m/100ft dip then separates you from a final, steep, rocky 150m/500ft rise to Narnain's summit, and it is on this section that the real fun begins.

The gritty path calls for occasional handwork as it weaves a way up among the crags. At first it traverses to the left, quite exposed in places and a bit of a clamber in others, but fortunately never at the same time. Then it climbs back right to the foot of

Below The Spearhead

In Spearhead Gully

a final 20m/65ft rock fang, known as The Spearhead.

The path avoids the rock obstacle on the right to finish up a worn gully and deposit you on Narnain's summit plateau a couple of hundred metres from the ▲summit. The gully is nowhere difficult or exposed, but don't expect to keep your hands in your pockets. There are three substantial cairns on the summit plateau (as well as another atop The Spearhead). The highest spot seems to be the trig. pillar just before the centre cairn.

Beyond the summit, heading directly for Beinn Ime, most people cross the plateau to the cairn at its north-west end, then negotiate an awkward boulder field to reach a path that descends the grassy hillside to the Bealach a' Mhaim. The most hassle-free way down through the boulders, however, follows an initially indistinct path that goes left from the centre cairn on the plateau.

The two paths join lower down to make the 289m/948ft descent. Nearing the bealach, the (now) single path becomes eroded then indistinct. If (when?) you lose it, aim for the stile in the fence that crosses the bealach at right-angles (from west to east).

At the stile you'll join a path that comes in from the left over the Narnain–Cobbler bealach. This is a continuation of the Cobbler Path, which you left earlier and which will form the return route. Continuing northwards from the Bealach a' Mhaim, the ascent of Beinn Ime is now little more than a 374m/1227ft aerobic workout on uniform grass slopes. The path is eroded and quite boggy at first but, after reaching a small plateau at the junction with the north-east ridge, it becomes rockier and firmer for the final push to the rocky nipple of a ▲summit (pic on Page 22).

After returning to the Bealach a'

Mhaim, bear right to follow the boggy main path across the western hillside of Beinn Narnain to the Narnain–Cobbler bealach, where you'll meet the new Cobbler Path for **a rollicking jaunt** back down to your starting point. In its upper reaches especially, the new path, built at a cost of £300,000 in the 2000s, is **a wonderful and welcome piece of engineering** that replaces the former execrable bog-trot. The Arrochar Alps may have little in common scenically with their European counterparts, but this path is the equal of any Swiss Alpine Hut approach.

A swift jog down beside the Allt a' Bhalachain brings you to the junction with the main approach path to the summit of The Cobbler, which branches back sharp right across the stream. Next you pass two giant rocks known as the Narnain Boulders, which were once a famous howff (natural shelter) used by early twentieth century rock climbers.

Further down, the path reaches the small dam noted above, after which a Land Rover track continues down beside the stream to a radio mast on a forest road. Following red waymarks on posts, turn left, then right again after c.60m, to find the continuing path down to the car park. This latter section of path is well-surfaced but takes such a convoluted route that short-cut paths are already developing between zigzags.

GiGi: If you're looking for a way to climb the two Munros without putting hand to rock, avoid the Narnain path and go up and down via the Cobbler Path and the Bealach a' Mhaim. The route is a couple of miles further but rivals the Ben Lomond Tourist Path (Route 1a) for ease of ascent. (10ml/16km, 1300m/4250ft G1 ****) Alternatively, use the shorter but less scenic Route 2b (Page 15).

Needlepoint: The main navigational problem in cloud is the broad, flat, featureless Bealach a' Mhaim between Beinn Narnain and Beinn Ime. The fence that crosses it from west to east is a useful marker but, on the return journey, finding a correct line across the hillside from the Bealach a' Mhaim to the Narnain–Cobbler bealach is not easy. If you lose the path on one of its indistinct sections, **expect some excellent navigational exercise**.

Chilly Willy: Both Munros are relatively benign winter mountains, especially if tackled from Glen Croe (Route 2b) or Glen Kinglas (Route 2c). On the ascent of Narnain from Loch Long via Route 2a, the vicinity of The Spearhead may give a few short snow and/or ice problems with some exposure. Whether you view these as good sport or a best-forgotten-soonest-mended ordeal will depend on your competence with ice axe and crampons.

BEN LOMOND

BEINN NARNAIN

NE Ridge

BEINN IME

Terminator: Left of The Spearhead (as encountered on ascent), the redoubtable rock face of Spearhead Buttress skirts Beinn Narnain's summit plateau. At its foot is a shelf of giant jumbled boulders that is well worth exploring (as long as you don't fall into cave-like holes in the ground).

If you fancy an easy wee scramble on the way up, quit the main path before it climbs the gully to the right of The Spearhead and instead go left around the foot of the rock face. Beyond Spearhead Arête, as the direct route up the front of

the rock tower is known, you'll pass Spearhead Chimney, then Jamblock Chimney (look for the jammed block) and Restricted Crack (only slim climbers admitted). Jamblock Chimney especially is so deeply cut into the mountain that its ascent is almost **a subterranean rock climb**. Such features may give the mountain its name.

Continuing around the foot of the rock face, you'll come to a short gully that, with only a few easy scrambling moves, will put you atop Beinn Narnain's summit plateau.

The Cobbler M8

Although not a Munro, The Cobbler is **a real mountain** – the favourite Arrochar Alp of both Terminator and whole generations of Glasgow climbers. Nevertheless, the 884m/2901ft summit lies only 256m/840ft above the Bealach a' Mhaim and is easily reached from Route 2a if you have time and energy to spare. After returning to the Narnain-Cobbler bealach from Beinn Ime, instead of turning left to follow the new Cobbler Path down the glen of the Allt a' Bhalachain, turn right to follow the renovated path up The

Cobbler's steep but easy north-east slopes. Once up, the equally well-renovated main Cobbler approach path descends via the eastern corrie to join the Allt a' Bhalachain path.

Of the three tops of The Cobbler, the North Top is a walk, the Centre Top (summit) is an easy scramble (see below) and the South Top is a hard scramble-cum-rock-climb. It is the North Top, viewed in the 'right' way from Arrochar, that looks like a cobbler bent over his last and gives the mountain its popular name (its proper name is Ben Arthur).

The Cobbler viewed from Arrochar

The ascent of the anvil-like block of rock that forms the Centre Top and summit is a test of nerves. It requires a short, easy but very exposed scramble through a hole in the rock (Argyll's Eyeglass) and up a couple of sloping ledges to a flat roof. It can always be left for another day.

F-Stop: Beinn Narnain's summit crags are perfectly positioned to add dramatic foreground to **photogenic views** of The Cobbler and Ben Lomond.

Unfortunately, morning is the best time to photograph The Cobbler, while evening is the best time for Ben Lomond.

Route 2b Beinn Narnain and Beinn Ime from Glen Croe

G1 ** NN 242060, 5ml/8km, 1160m/3800ft M8

If you need a couple of quick ticks on your list, an approach from Glen Croe gives the shortest round of the two Munros and, like an ascent via the Cobbler Path (see Page 12), offers a way up for those allergic to rock. However, it's a **criminally unscenic** way of reaching the summits. In fact, it's hard to believe the Arrochar Alps can look so dull.

While the Cobbler Path begins at sea-level on the south-east side of the Bealach a' Mhaim, the Glen Croe approach begins at a height of 170m/550ft on the south-west side, at the foot of Coire Croe (unnamed on OS map). There are parking spaces on the A83, beside the bridge over the stream that flows down the corrie, 5ml/8km outside Arrochar.

BEINN IME

NE Ridge

Bealach a' Mhargaidh

Bealach a' Mhaim

Coire Croe

BEINN NARNAIN

The start is confusing. White posts and a stile over a fence point the way up the right-hand (south) side of the stream, but the path there soon becomes boggy and indistinct.

Instead, go through the gate on the left and cross a bridge to find a better path up the left-hand (north) side of the stream. It climbs steeply up the hillside before easing off into grassy,

V-shaped Coire Croe, where you'll reach a small dam, half-way up to the bealach, at NN 252067.

Nondescript hillsides rise all around

BEINN IME   BEINN NARNAIN

Coire Croe

as the path continues to make its way up the corrie, eventually to become lost in thick grass as it nears the bealach. Once on the bealach, join Route 2a to knock off ▲Beinn Narnain and ▲Beinn Ime in turn.

NB If you wish to bag The Cobbler on the way back, you won't then have to retrace steps to the Bealach a' Mhaim as, from the summit, easy slopes descend directly north-west beside a stream to the dam in lower Coire Croe.

BEINN NARNAIN

Bealach a' Mhaim

BEINN IME

Needlepoint: Despite the featurelessness of the Bealach a' Mhaim, the Glen Croe approach gives more room for navigational error than Route 2a from Loch Long. On descent from the bealach in cloud, head south-west down the grassy hillside and you should meet the stream leading down to the roadside at some point.

Chilly Willy: Even when the mountains are snow-covered, this route lacks technical difficulty and is a more straightforward winter option than Route 2a. An ascent from Loch Long via the Cobbler Path and the Bealach a' Mhaim, as noted on Page 12, is equally easy and far more scenic, but twice as long.

Route 2c Beinn Ime alone from Glen Kinglas
G2 * NN 237093, 4ml/6km, 810m/2650ft M8

On the north-west side of the Arrochar Alps, the A83 swings left over the Kinglas Water at Butterbridge, at the foot of Beinn an Lochain's north-east ridge. Above the roadside, Beinn Ime **rises majestically** as a symmetrical cone, although unfortunately it flatters to deceive. There are two routes up the mountain from here, but both are tiresome plods that have little to recommend them beyond the exercise. Save them for a short sharp shock to the system when you're pressed for time and desirous of the quickest way up an Arrochar Alp... *any* Arrochar Alp.

BEINN IME

Glas Bhealach

Bealach a' Mhargaidh

Butterbridge

F-Stop: Butterbridge is the still-standing single-arched bridge by which the original eighteenth century military road crossed the Kinglas Water. There's a car park beside the bridge at NN 234095, just around the corner from the start of Route 2c. After returning from Ben Ime, take time to view the mountain at its best, rising photogenically behind the bridge in evening light.

One ascent route goes via the Bealach a' Mhargaidh (*Byalach a Varky*, Pass of the Market, unnamed on OS map), which lies to the south-west of the summit, between Ime and Beinn Luibhean (*Ben Livven* or *Ben Li-yen*, Mountain of Herbs or Plants). The other ascent route goes via the Glas Bhealach (*Glass Vyalach*, Green Pass), which lies to the north of the summit, between Ime and Beinn Chorranach (*Ben Chorranach*, Mountain of the Lament).

The Bealach a' Mhargaidh option carries a path of sorts, but there is so little to choose between the two routes that we suggest making a round by going up one and down the other. As the path is more of an aid on ascent than descent, an anti-clockwise round, beginning with a climb to the Bealach a' Mhargaidh, is recommended.

Begin 100m before the bend in the road at the Kinglas Water, 200m/650ft above sea-level, at the foot of a forest track that climbs the hillside through felled trees. The path itself actually begins at the near end of the bend, beside a road sign. From here, it passes a ruined building and climbs

BEINN IME

SW Spur

Scramblers' route

Baffies' route

the right-hand side of the stream that comes down from the Bealach a' Mhargaidh, but its initial section is overgrown and crosses very rough ground. It is much less aggravating to begin on the forest track and join the path higher up, even though the overgrown track climbs only 60m/200ft up the hillside.

Follow the track until it peters out near a fence that runs up the right-hand bank of the stream. You'll find the continuing path beside the stream, but don't harbour high hopes of it as it is boggy and climbs through rough ground strewn with felled trees. You may prefer the better going to be found on the tree-free grassy hillside on the left-hand side of the stream.

In the bowl of the corrie at the foot of Beinn Ime's western slopes, the stream divides. Northern branches rise ahead to the Glas Bhealach (the descent route), while the main stream bends right to carry the ascent route to the Bealach a' Mhargaidh. You can continue along either streambank, but you'll probably be seduced by the continuing path on the right-hand

bank, especially as it eventually dries out on the steeper grass slopes that make the final climb to the bealach.

Above the Bealach a' Mhargaidh, Beinn Ime's crag-littered south-west spur rises to the summit. The crest gives a very steep ascent on grass slopes among sizeable outcrops (or over them if you wish to seek scrambling). The angle lessens further right, where slopes of boulder-strewn grass rise to the south-east ridge to meet the path from the Bealach a' Mhaim to the ▲summit.

Over the summit, a path begins the steep descent of Ime's uniform northern slopes to the Glas Bhealach. Scattered rocks and short grass give way to marshier ground, where the path eventually becomes lost. Avoid the temptation to descend before reaching the bealach as there is a rocky buttress just below it. At the far end of the bealach, descend the right-hand side of the buttress and you'll find a stony little path that takes you down into the corrie below. Keep going down the grassy hillside to rejoin the outward route at the bend in the stream.

The Cobbler

N Top

Centre Top (summit)

Viewed from Beinn Ime

Torpedo: If, having decided to do this route in order to leave Beinn Narnain for another day, you yet find yourself at the summit of Beinn Ime with energy to spare, you can bag Beinn Narnain and return to Butterbridge without having to climb back over Beinn Ime.

From the Bealach a' Mhaim, bypass the summit of Beinn Ime by traversing grass slopes directly to the Bealach a' Mhargaidh, which is only 40m/130ft higher than the Bealach a' Mhaim (see pic on page 15). It's a bit of a traipse but will take less than an hour. (Add-on Beinn Narnain: 3ml/5km, 330m/1080ft)

Needlepoint: The broad Bealach a' Mhargaidh is difficult to navigate in cloud. Make sure you've fully reached the bealach before cutting left up Beinn Ime or you could end up on the steep craggy ground of the south-west spur. On the return route, the Glas Bhealach may also cause difficulties if you attempt to descend from it before reaching its lowest point.

Chilly Willy: The Butterbridge approach gives no especial winter problems, but competence on steep snow is required on the slopes above the Bealach a' Mhargaidh and below the Glas Bhealach.

Beinn an Lochain

Butterbridge

BEINN IME

GiGi: There used to be five Munros in the Alps but, after a re-survey gave Beinn an Lochain a height of 901m/2957ft, that mountain lost its Munro status in 1981. It still merits the short ascent from near Butterbridge to the summit, only 700m/2300ft above the Rest and Be Thankful pass on the A83 west of Arrochar.

Route 2d Beinn Narnain and Beinn Ime from Inveruglas (via Coiregrogain): Beinn Ime North-east Ridge

G4 **** NN 318093, 12½ml/20km, 1300m/4250ft M8

For a description of the special place that is Coiregrogain, see ▲4 Ben Vane (Page 25). The knobbly north-east ridge of Beinn Ime bounds the upper corrie on the right, bristling with tiers of rock that are generally too difficult or too vegetated to offer clean scrambling lines. Despite or because of this, the ridge is a challenging scramble that gives the most **adventurous ascent route** in the Arrochar Alps.

The ascent is something of a prolonged thrutch up lines of least resistance, often employing clumps of grass as handholds (please leave some behind for the next person). A sense of humour, plus an ability to distinguish well-rooted vegetative matter from tender growth that is as delicately poised as you are, is essential. Additional amusement may be derived from routefinding misjudgements, as the optimal way up each rock tier is not always immediately discernible.

The easiest line barely rates as a scramble, but in several places you'll require multiple points of contact to heave yourself up the green stuff, and there is some exposure towards the top, so we grade the route G4. Only you can decide whether such a prospect fills you with anticipation or dread.

The rocks begin... but which way up?

To reach the ridge, follow Route 4a up Coiregrogain to the foot of Ben Vane, then continue along the Land Rover track until it reaches a small dam below a waterfall on a side stream (NN 279090). Here the track bears left into a forestry plantation and will form the return route.

On the far side of the dam, a rough path climbs steeply around rocks to reach the streamside above and follow it to the foot of the ridge, where the first **tiers of crags explode out of the moor**. We could tell you the best way up, but we're not going to, because that would spoil the fun. (If truth be told, we're not sure we know the best way up, but please don't rat on us.)

Above the first tiers is a small levelling then... well, there's more of the same. Unless you're as

Rock Tower

BEINN IME →

Exposed Bypass path

Easier Bypass route

navigationally challenged as Needlepoint, you should experience no real problems until, beyond a small dip, you find yourself at the foot of a final rock tower. And an intimidatingly steep, exposed and vegetated beast of a thing it is too. You may well choose to sit here awhile and ponder.

Only the brave will tackle this **mother of all thrutches** direct, but the seemingly formidable upper rocks do have two lines of weakness – one in the centre and an easier one to the right.

Caution: Do not attempt a direct ascent of the rock tower unless you are a capable Grade 5 scrambler inured to exposure.

Fortunately there is an easier way to surmount the obstacle. Look for a small path that traverses left to climb around the tower and regain the ridge above. This path crosses very steep grass, is quite exposed and is not recommended to anyone too delicate to get their fingernails dirty, but it is much easier than a frontal assault. And there is a still easier option for those unconvinced of the adhesive properties of grass. From the dip before the tower, a developing path descends a hundred metres or so down stony slopes on the right, then climbs back around the side of the tower to regain the ridge.

BEINN IME
summit 'nipple'

Above the tower, the ridge levels and merges with Beinn Ime's southern hillside, where Route 2a is joined for the final spurt to the ▲summit.

After bagging ▲Narnain in turn, return to the Bealach a' Mhaim and descend north-east from there, back into Coiregrogain. As long as you avoid the deep-cut sides of the stream that tumbles down from the north (Beinn Ime) end of the bealach, the grassy hillside is steep but negotiable anywhere. For a line that's as good as any (especially in cloud), descend beside the fence that crosses the bealach from west to east.

Lower down, after the fence meets the stream, a developing path runs along the left bank through sparse tree cover. Near the start of the Land Rover track in Coiregrogain, a few metres of easy bushwhacking may be required. Once on the track, it's a 4ml/7km jog back to the roadside.

Needlepoint: In cloud, keep climbing Beinn Ime's north-east ridge and you should eventually reach its top, but you'd be better advised to give it a body swerve until the grass and rock are dry and you can see the best way up.

Chilly Willy: In winter, the north-east ridge becomes an exposed snow and ice climb. The final rock tower is a formidable obstacle if tackled direct, and any attempt to bypass it is likely to lead onto equally difficult ground.

A' Chrois

BEINN NARNAIN

Terminator: From the summit of Beinn Narnain, the aesthetic return route would be to complete a horseshoe of Coiregrogain by wandering out along Narnain's rugged little north-east ridge to its end at the viewpoint of A' Chrois. Unfortunately the lower slopes of A' Chrois are thickly forested. By continuing over the top of A' Chrois, it is just about possible to descend left into a steep basin on vertiginous grass, then continue down a gully beside a stream on equally steep but even rougher grass, then bushwhack down through dense conifers, then cross the Allt Coiregrogain to regain the Land Rover track. But you'd have to be a masochistic combination of mountain goat and mole to get the full benefit of it.

▲4 Ben Vane 282 915m/3002ft (OS 56, NN 277098)
Middle Mountain (from Gaelic *Mheadhoin*)

BEN VANE

F-Stop: Morning is the prime time for photography in Coiregrogain, but you'll need a panoramic lens to capture the complete vista.

Peak Fitness: No change since 1891 Tables. In the latest (1997) edition of the Tables Ben Vane was the second lowest Munro, lower than Beinn Teallach (▲109) but higher than the Munro Sgurr nan Ceannaichean in the Western Highlands.

Re-surveying in 2009 resulted in the demotion of Ceannaichean to Corbett status. Ben Vane's height was re-measured as 915.76m (3004.60ft) but Beinn Teallach's was re-measured as 914.60m (3000.80ft), leaving Ben Vane still second bottom.

This most distinctive of the Arrochar Alps' Munros (unlike The Cobbler, it just scrapes over the 3000ft mark) is **a crag-spattered dome of a mountain** that stands apart from its neighbours at the head of Coiregrogain. Its main line of weakness is its steep south-east spur, and it is this that carries the path to the summit. The relentless steepness of the ascent makes it something of a lung-buster, but the scenery and the intricacy of the terrain provide constant diversion.

Baffies: Ben Vane is one steep hill, but it compensates with a cornucopia of natural rock seats, human posteriors for the benefit of, scenery for the perusal of.

Coiregrogain M26

At the wild heart of the Arrochar Alps, Coiregrogain is **one of the most scenic secret places in the Southern Highlands**, unknown to the majority of car-bound touros crawling past its mouth along traffic-jammed Loch Lomondside. If you can't get to Glacier National Park, Montana, to view arrowhead peaks towering over trench-like valleys, the great hidden basin of Coiregrogain is the next best thing.

As you enter, between the craggy portals of A' Chrois (*A Chrosh*, The Cross) and Ben Vorlich, the view ahead to volcano-like Ben Vane is **unique in Scotland for both its form and symmetry**. Even hydro-electric works and a private road up to Loch Sloy, situated in the trench between Ben Vane and Ben Vorlich, cannot detract from the majesty of the place.

The paved road into Coiregrogain leaves the A82 Loch Lomond road at the foot of the Inveruglas Water, 3½ml/6km north of Tarbet. There is a car park at Inveruglas Visitor Centre, 400m further north, from where there is a connecting path. On leaving the A82, walk under the railway bridge, take the path that short-cuts the first hairpin bend and follow the road up into the corrie.

BEN VANE

Route 4a Ben Vane from Inveruglas (via Coiregrogain)

G3 **** NN 318093, 6ml/10km, 880m/2900ft

From Inveruglas, walk up the Coiregrogain road to the foot of Ben Vane, then branch left on a Land Rover track that crosses a bridge and continues into the forestry plantation at the head of the corrie. The paved road continues right of Ben Vane to Loch Sloy dam and is a possible return route (see Alternative Descent).

About 500m along the track from the road, at the bridge over the first stream, the obvious path up the mountain takes to the hillside. It is boggy for the first couple of hundred metres, but take comfort in the knowledge that it will never be quite as bad higher up. It climbs steeply around a crag to gain the south-east spur at a levelling, then it climbs past a second levelling to reach more outcroppy terrain that will be with you for the remainder of the ascent.

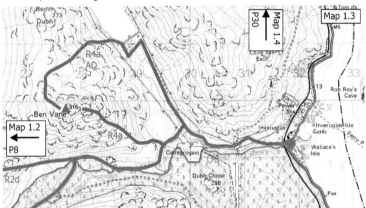

At the foot of the first major outcrop, the path veers right and becomes more eroded and stony. You may well use hands for balance here and there as it ascends to a **viewpoint** overlooking Loch Sloy, before climbing back left to regain the crest of the spur.

At this point, with the previously hidden upper slopes of the mountain coming into view at last, you may well think there's still a disappointingly long way to go, and there's no respite either as the path continues its **relentlessly steep upward trajectory**. Numerous small outcrops give ample opportunities for off-path scrambling, and good luck to anyone who has the energy. As distraction, there are ever-expanding views eastwards over Loch Lomond, Loch Arklet and Loch Katrine.

Only after reaching the skyline seen above does the angle ease at last over a succession of levellings fronted by sizeable crags. The path threads a convoluted line around and over the rocks with several variations. Even on the easiest line you'll probably use hands in one or two places, but there's no exposure or danger. Other lines may require occasional thrutches that,

to the grateful amusement of companions, will be difficult to achieve with any semblance of dignity. A final rock step pops you out onto the small table-top ▲summit.

It is now apparent how the mountain derives its name, as it lies directly between Ben Vorlich and the rest of the Alps. Ben Lomond is also visible across Loch Lomond.

Needlepoint: In cloud you may never quite know where you are amid all the rock outcrops, but there are no subsidiary tops or ridges to mislead and the well-worn path should make the ascent fairly foul-weatherproof.

Chilly Willy: Ben Vane is no place to learn how to use ice axe and crampons. Under snow, the slopes of the south-east spur become intimidatingly steep and exposed, such that in some places a slip would be difficult to arrest.

GiGi: After rain an odd phenomenon occurs: a small lochan forms on Ben Vane's summit table-top.

Route 4a Alternative Descent: Loch Sloy
G2 *** Add-on: 1½ml/2km, zero ascent

If you are unfazed by pathless grass slopes that can be quite steep in places, this alternative descent route is well worth consideration. It avoids the retracing of steps down the south-west spur and passes a number of features of interest.

From Ben Vane's summit, stroll along the turf ridge that heads north-west around the skyline, aiming for the saddle below the subsidiary peak of Beinn Dubh (*Ben Doo*, Black Mountain). Before reaching the saddle, descend right into the **attractively**

BEN VORLICH

Loch Sloy

Rocky
Basin

BEN VANE

**rugged, ice-scoured, lochan-filled
basin** between the two peaks.

This basin is so wide-open and
complex that the way out of it is
ridiculously difficult to spot. Aim left of
the rocky highpoint seen on the lower
basin lip to find a stream descending
to Loch Sloy (N.B. *Not* the stream at
the far right-hand side of the basin).
As the stream tumbles down from the
lip, a path on its left eases the initial

steepening and passes a jumble of
giant boulders that harbour **a
labyrinth of deep fissures** – well
worth a careful look.

Below the boulders, yomp down the
grassy hillside beside the stream until
you can take an easy diagonal line
down to Loch Sloy dam. Here you'll
meet the paved road that will take you
back down Coiregrogain to your
starting point.

GiGi: The maze of fissures
passed on the Alternative
Descent is among a
number of 'underground'
features found around the
Arrochar Alps. There are
caves on The Brack, Beinn
an Lochain and A' Chrois,
numerous howffs such as
the Narnain Boulders (see
Route 2a), and more fis-
sures high on the south-
west side of Ben Vorlich
above Loch Sloy dam.

Evening at Ben Vane
summit with The Cobbler
in silhouette behind the
Bealach a' Mhaim

▲5 Ben Vorlich 229 943m/3094ft (OS 56, NN 295124)

The meaning is a problem. The *Vor* part could derive from the aspirated Gaelic *Mur* (Wall), *Muir* (Sea) or *Mor* (Big). The *lich* part could derive from an even greater variety of Gaelic words. The name is often translated as Mountain of the Sea-bag or Bag-shaped Bay (from *Muir-bhalg*), but equally possible are Big Mountain (from *Mhor-thulaich*) and Mountain of the Moor of the Hollow (from *Mhur-luig*). There's also another possibility: *Mhuirlaich* means kingfisher.

△**North Top** 931m/3055ft (OS 56, NN 294130)

BEN VORLICH

Loch Sloy

Ardlui

Inveruglas

Loch Lomond

Viewed from
Ben Lomond

Peak Fitness: No change since 1891 Tables. The North Top remains a Top despite a dip of only 27m/88ft between it and the summit (South Top).

Between Coiregrogain and Ardlui at the north end of Loch Lomond, the sprawling mass of Ben Vorlich covers about as much ground as the other three Arrochar Munros combined. It is separated from them by the trench of Loch Sloy to the west and boasts its own brand of hillwalking on **three panoramic ridges** that jut north-east, east and south-east above Loch Lomond.

The middle (east) ridge climbs over two steep cones known as the Little Hills to divide the Lomond side of the mountain into two great corries: the southern Coire na Baintighearna (*Ben-tyurna*, Lady) and the northern Coire Creagach (*Craikach*, Craggy).

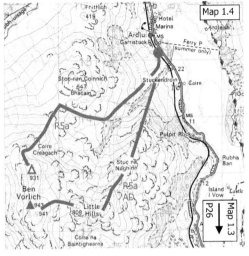

Map 1.4

The south-east ridge, which rises around the south side of Coire na Baintighearna, gives a pleasant enough ascent, yet it can hardly be recommended over the north-east ridge, which rises around the north side of Coire Creagach. An ascent of this latter ridge has the benefit of an approach path and gives you the option of returning via the east ridge over the Little Hills, so making **a scenic skyline circuit** of Coire Creagach.

Little Hills

2   1

Coire Creagach

BEN VORLICH

Loch Lomond

Ardlui

Viewed from Cnap Mor

GiGi: Do not confuse this mountain with its namesake ▲18. Such a whimsical aberration would result in a navigational indiscretion of risible proportions.

Route 5a Ben Vorlich from Ardlui
G1 *** NN 319151, 6ml/10km, 980m/3200ft

The path to the mountain begins on the A82 at the north end of Loch Lomond, at the *second* railway underpass south of and 300m from Ardlui railway station. Park in the lay-by opposite the station.

The path rises across the hillside into Coire Creagach and can be infuriatingly boggy after rain, so leave the ascent for a dry spell. Without incident, it climbs uniform slopes of grass and bracken to a small dam high up in the corrie, on the first stream that comes down from the saddle on the north-east ridge (NN 308139).

Leave the path at the dam (it soon ends anyway) and follow the stream up the grassy hillside to the saddle, situated between Ben Vorlich's North Top and Stob nan Coinnich Bhacain (*Stop nan Coan-yich Vach-kan*, poss. Peak of the Mossy Notch). The north-east ridge climbs from here to the North Top, becoming increasingly rocky with height. For a spot of easy scrambling, stay left near the rim of Coire Creagach, otherwise keep right on a path that finds easier going on more broken slopes. Beyond the ∆North Top, a short, **very pleasant sky-high stroll** takes you across a shallow saddle to the ▲summit.

BEN VORLICH   Summit   BEN LUI
                                                          BEN OSS
                                                    N Top

F-Stop: Like Ben Lomond, Ben Vorlich gives extensive views northwards across lower hills into the heart of the Southern Highlands, with the Tyndrum and Crianlarich groups prominent. Before you leave the summit area, it is worth strolling across a shallow dip to a nearby trig. point and viewpoint overlooking the vast southern reaches of Loch Lomond. For close-up views of the loch's narrow northern reaches, return via the Alternative Descent over the Little Hills.

Needlepoint: The north-east ridge route is fairly foul-weatherproof, but the Alternative Descent may prove more problematic. The craggy terrain of the Little Hills forces deviations that make it difficult to keep to the correct line.

Chilly Willy: Under normal conditions, the standard north-east ridge route gives a straightforward winter ascent for those competent on snow. Steeper snow may be encountered on the Alternative Descent.

Route 5a Alternative Descent: The Little Hills
G2 **** Add-on: zero mileage, 190m/600ft ascent M30

The middle (east) ridge on Vorlich's Lomond side divides the mountain into its two great eastern corries and sports goodly amounts of rock on its abrupt twin tops – the two Little Hills. A return over these misleadingly named protuberances adds some spice to the return trip. Hidden tiers of cliffs make for **entertaining routefinding**, although there's no difficulty once you've found the line of least resistance.

From Vorlich's summit, the ridge runs directly east before turning north-east at the second Little Hill to descend to Ardlui. The initial descent from the trig. point is quite steep, so you may prefer to take a more gentle, curving line down, trending left (north) then back right, to reach the gap below Little Hill No. 1 (Point 808 on OS map). On the descent, grass slopes give way to craggier ground where, if you're lucky, you'll come across a useful path.

On the far side of the gap, tiers of crags bar the 45m/150ft direct ascent of No. 1... And hidden over the top, on descent to the gap below No. 2, two more tiers bar the way down. The easiest line is unfailingly to the left. A steep 54m/180ft ascent from the second gap then puts you atop 793m/2601ft Little Hill No. 2 for **a stunning view over Loch Lomond**.

The ridge now turns north-east to head back down to Ardlui, steeply at first but easing off lower down. There are no more major crags to avoid, but the stepped nature of the descent makes it difficult to spot the best line except from that most frustrating of viewpoints: retrospect.

That's not to say that all the fun is over. Obstacles lower down include an electric fence (hopefully the stile is still there!) and the river that runs through the deep-cut glen below Coire Creagach. The river can normally be crossed dryshod further down, once the glen flattens out onto the moor, to regain the approach path. Good luck!

BEN LOMOND

Loch Lomond

On Little Hill No. 2

▲6 Beinn Bhuidhe 216 948m/3110ft (OS 50 or 56, NN 203187) *Ben Voo-ya*, Yellow Mountain
(probably named for the subdued colouring of its vegetation)

BEINN BHUIDHE

Viewed from
Beinn Ime

Peak Fitness: No change since 1891 Tables.

The nondescript country to the north-west of Arrochar contains only one solitary Munro and is little visited. Even Beinn Bhuidhe itself, despite being the highest point, fails to stand out on the map. It fares little better on the ground. In fact, it is difficult to see at all behind the all-encompassing high moorland that surrounds it.

But don't let that fool you into thinking the mountain is easy pickings. The approach is tiring, the summit is guarded by crags, the ascent is steep, the route is vertiginous in places, the path crosses a number of rocky steps, routefinding is complex...

In short, Beinn Bhuidhe is **one awkward customer**.

Route 6a Beinn Bhuidhe from Glen Fyne
G3 *** NN 194125, 13ml/21km, 950m/3100ft M33

The route begins with a 4½ml/7km walk along Glen Fyne, most of it on a paved private road. There's a car park at the beginning of the road, just off the A83 at the head of Loch Fyne. The walk follows the river all the way, passing flat green fields between steep grassy hillsides. **Choose to enjoy it** - you won't be seeing Beinn Bhuidhe's retiring summit for some time yet.

After 3ml/5km, the paved road crosses the river to climb to a hidden reservoir. Leave it at this point to stay on the near (west) bank, where a Land Rover track continues to the locked bothy at Inverchorachan, at the foot of the mountain. At a gate just beyond the bothy, the climb to the summit begins on the near (south) bank of the Allt na Faing (*Owlt na Fank*, Stream of the Sheep Fank or Enclosure).

A path climbs steeply beside the stream into a small gorge, where it becomes quite exposed on steep grass slopes. Above, a two-tiered waterfall tumbles from the skyline. Bhuidhe's summit, of course, remains well out of sight above there. The path negotiates a few rocky steps as it clings to the side of the gorge and, just before a levelling at the foot of the waterfall, **a granny stopper of a rock outcrop** may well give sensitive souls pause for thought. (NB It's not at all difficult.)

The path surmounts the waterfall by climbing diagonally left of it then cutting back right to the riverbank above, after which it leaves the Allt na Faing for good to veer left again into an ill-defined, knolly, confusing corrie. The path becomes indistinct but you

The Rock Outcrop

should be able to follow it up to a broad grassy shelf at the foot of the craggy south-east face of Beinn Bhuidhe's north-east ridge.

As you face the face, the summit is up there to the left somewhere (still hidden of course), while to the right is a bealach between the summit and a minor north-east top (Point 901 on OS 1:50,000 map). The route to the ridge crest lies straight ahead, via a steep grassy gully that twists its way up to an obvious nick on the skyline. Once into the gully, a developing path will give you confidence that it does in-deed *go*, and there's a cairn at the top to doubly convince you that you're on the right track.

On the skyline, a better path continues up the ridge but the going remains stiff, with the summit still playing hide and seek above. The path runs across grass slopes below (left of) the knobbly ridge crest and is quite exposed in parts above steep drops. Only when you run out of ground to ascend can you be assured that you're finally at the ▲summit.

NE Ridge

Top of gully

On the return trip, a descent of the gully can be avoided by continuing past its top to the bealach at the foot of the ridge, below the north-east top. Beyond the cairn at the top of the gully, the path switches from one side of the ridge crest to the other and continues all the way down to the bealach, from where you can at last look back and gain some perspective on what the summit actually looks like.

The route down from the bealach is complex (no change there, then), carries no more than occasional traces of path and requires constant shifts of direction to avoid hidden craglets. In its favour, it is much less steep than the grassy gully route and, with that bring-it-on spirit we know you have in you, can be fun.

Lower down, rejoin the outward path above the waterfall and look forward to yet more fun on the granny stopper and the stroll out.

F-Stop: The view from such an isolated peak is extensive, although there is little to see to the south except moor and sea-loch. To the west, the Loch Awe Munros are prominent, while eastern and northern views give unfamiliar perspectives on the backsides of the Arrochar Alps and the Tyndrum Munros.

BEINN BHUIDHE

NE Ridge

Needlepoint: Beinn Bhuidhe's summit shies away atop such complex terrain that a direct approach is difficult even in *good* visibility. The path helps, but it is indistinct in parts and, if cloud obscures the grassy gully that is the key to reaching the north-east ridge, you're going to have problems. This is one mountain whose ascent is best left for fair weather .

Chilly Willy: If Beinn Bhuidhe is an awkward little mountain in summer, it is doubly so in winter. Not only is routefinding far more complex when the path is under snow, but you'll face major problems higher up. The grassy gully becomes a snow climb and the exposed slopes of the upper north-east ridge require care above considerable drops.

Terminator: When the paved approach road crosses the River Fyne after 2ml/3km, a wooded ravine splits the hillside to the east. Above this ravine, hidden from sight, is **Eagle's Fall**, a 50m/160ft waterfall that would be a major tourist attraction were it less awkward to reach. Some of the water is today diverted into Loch Sloy reservoir, but anyone in search of adventure will still find a visit worthwhile. Not to say challenging. **Fancy a spot of canyoneering?** After surmounting the ravine, the only way to reach the waterfall is by scrambling up the bed of the stream.

2 TYNDRUM

North of the Arrochar Alps and west of the A82 Crianlarich-Tyndrum road, half-hidden behind lower hills, a twisting east-west line of four Munros forms one of the most distinctive mountain groups in the Southern Highlands. Ben Lui, the highest of the four peaks, is a **Southern Highland classic**, of such superior stature that its neighbours suffer by comparison.

Hillwalking in the group is similarly diverse, with both some of the hardest and some of the easiest routes on offer in the whole region. Ben Lui is the main draw and has ascent routes

to satisfy all tastes. Its dull but straightforward western slopes carry the standard ascent route and enable the adjacent satellite Munro of Beinn a' Chleibh to be bagged without much further ado while you're up there (Route 7a). For those seeking more adventure and excitement, an ascent from the east will meet all requirements (Route 7b).

Like Beinn a' Chleibh, the two other Tyndrum Munros (Ben Oss and Beinn Dubhchraig) are overshadowed by Ben Lui but can conveniently be climbed together via their high intervening bealach (Route 9a).

Ben Lui viewed 'in winter raiment'

▲**7 Ben Lui** 28 1130m/3707ft (OS 50, NN 266263)
Ben Loo-y, Calf Mountain (from Gaelic *Laoigh*) or Lead Mountain (from Gaelic *Luaidhe*). Both meanings have claim, although the mountain was named before Tyndrum became a lead mining village in the eighteenth century. Some profess to see the shape of a horned calf in Lui's twin summits, but the name Calf Mountain most likely derives from times when cattle were a mainstay of clan life.

▲**8 Beinn a' Chleibh** 281 916m/3005ft (OS 50, NN 250256)
Ben a Chlave, Mountain of the Creel or Basket

Peak Fitness: No change to existing Munros since original 1891 Tables, although Ben Lui's north-west top has courted controversy in recent years. It erroneously became a Munro in 1974, at the expense of the nearby south-east top (the true summit). Once the error was discovered, it was demoted to Top status in 1981 and deleted completely from the Tables in 1997, after 23 glorious but spurious years in the Big League. This has left no extant Tops in the whole Tyndrum Group.

Ben Lui is one dramatic mountain, of such character that **it begs to be climbed**. Take one glance at it from the east, from near Dalrigh on the A82 Crianlarich-Tyndrum road, and you'll be hooked. Its height, symmetry and isolation, especially when seen 'in winter raiment' (as old-style guidebooks used to say), give it a positively **Himalayan grandeur**. We kid you not.

The Munro larges it over its hinterland at the end of lengthy Glen Cononish, sporting **airy twin tops** that drop steep ridges to enclose Coire Gaothach (*Corra Geu-ich*, Windy Corrie). From the bowl of the corrie, Central Gully rises to the skyline between the two tops.

The south-east top (the left-hand top when viewed from Dalrigh) is the summit. The ridge that drops from it, bounding Coire Gaothach on the left, is the corrie's south-east arm. The ridge that drops from the north-west (right-hand) top, bounding Coire Gaothach on the right, is the corrie's north-west arm. Both arms give adventurous ascent routes, while to each side of Coire Gaothach are smaller corries bounded by easier ridges: the enjoyable north-west ridge and the gentle south-east ridge (which connects Lui to Ben Oss).

The 'backside' of the mountain, above Glen Lochy to the west, is less impressive. Let's be blunt: its uniform grass slopes are determinedly dull. Not coincidentally, the most straightforward ascent route is found here (Route 7a). And there's more... an approach from this side makes lowly Beinn a' Chleibh, little more than a flat-topped appendage on Lui's featureless western flanks, a readily baggable add-on.

There's no question, though, that as long as you don't suffer from vertigo, the longer eastern approach from Dalrigh gives a correspondingly more rewarding ascent (Route 7b). Beinn a' Chleibh is a more awkward add-on from this side, but you could always leave that for another day. Some mountains deserve to be seen at their best. Ben Lui is one of them.

Torpedo: Dalrigh is the starting point not only for the classic approach to Ben Lui but also for the ascent of the group's two other Munros - Ben Oss and Beinn Dubhchraig (Route 9a). Lui is separated from Oss by such an easy bealach that the three mountains could be climbed on the same trip (plus Chleibh?) to make a memorable round (see Route 9a Extension 1 on Page 60). Pardon? Of course you can.

BEN LUI

Coire an t-Sneachda

Stob Garbh

Coire Gaothach

Stob an Tighe Aird

Viewed from Ben Oss

GiGi: Tyndrum (*Tyne-drum*, from the Gaelic *Tigh an Druim*) means House on the Ridge. Dalrigh (*Dal-ree*, from the Gaelic *Dal Righ*) means King's Field. During his long campaign to impose himself as King of Scotland, Robert Bruce fought the MacDougalls of Lorn here in 1306. And lost.

He didn't get his own back until a rematch on the slopes of Ben Cruachan two years later. Lochan nan Arm (Lochan of the Weapon), on the south side of the River Cononish, derives its name from the legend that, during the retreat, Bruce threw his sword into it.

Route 7a Ben Lui and Beinn a' Chleibh from Glen Lochy (western approach: Fionn Choirein) NN 239278

Ben Lui and Beinn a' Chleibh: G2 *** 7ml/11km, 1100m/3600ft
Beinn a' Chleibh alone (for the pure of heart who have already climbed
Ben Lui by Route 7b): G2 * 5ml/8km, 730m/2400ft

The western approach route offers the shortest way up Lui but manages to avoid completely all the best scenery. We give it a three-star rating for the summit environs, but only if you promise to **sit awhile at the cairn and meditate on why you came up this way**. However, unless you're allergic to the touch of rock beneath your fingers, you can go some way to redressing the balance of missing out on the east side of the mountain by taking a scrambly detour up the enjoyable north-west ridge (see Alternative Approach).

On their west sides, the summits of Ben Lui and Beinn a' Chleibh enclose the deep green bowl of Fionn Choirein (*Fyoon Chorran*, White Corrie). The corrie's main stream flows into another stream, confusingly named the Eas Daimh (*Aiss Daff*, Stag Waterfall), which eventually enters the River Lochy in Glen Lochy. Near the confluence with the Lochy, 6½ml/10km west of Tyndrum on the A85 road through the glen, the route begins at a Munro baggers' car park.

Both Munros rise stoutly out of the forest above the car park. Lui's north-

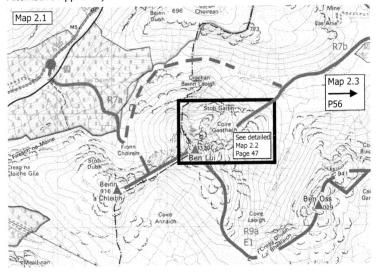

west top appears as a steep pyramid, hiding the true summit. Chleibh appears as a bold grassy dome encrusted with crags above Fionn Choirein. The forest and crags dictate that the only practicable route up Chleibh is via the corrie and the bealach between the two Munros.

Separating car park from open ground is a variety of obstacles: the River Lochy, the West Highland Railway line and blanket forestry cover. A grassy path runs down to the river and along the bank to the confluence with the Eas Daimh. Unless the water is very low, the only way to cross the River Lochy is to paddle.

Tip: Carry your boots down to the river and cross it in old trainers, then boot up and leave your trainers for the return crossing. NB There is a footbridge ½ml/1km downstream, but using it would necessitate a frustrating detour and an illegal walk back along the railway line.

On the far bank of the river, the railway line bridges the Eas Daimh. Paddle under the bridge (it is illegal to cross the line) to find a well-worn path along the left-hand (north) bank of the Eas Daimh between forest and stream. Don't just put your head down and walk or you'll miss an important path fork after c.400m, where the tributary stream descending from Fionn Choirein leaps into the Eas Daimh at a small waterfall.

While the left-hand path continues along the Eas Daimh, the right-hand path heads for Ben Lui, crossing the Eas Daimh on stepping stones and climbing the left-hand side of the tributary stream all the way to the upper forest fence (NN 249266) and into Fionn Choirein.

Like most paths of its ilk, it is amusingly boggy in parts. That said, it is nowhere near as glutinous as the Beinn Dubhchraig path (Route 9a), while numerous small cascades offer distraction. NB At the time of writing, the Forestry Commission hopes to upgrade the whole route.

After exiting the forest at the 470m/1550ft contour, you find yourself in the bowl of Fionn Choirein, where the going improves dramatically. There's even a large wooden monolith, like something out of the film *2001*, to welcome you to Ben Lui National Nature Reserve.

To the left, grassy slopes rise to Ben Lui's north-west ridge. To the right is the precipitous north-east face of Beinn a' Chleibh. On the skyline ahead is the bealach between the two Munros. The improved path continues up beside the stream into the upper corrie. You can follow it all the way to the bealach or opt instead to climb Ben Lui's north-west ridge (see Alternative Approach).

To avoid steep terrain, the path doesn't head directly for the bealach, but instead climbs well left beside a minor stream before cutting back right across easier ground. It becomes indistinct on wet ground in the upper corrie but improves again to make the final diagonal climb up to the bealach.

On the bealach itself, the path splits – left to Lui and right to Chleibh. We suggest you climb Lui first, as it's quite a slog, and leave the quick jaunt up Chleibh for later. The 370m/1200ft climb up Lui's broad south-west shoulder begins well on grass and rocks but deteriorates higher up on steep, stony ground that requires determination.

The path emerges onto the skyline at the dip between the twin tops for **a sudden and dramatic change of scenery**. Beneath your feet, over the lip of Central Gully, is the abyss of Coire Gaothach.

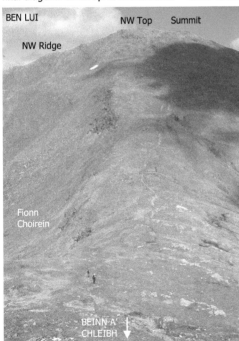

To the left is the north-west top. To the right, crowned by a large cairn, is the castellated chunk of rock that forms the 3m/10ft higher ▲summit (south-east top). You'll want to spend some time here.

After returning to the bealach, you'll find Beinn a' Chleibh so easy to bag that you'll almost begrudge its status as a Munro. Surely they shouldn't be this easy?

Follow the obvious path 160m/500ft up the broad, grassy north-east ridge to the flat ▲summit, then retrace steps to the bealach. Now... look forward with renewed vigour to that fun re-descent through the forest.

F-Stop: As befits such an outstanding peak, Ben Lui's rocky summit eyrie commands **extensive views** in all directions. Most prominent are the Arrochar Alps to the south, the Crianlarich hills to the east, Ben Cruachan to the west and Glen Coe and Ben Nevis to the north.

From the summit of Beinn a' Chleibh, you can stroll north-west across the summit plateau, following cairns, to an uninterrupted view of Cruachan and the other Loch Awe Munros.

Needlepoint: If you can stay on the path, the route is fairly foul-weatherproof. Routefinding difficulties occur mainly when low cloud hangs in upper Fionn Choirein, where the path is indistinct. If you try to reach the bealach without the aid of the path, you could easily end up on steep, craggy ground that could lead anywhere!

Chilly Willy: The Fionn Choirein approach to Ben Lui poses no specific problems in winter, but that doesn't necessarily mean it is a straightforward ascent option. Without a path to follow, you'll most likely face steep exposed snow on the corrie's headwall and again on the approach to the summit of the mountain. There is no doubt, however, about what constitutes the most enervating part of the route: the **icy paddle** across the River Lochy.

In a good winter, **a mighty cornice** forms at the deeply incised head of Coire Gaothach's Central Gully. Take care near the lip to avoid inadvertently stepping over the abyss.

Route 7a Alternative Approach: Ben Lui North-west Ridge

G3 **** No extra mileage or ascent M40

If you deem the eastern approach to Ben Lui from Dalrigh (Route 7b) to be outwith your comfort zone, yet nevertheless enjoy a spot of clambering over rock, you'll find the north-west ridge **the most enjoyable ridge on the mountain**. Its upper section rises in a fine situation between Fionn Choirein and Coire an Lochain (Corrie of the Lochan), a high little corrie that separates Fionn Choirein from Coire Gaothach. Best of all, a couple of rock steps, neither difficult nor exposed, nor barely rating a scramble, add spice to the ascent.

In its lower reaches, the ridge broadens onto two huge buttresses, one above the other, fancifully known as Ciochan Beinn Laoigh (*Kee-ochan*,

Breasts). Don't worry – you'll join the ridge well above these. Once out of the forest in Fionn Choirein, instead of following the continuing path up the corrie, bear left and go straight up the grassy hillside to reach the skyline at the foot of the upper ridge. It's a pretty relentless ascent but, once you're on the ridge, a good path runs all the way up to Lui's north-west top, giving good views over Coire an Lochain to the steep north-west arm of Coire Gaothach.

With those couple of crampon-scratched rock steps to add to the fun, the main drawback to the ascent is its brevity. NB The north-west ridge is also an ascent option from Dalrigh (see Route 7b Option 2 on Page 49).

BEN LUI
NW Top

NW Arm

NW Ridge

rock step

Needlepoint: In cloud, the grassy hillside that climbs to the north-west ridge requires precise navigation if you hope to hit the skyline at the right point. Routefinding on the ridge itself remains pretty straightforward, but the route as a whole is best saved for a fine day.

Chilly Willy: In winter it can be easier to climb to the north-west ridge than to the bealach at the head of Fionn Choirein, but the ridge itself may well sport exposed snow slopes and iced rock. The crampon scratches on the rock steps are not there for no reason.

Route 7b Ben Lui alone from Dalrigh (near Tyndrum) (eastern approach via Glen Cononish and Coire Gaothach)

G2, G3, G4 or G5 ***** NN 344291, 11½ml/18km, 950/3100ft M40

Okay, so it's a longer walk-in. Okay, so you'll probably want to leave Beinn a' Chleibh for another day. Okay, so there are some routefinding decisions to be made. It's worth it. The eastern approach to Ben Lui is **the classic approach**. The Land Rover track that leads to the foot of the mountain is infinitely less aggravating than the current path through the forest from Glen Lochy, imposing Coire Gaothach is in front of you the whole way and you'll have a choice of four scenic ascent options, ranging from easy to hard.

From the car park at Dalrigh, just off the A82 2ml/3km east of Tyndrum, the route begins with a 4½ml/7km walk-in along Glen Cononish, following a Land Rover track to a height of 350m/1150ft on Lui's north-east flank below Coire Gaothach. (A second route in from Tyndrum Lower Station at NN 327301 joins this track after a couple of miles but requires more uphill/downhill work on both outward and return journeys.)

The track begins at Dalrigh House, a short distance down a paved road below the car park. Immediately beyond the house, the track forks.

Both branches cross a stream and rejoin, but it is better to stay right as only that branch carries a bridge (but see Baffies on Page 53).

At first, views of Ben Lui are obscured by Beinn Dubhchraig's northern shoulder, but there are good views of Dubhchraig itself, seen across the pine trees of Coille Coire Chuilc. That all changes after a couple of miles, on approach to Cononish Farm, where a sign marks the entrance to Ben Lui National Nature Reserve and the whole symmetrical north-east face of the mountain presents itself for your delectation.

At the centre, beneath the twin tops, is Coire Gaothach and its enclosing south-east and north-west arms, but on a dull day or if the sun is in your eyes these can be difficult to distinguish.

BEN LUI

The ridges that form both left and right skylines lie outwith the corrie. The gentle left-hand skyline is the south-east ridge (connecting to Ben Oss), while the similar right-hand skyline is the north-west ridge.

The two arms of the corrie drop more steeply towards you, terminating abruptly at rocky noses that form portals at the corrie entrance. On the left, the south-east arm drops from the summit to Stob an Tighe Aird (*Stop an Ty Airj*, Peak of the House on the Point – now a ruined building at the foot of the mountain). On the right, the north-west arm drops from the north-west top to the more prominent rocky pyramid of Stob Garbh (*Stop Garrav*, Rough Peak).

Beyond Cononish Farm, the track rises gradually across the hillside well above the river. As it draws nearer to the mountain, the crags of Coire Gaothach, framed by the two Stobs,

become increasingly foreshortened, while the summit becomes ever more **neck-craningly imposing**.

When the track ends at the Allt an Rund, cross the stream on stepping stones and continue up the hillside ahead on a good baggers' path right of the Allt Coire Gaothach (the stream that comes down from its eponymous corrie). The path climbs into the sloping bowl of the crag-bound corrie – **a true high mountain sanctuary** that, if we're being picky, lacks only flat ground and a lochan to make it a truly outstanding spot.

On each side, the corrie's embracing arms climb to Lui's twin tops. Each arm can be reached relatively easily at its low point, immediately behind its respective Stob, but which way to go? There are in fact *four* ways to reach the ▲summit, all of which carry paths of varying difficulty: see Options opposite.

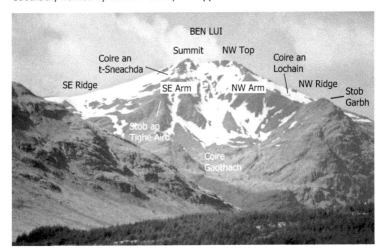

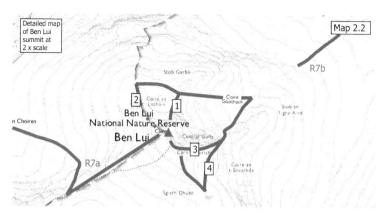

Option 1: North-west Arm Direct (G3). The north-west (right-hand) arm is regarded as the standard ascent route. The path up it is steep, stony and exposed, but it keeps you close to the scenery and requires no more than minor handwork.

Option 2: North-west Ridge via Coire an Lochain (G3). The north-west ridge lies over the right-hand skyline, beyond the north-west arm, on the far side of hidden Coire an Lochain. It is gentler and less exposed than the north-west arm, with a couple of easy rock steps to add interest.

Option 3: South-east Arm Direct (G4/G5). For expert scramblers in search of an adrenaline rush, the south-east (left-hand) arm gives a gravity-defying ascent up the narrow rock rib that separates Coire Gaothach from a hidden eastern corrie (Coire an t-Sneachda).

Option 4: South-east Ridge via Coire an t-Sneachda (G2). The easiest ascent route out of Coire Gaothach traverses left of the south-east arm to find an easy way up over the left-hand skyline via hidden Coire an t-Sneachda.

Which option to choose?

If you're in search of a testing scramble, consider going up the SE Arm Direct (Option 3) and down the NW Ridge (Option 2). If you enjoy a spot of handwork but nothing too demanding, and you don't mind a bit of exposure, go up the NW Arm Direct (Option 1) and down the NW Ridge (Option 2). If you want to avoid as much exposure and rockwork as possible, go up and down via Coire an t-Sneachda (Option 4), but take a look down the NW Arm (Option 1) and the NW Ridge (Option 2) and consider them as possible descent routes. To help you in your decision, we describe each option in detail.

Option 1: North-west Arm Direct (G3) M47

From the floor of Coire Gaothach, your first objective is the low point on the right-hand skyline, at the head of an open gully of grass and rocks behind Stob Garbh. There's a side path to the gully, but it is non-existent at first and therefore difficult to locate.

After reaching Coire Gaothach, the stream splits and, just above the confluence, the main path you've followed from the Allt an Rund crosses the main stream. At this crossing,

you've already missed the line of the side path to the gully 100m back. To find it, leave the main path at the stream crossing and climb the hillside on the right.

The side path makes a diagonal beeline for the top of the gully on grassy slopes to its right. Nearing the skyline, it no longer has any choice but to enter the steep, stony gully itself, but the going is neither exposed nor difficult and the skyline cairn is reached without much ado.

BEN LUI
NW Top
Summit
NW Ridge
SE Arm
Coire an Lochain
Coire Gaothach
NW Arm

Once on the skyline, the view west opens up over the small lochan-floored Coire an Lochain to Lui's north-west ridge, with Ben Cruachan visible beyond. Above, the north-west arm rears up to the north-west top, promising **an adventurous finish to**

the ascent. The path is steep, stony and occasionally exposed above big drops left into Coire Gaothach. With lots of rock around, there are one or two places where hands will prove useful. It's not difficult, but it requires care and concentration. The ridge tops out near the north-west top for a short walk to the ▲summit.

Note on descent: If you descend this way, the gritty path requires even more care than on ascent, and the fact that you'll be looking over the drops adds to the feeling of exposure. You may well discover backside holds you missed on the way up. If you don't fancy it, you'll have more fun going down the north-west ridge (Option 2) and crossing Coire an Lochain to regain the path at the low point on the skyline near the top of Stob Garbh.

Stob Garbh

Looking down
The NW Arm

Option 2: North-west Ridge via Coire an Lochain (G3)
NN 265267, unnamed on OS 1:50,000 map M47

The north-west ridge lies across Coire an Lochain from the north-west arm. Compared to the latter, its angle is more gentle, there is less exposure and the path is more stable. A couple of rock steps require handwork, but they are easy, clean and non-exposed. Although technically harder than anything on the north-west arm, they are decidedly less unnerving than some sections of that route's gritty, exposed path. In fact they're fun.

After climbing from Coire Gaothach to the low point on the right-hand skyline, as described in Option 1, cross grassy Coire an Lochain with its tiny lochan to reach the upper north-west ridge (described as Route 7a Alternative Approach on Page 44).

Option 3: South-east Arm Direct (G4/G5) M47

The direct ascent of the south-east arm of Coire Gaothach gives **a pulse-pumping scramble** on the edge of the abyss. If you're an adrenaline junkie in search of excitement, as well as an experienced scrambler immune to exposure, this might be the one for you.

Caution: This is no place to practice rock skills. Expect loose rock, gritty stances and great exposure. As the ground is occasionally vegetated and the path loose, avoid when wet and manky (the route, not you).

SE Arm
upper section

Your first objective is the low point on the left-hand skyline, at the far left-hand corner of the corrie, at the very foot of the steep south-east arm. In the bowl of Coire Gaothach, the main path crosses the main stream and heads for that very spot. It soon becomes indistinct but, if you lose it, you'll pick it up again higher up. It climbs steep grass slopes left of a boulder ruckle to a short grass ramp, clearly seen from below, which cuts back left onto the low point of the skyline. You may choose to use hands for balance on the steep grass but it's not difficult.

Once on the skyline, the rocky south-east arm towers overhead. The ascent begins on a gritty path that climbs steeply to the foot of a nose of outcrops and vegetated ledges. The crest (G5) has the cleanest rock but is hard and very exposed above Coire Gaothach. The path (G4) manages to find an easier route to the left, away from the edge, but it too is exposed and loose enough in places to concentrate the mind.

Above the nose, the path climbs an easier central section of ridge, passing abysmal drops, to reach the foot of a final rock band immediately beneath the summit. On this final section, the rock is cleaner and generally less exposed, giving a more entertaining scramble than down below. Much of it requires little more than G3 handwork, but there's a sting in the tail of two rock steps, one immediately above the other. Both are easy scrambles of only a few moves, and the scratched rock is clean and mottled – would that it were so lower down. The first step is steep but not exposed; the second is easier but more exposed. The summit lies just above.

Glen Cononish

Looking down The SE Arm

Stob an Tighe Aird

Coire Gaothach

Option 4: South-east Ridge via Coire an t-Sneachda (G2)
NN 269262, unnamed on OS 1:50,000 map M47

The easiest route from Coire Gaothach to Lui's summit climbs left of the south-east arm into hidden Coire an t-Sneachda (*Corran Drechka*, Snow Corrie). First reach the low point on the skyline of the south-east arm, as for Option 3. From here, a distinct path traverses left across easy slopes of grass and rocks below crags into the shallow basin of Coire an t-Sneachda. Continuing across the corrie in the same direction, the path climbs an open, grassy gully to a levelling on the south-east ridge, from where easy slopes of grass among boulders lead to the summit.

The summit of Ben Lui

Needlepoint: In Coire Gaothach in cloud, it is better to be safe than sorry. The only well-defined path is that up the north-west arm (Option 1).Take note of the route on the way up so that you can follow it on the way down. If you've come up by one of the alternative ascents, a few pointers may prove useful on descent.

After crossing from the summit to the north-west top, continue c.20m further along the cliff edge in the same direction. Here you'll find a flattened cairn, and another one less than 20m beyond that.

From the second cairn, the path cuts back diagonally down shattered ground to the crest of the north-west arm. At the foot of the steep stuff, before the short ascent to Stob Garbh, a small cairn marks the start of the path down to Coire Gaothach (see pic on Page 49).

Chilly Willy: Coire Gaothach in winter is **a magical place** but a cul-de-sac for non-climbers. On any attempt to climb out of it, any or all of these may be encountered: avalanche danger, steep snow and iced rock in exposed situations and corniced exits onto the low points of the south-east and north-west arms. Even the easiest summer route (Option 4) involves a very steep snow climb to the low point on the south-east arm, followed by an exposed traverse to Coire an t-Sneachda.

The easiest winter route is in fact the north-west ridge (Option 2), but even that involves another very steep (possibly corniced) snow climb to the low point on the north-west arm and, once you've crossed to the ridge itself, more steep snow and ice-glaze on the rock steps.

A good time to visit Coire Gaothach is springtime, when there is still snow in Central Gully but not on the corrie's two bounding arms. The floor of the corrie is often carpeted with avalanche debris from the great cornice that forms at the head of Central Gully. The 1891 ascent of the gully by members of the newly formed Scottish Mountaineering Club traditionally marks the beginning of winter climbing in the Highlands.

Route 7b Extension 1: Beinn a' Chleibh
G1 ** Add-on: 3½ml/6km, 160m/500ft M40

As Beinn a' Chleibh lies west of Ben Lui, it is not readily appended to an ascent of Lui from Dalrigh to the east. We nevertheless describe it for the benefit of those who reach Lui's summit with energy to squander and motivation to spare. Of course, a continuation to Chleibh would entail missing one of the interesting descent routes from Lui into Coire Gaothach...

From the dip between Lui's summit and north-west top, descend the path down the south-west shoulder to the bealach below Beinn a' Chleibh and follow the path to the ▲summit as described in Route 7a. Return to the bealach and descend the path into Fionn Choirein but, instead of following it all the way down to the forest, traverse right across the grassy hillside above the trees.

Eventually you'll reach the bealach at the head of the Eas Daimh, beyond which the gentle green glen of the Allt an Rund will lead you down to the start of the Land Rover track back to the car park at Dalrigh.

The path up Beinn a' Chleibh

GiGi: Above Cononish Farm, on the south-east shoulder of Beinn a' Chuirn (*Ben a Choorn*, Mountain of the Cairn), are the remains of some old mines. Lead was first worked in the Tyndrum area in 1739 and last worked in 1925. In the 1980s and 1990s, gold was also discovered in the area. Plans to re-open the Cononish mine for gold extraction were approved by Loch Lomond national park in 2011, with the first gold production taking place in 2014.

Some regard the workings as an eyesore, but we like the notion of passing Scotland's only gold mine *en route* to our Munro. And it might be worth your while taking a peek in any burns you cross...

To the left of the mine is a deep dark gorge containing a hanging waterfall (the Eas Anie), which according to Chilly Willy makes a good winter ice climb.

Baffies: At the junction of tracks near Dalrigh House, the unbridged branch leads to a fine stretch of the River Cononish, complete with pools and cascades that are **very seductive** on a hot day.

Try it on the return trip... or for a short afternoon stroll from the car park. The unbridged tributary stream that the track fords can usually be crossed dryshod on stepping stones.

▲9 Ben Oss 101 1029m/3376ft (OS 50, NN 287253)
Elk Mountain (The last elk in the Highlands disappeared more than 700 years ago)
▲10 Beinn Dubhchraig 175 978m/3209ft (OS 50, NN 307254) *Ben Doo-chraik*, Black Crag Mountain

Peak Fitness: No change since 1891 Tables.

When travelling along the A82 from Crianlarich to Tyndrum, you may be forgiven for not giving this pair a second glance. That **squashed pudding of a hill** lurking in the shadow of majestic Ben Lui can't be a Munro, can it? Indeed it can. You're looking at the mountain-out-of-a-molehill that is Beinn Dubhchraig. Barely more exciting Ben Oss cowers sheepishly behind it, equally overawed by Lui's presence.

BEN OSS   BEINN DUBHCHRAIG

Viewed from the south

The duo's best features lie on their hidden south side, where their connecting ridge, fringed by crags, forms a horseshoe around remote Loch Oss. Unfortunately the walk-in to the loch is long, featureless and pathless, and can scarcely be recommended over the northern approach from Dalrigh near Tyndrum.

It's a shame, because the northern view hardly sets the spirits soaring. And there's worse. We're talking bog. Not just any old bog. We're talking **Slough of Despond**. After rain the going is execrable. Until the approach path is replaced by an escalator, you may prefer to leave the bagging of the two Munros for a drought.

On the plus side, the bealach between the two mountains is high enough to facilitate a joint bagging trip, while the connecting ridge and its views would merit more stars were it not for the demerit of reaching it.

Route 9a Ben Oss and Beinn Dubhchraig from Dalrigh

G3 ** Route Rage Alert NN 344291, 10½ml/17km, 1170m/3850ft M56
(*** if you have a helicopter to bypass the approach wallow)

Begin at Dalrigh car park (as for Route 7b). Steps at the far end of the car park descend to a road that leads to a bridge over the River Cononish. On the far side of the bridge, turn immediately right on a Land Rover track that leads to a bridge over the West Highland Railway line at NN 336285.

On the far side of the railway bridge, a boggy path branches right to a footbridge over the Allt Gleann Auchreoch at NN 333284. You can avoid the boggy going by continuing up the track to a left-hand bend, from where drier paths lead back down to the footbridge. On the other hand, you might as well accustom yourself to the boggy stuff now.

On the far side of the footbridge, a path goes up the right-hand side of the Allt Gleann Auchreoch and then the right-hand side of the Allt Coire Dubhchraig, climbing all the way through Coire Dubhchraig to two lochans on Beinn Dubhchraig's summit ridge. We trust your boots are waterproof and advise you to **pack a snorkel**. If you want to detour around the worst of the bog, check out the Alternative Approach.

The sodden path passes through the **beautiful old pine forest** of Coille Coire Chuilc (*Cull-ya Corra Cool-ak*,

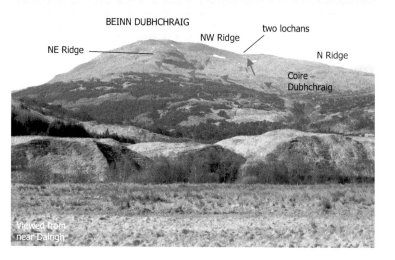

BEINN DUBHCHRAIG

two lochans

NW Ridge

NE Ridge

N Ridge

Coire Dubhchraig

Viewed from near Dalrigh

Wood of the Reedy Corrie), although, conditions underfoot being as they are, you may find its beautiful oldness hard to appreciate. You may find it even harder to understand how Dubhchraig acquired its imposing name (the 'black crag' is on the south side of the mountain).

The underfoot morass deteriorates still further as you leave the wood and climb through newer forestry plantations. When the trees finally begin to thin out at their upper boundary, don't let quagmires draw you away from the streamside path as it makes its way into the vast open spaces of shallow Coire Dubhchraig.

Here at last matters start to improve. The stream itself forms **an attractive series of cascades** as it drops over a long staircase of ledges. The path remains boggy in parts but

feels like baked earth compared to what you've just negotiated.

Should you have made it this far, there is a choice of ways out of the corrie. Dubhchraig's summit is on the left, at the head of the north-east ridge, but the path follows the stream right to climb diagonally across the corrie to two skyline lochans at the junction of north and north-west ridges. The path has one steep section beside a waterfall before it peters out near the lochans, from where an indistinct path continues up the broad north-west ridge to the summit.

The shorter north-east ridge, which starts steeply but eases with height, carries no more than traces of path but is equally easy and has better views and better going on grass and boulders. In addition, by ascending this way, you won't have to retrace

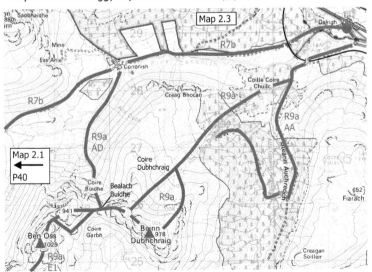

steps to reach Ben Oss.

At the gentle ▲summit you can put all thoughts of the boggy approach behind you, enjoy the view and prepare for more interesting fare. The north-west ridge descends to the two lochans and divides. To the right, the easy north ridge rims the west side of Coire Dubhchraig, while to the left the craggy west ridge drops steeply to the bealach below Ben Oss. Seen from here, Ben Oss's steeper slopes give it a shapelier outline than Beinn Dubhchraig, but it remains a heap compared to the ever more unlikely shark's fin of Ben Lui behind it.

A stony path winds down the west ridge among the rocks. There are one or two places where you'll find hands useful, but the descent is without

difficulty, much easier than it seems from above. The bealach is the Bealach Buidhe (*Byalach Boo-ya*, Yellow Pass, 820m/2700ft), named after the corrie to its north although unnamed on the OS map. On its far side, the 270m/700ft climb to the summit of Ben Oss offers a choice of two ways up.

The obvious route goes straight up the north-east ridge, on steep grass whose angle eases with height. The main path takes a less obvious route, initially making a rising traverse left into Coire Garbh (*Corra Garrav*, Rough Corrie), a high little corrie floored by a reedy lochan on the east side of the mountain. From here, a less distinct path climbs grass slopes beside a stream to the low point on the skyline,

See also pic on Page xxiv

BEN OSS

NE top

BEN LUI

Coire Garbh

Bealach Buidhe

BEINN DUBHCHRAIG

between the summit and a minor north-east top (Point 941 on OS map).

The two routes join here for the final climb up a stony path to the small plateau ▲summit. Which route to choose? We'd go up via the corrie and down by the north-east ridge (the path between corrie and bealach is harder to find on descent).

To return to Dalrigh, there are more choices to be made. The usual option is to re-climb the 80m/250ft from the Bealach Buidhe to the two lochans on Dubhchraig's north-west ridge then re-descend the approach path. If you choose this option, it is unlikely that you will view with relish the prospect of revisiting the Slough of Despond, so you'll need no recommendation from us to avoid it via the Alternative Approach (Page 59). A second, off-path option is to descend from the Bealach Buidhe into Glen Cononish (see Alternative Descent, Page 60).

BEN OSS

BEN LUI

BEINN
DUBHCHRAIG

Chilly Willy: When the boggy ground is hardened by frost, Beinn Dubhchraig is one of those estimable mountains whose ascent is made less taxing by winter conditions. The generally easy-angled terrain makes the mountain **a good winter training ground for beginners**.

Patches of steep (perhaps cramponnable) snow may be encountered on both the north-east ridge and the main path out of Coire Dubhchraig, but there is no great exposure. The slopes leading up to the north ridge, on the west side of the corrie, offer an even more benign way up.

The continuation to Ben Oss is a more serious proposition, with steep, icy drop-offs that are definitely no place for the inexperienced.

Needlepoint: These are dreary hills to climb in cloud. The junction of Beinn Dubhchraig's north and north-west ridges, in the vicinity of the two ridge-top lochans, is a prime location for routefinding error. The featureless, knolly terrain here calls for expert navigation.

F-Stop: In defence of these maligned mountains, it must be said that the summit of Bheinn Dubhchraig offers **sublime views** of Ben Lomond and Loch Lomond, while the summit of Ben Oss offers **dramatic close-ups** of Ben Lui's vertiginous ridges.

Route 9a Alternative Approach (avoiding the Slough of Despond)
Add-on: 2ml/3km in each direction, zero extra ascent M56

The Land Rover track that crosses the West Highland Railway line at the start of the route becomes a forest track that climbs almost all the way to the upper forest boundary in Coire Dubhchraig. It makes a long, sweeping, easy-angled ascent that adds a couple of miles to the ascent/descent, but you'll probably cover that extra distance anyway in order to avoid bog on the time-dishonoured traditional route. Most people take the traditional route on ascent, but on descent it's surprising how those extra couple of miles suddenly don't seem to matter so much.

To find the track on descent, cross the Allt Coire Dubhchraig when you reach the upper forest fence, then follow the right bank down for a few hundred metres, to an indentation in the forest perimeter, where the track starts on open ground a short distance from the stream.

BEINN DUBHCHRAIG

BEN MORE

STOB BINNEIN

two lochans

Bealach Buidhe

Loch Oss

Coire Garbh

BEN OSS

Route 9a Alternative Descent: Coire Buidhe
Add-on: negligible mileage; Save: 80m/250ft ascent M56

O n the north side of the Bealach Buidhe the verdant bowl of Coire Buidhe offers a route down to Cononish farm and the track back to Dalrigh (described in Route 7b). This return option turns the bagging of Dubhchraig and Oss into a round trip for no extra mileage. Also in its favour, it saves the 80m/250ft climb back up to the two lochans on Dubhchraig's north-west ridge, to say nothing of the boggy descent thereafter. In the cons column, the initial descent from the bealach is steep, Coire Buidhe is pathless and the River Cononish has to be forded.

The headwall of Coire Buidhe, immediately below the bealach, is beset with discontinuous crags. There is more than one way down through them, but the following should be foolproof. From the extreme east end of the bealach, hard under Beinn Dubhchraig, descend diagonally left on steep grass beneath a line of small crags. You'll soon come across traces of a path (thank you, sheep), which leads past all difficulties onto steep grass slopes that ease with descent.

Once in the bowl of the corrie, follow the stream to its confluence with the River Cononish, then follow the riverbank to Cononish Farm and cross to pick up the track back along the glen to Dalrigh. The river crossing usually requires a paddle as the bridge marked on older maps at NN 304283 no longer exists.

Route 9a Extension 1: Ben Lui
G1 **** Add-on: 3ml/5km, 260m/850ft (The ascent from the Oss-Lui bealach to the summit of Ben Lui is 340m/1100ft, but the route avoids the 80m/250ft re-ascent to Beinn Dubhchraig's north-west ridge on the normal return route)
+ Beinn a' Chleibh: The Tyndrum Grand Slam
All four Tyndrum Munros: G3 **** 17ml/27km, 1550m/5100ft M40/56

B en Oss is connected to Ben Lui by a broad curving ridge that crosses a low (690m/2250ft) bealach. An indistinct path comes and goes, but easy slopes of grass among rocks make for straightforward going with or without it. From the summit of Oss, it seems a long way down and up again to the summit of Lui, but a steady plod will get you there.

The ridge descends to a grassy levelling and then to the long bealach itself, from where Lui's ▲summit is initially hidden behind a shoulder. After surmounting the shoulder, the route joins the path from Coire an t-Sneachda for the remainder of the ascent (Route 7b Option 4).

Descend to Dalrigh as per any of Route 7b options... or add ▲Chleibh to the trip to complete the Tyndrum Grand Slam (Route 7b Extension 1)!

3 CRIANLARICH

East of the Lui group described in Section 2, a cluster of seven Munros huddles on the south side of the village of Crianlarich at the heart of the Southern Highlands. Their steep, grassy mountainsides give an impression of great height, while **widespread rock outcrops enliven ascents**. The main trade routes carry obvious paths that minimise routefinding complications, but even they can't completely avoid the outcrops, while off-path routes require surprising invention.

Unless you break out in a nervous rash at the idea of a close encounter with rock, the seven Munros and their four Tops offer a smorgasbord of savoury hillwalking delights both individually and in combination. Approaches can be uninspiring on occasion, courtesy of afforestation in the corries and rough terrain on the steep hillsides, which prompts us to reduce the star rating of several routes. Nevertheless, arboreal aberrations will soon be forgotten when you stride out along the summit ridges. As further compensation on ascent, you'll pass some of the most interesting mountain features in the whole Southern Highlands.

Ascents are usually made from the Crianlarich side to the north and west, where main roads give easy access to a number of ridges that climb to the summits. To the south and east, access is also possible via the road through Balquhidder village. Ascents from this side, however, are generally steeper and pathless, with the single exception of the fine south ridge of Stob Binnein (Route 16d).

The three eastern Munros (An Caisteal, Beinn a' Chroin and Beinn Chabhair) form a subgroup that boasts an enormous variety of route options, both for single and combined ascents (Routes 11a – 11f). The four western Munros are usually climbed as two pairs: wedge-shaped Cruach Ardrain with its satellite Beinn Tulaichean (Routes 14a and 14b), and the great twin domes of Ben More and Stob Binnein (Routes 16a – 16d).

BEN MORE

STOB BINNEIN

The Glen Falloch Group:

▲**11 An Caisteal** 147 995m/3264ft (OS 50 or 56, NN 378193)
An Cash-tyal, The Castle

▲**12 Beinn a' Chroin** 233 942m/3089ft (OS 50 or 56, NN 388186) *Ben a Chroa-in*, often translated as Mountain of Harm (from Gaelic *Cron*), but more probably Mountain of the Sheepfold (from Gaelic *Chrothain*)
△East Top 940m/3084ft (OS 50 or 56, NN 394186)

▲**13 Beinn Chabhair** 244 933m/3060ft (OS 50 or 56, NN 367179) *Ben Chav-ir*, Antler Mountain

AN CAISTEAL

BEINN CHABHAIR ◀

BEINN A' CHROIN

Peak Fitness: No change in Tables 1891-1997 but, uniquely, there has been change since then. In the latest (1997) edition of the Tables the East Top of Beinn a' Chroin is listed as the Munro (940m), while the West Top (938m, at NN 385185) is listed as a Top. Subsequent resurveying has uncovered a higher point (941.5m) some 100m east of the latter, so this is now the Munro (rounded up to 942m), the East Top is now a subsidiary Top, and the former West Top no longer figures. Better climb all three, just in case? Ronald Burn, the first Compleat Munroist, finished his 1923 round on Beinn a' Chroin. Let's hope he too bagged the true summit.

With grassy lower slopes rising to crag-spattered upper slopes, this compact subgroup dominates Glen Falloch on the south-west side of Crianlarich, forming **a triangular triumvirate of trampers' tops** with odd spots of excitement to add spice to ascents. As a bonus for readers who revel in *schadenfreude*, the three Munros can be tackled in so many ways that they constitute a nightmare for guidebook writers.

The summit of An Caisteal lies at the apex of three easy but entertaining ridges, each of which is worth exploring in its own right. By contrast, Beinn a' Chroin sports a number of tops dotted along a crescent-shaped summit ridge.

As the dip between the duo is only 137m/450ft, they are traditionally bagged together (Route 11a). Those of a genteel disposition, however, should note that there's a rock step (albeit easy) on the connecting route. If you wish to avoid this, you can bag each Munro individually by two easier rounds that enable a more extensive exploration of the mountains' many facets (Routes 11b and 11c).

Craggier Beinn Chabhair is separated from its two neighbours by a more awkward 314m/1030ft-deep bealach, so it is usually climbed on its own directly from Glen Falloch by its main line of weakness – its north-west ridge (Route 11d). Nevertheless, the bealach *goes*, such that anyone in search of a sterner test of fitness and routefinding ability can bag all three Munros together, beginning either in Glen Falloch to the west (Route 11e) or at Balquhidder road-end to the east (Route 11f).

Which route to choose? Settle down in an armchair with this book, read on and make up your own mind.

Sphinx Rock

Baffies: Beinglas farm, situated on the West Highland Way at the foot of Beinn Chabhair, has a restaurant and shop, as well as rooms, 'wigwams' and camping facilities. Open all day and all year. Tel: 01301-704281. Website: www.beinglascampsite.co.uk. Email: beinglas.campsite@virgin.net.

One of the best short walks in the area is to the wonderfully named Cnap Mor (*Crap Moar*, Big Knob), a 164m/538ft hillock situated 1½ml/2½km south of Beinglas along the West Highland Way. The lowly summit offers a great view along the northern reaches of Loch Lomond to Ben Lomond, and the best view from anywhere of Ben Vorlich (▲6), seen across the marinas of Ardlui (see Page 30).

Route 11a An Caisteal and Beinn a' Chroin
from Glen Falloch M67
G3 **** NN 369239, 9ml/14km, 1040m/3400ft (incl. Beinn a' Chroin E Top)

Map note: The whole route is on OS 50 but not OS 56.

Thanks to the high (805m/2640ft) bealach between these two mountains, appending the ascent of Beinn a' Chroin to that of An Caisteal adds a mere 137m/450ft to the trip, making a combined round an attractive proposition. In addition, the route has the merit of climbing An Caisteal via Twistin Hill, which sports a number of **interesting and unusual geophysical features**.

Caution: The ascent to the summit of Beinn a' Chroin is steep, is quite exposed and involves negotiating a rock step that, although easy, will not be to everyone's liking. If in doubt, bag each Munro separately using Routes 11b and 11c.

AN CAISTEAL

Twistin Hill
viewed from
Sron Gharbh

Begin at the lay-by at the foot of Coire Earb (*Erb*, Roe), just beyond the turn-off to Keilator farm, 1½ml/2km south of Crianlarich on the A82. Take the vehicle track that begins at the north end of the lay-by, tunnels under the West Highland Railway line, bridges the River Falloch and runs up the corrie. A tempting path, which begins at a stile in the lay-by, shortcuts an initial bend but is abysmally boggy.

The first objective of the day is Sron Gharbh (*Strawn Gharrav*, Rough

Nose), the grassy point seen ahead on the right-hand side of the corrie. The rock outcrops marked on the OS map are no obstacle but the boggy moor lower down is a nuisance. About 500m after the track crosses the River Falloch, it bends sharp left to cross a small stream. A path of sorts leaves the track here to follow the stream across the moor and tackle the ascent of Sron Gharbh direct. Unfortunately this path is little more than a hard-to-follow boggy ribbon that you'll spend more time off than on.

You may well prefer to continue up the track to a fence, which can be followed onto higher ground. Alternatively, continue even further up the corrie and climb Sron Gharbh's left-hand skyline. Whichever route you choose, boggy ground is unavoidable and makes for a less than exhilarating start to the day. But all that will be forgotten when, just before the top of Sron Gharbh, you reach a well-defined ridge with better terrain and a good path.

Over the top, a long saddle leads the eye to An Caisteal's north ridge, otherwise known as Twistin Hill. This steepens to the problematic-looking **rock 'castle'** that gives its name to the whole mountain. Don't worry – it's much less daunting than it looks. The path crosses the saddle and climbs the ridge on short grass among rocks.

Approaching the castle, you'll pass some **curious hollows and clefts**, the last of which is a deep fissure that completely splits the ridge in two. Clamber in and out (minimal handwork required) to reach the foot of the

castle itself, whose fierce appearance is designed solely to deter the errant tourist. It will happily yield tamely to the pure-in-heart hillwalker.

Two paths surmount it, both of them easy. The main path bypasses the rocks on the left and looks initially easier, but it soon becomes exposed and requires at least as much handwork. It is just as easy, and more satisfying, to clamber straight up. An Caisteal's ▲summit is not far beyond.

Continuing to Beinn a' Chroin, An Caisteal's south-east ridge gives an obvious and straightforward descent to the intervening Bealach Buidhe (*Byalach Boo-ya*, Yellow Pass, unnamed on OS map), although there's so much broken rock around that you'll use hands for balance in a few places. The route up Beinn a' Chroin's steep west face on the far side of the bealach takes a more

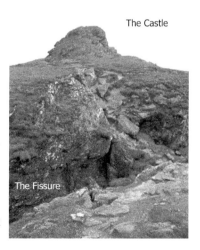

The Castle

The Fissure

BEINN A' CHROIN

AN CAISTEAL

determinedly whimsical line. Viewed from An Caisteal, the most obvious way up trends left on grassy rakes among outcrops, but it is steeper here than it looks. The path instead traverses well to the right, beneath crags and above steep drops, before cutting back left up a little gully.

This gully is usually wet and sports a rock step that requires a couple of what, in technical terms, are known as 'manky thrutches'. Unless erosion worsens it, the ascent remains perfectly practicable, but those of a nervous disposition may well need coaxing up with promises of sexual favours or the like. Above the rock

step, the going eases again and the path soon tops out on Beinn a' Chroin's summit ridge.

Over the years, confusion has reigned concerning the location of the true summit amid numerous undulations (see *Peak Fitness*), so we describe the summit area in some detail. The path first crosses a dip to a cairned point, just beyond a sphinx-like rock. This is the old 938m West Top. The path then crosses a lochan-filled hollow to reach the new ▲summit cairn atop an outcrop. Beyond here, the path crosses a deeper gap and climbs 63m/206ft to the ∆East Top.

The Thrutch

From the East Top, an easy ridge descends north to the head of Coire Earb to give a straightforward return route. A short distance before reaching the East Top, at a right-angled bend on the main path, a side path descends this ridge. It becomes indistinct for a while, but it points the way down.

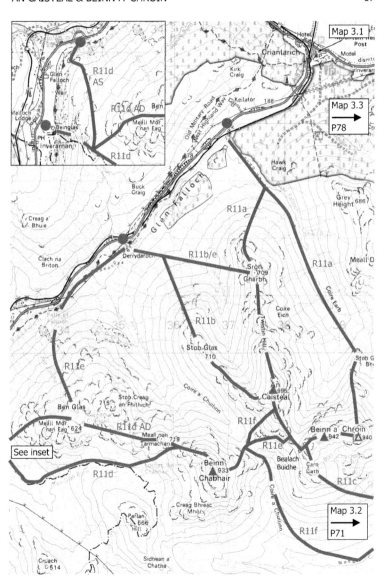

If you really *really* have an aversion to Top bagging, it is possible to bypass the East Top completely and traverse to the north ridge directly from the gap between it and the summit. Descend beside the stream for a few metres and you'll find a small path that runs across the hillside to the ridge.

From the junction of the path from the East Top and the path from the gap, a more distinct path descends the ridge to the corrie. But if you think that sounds like a perfect end to the day, you're in for a disappointment, because the path is both rough and boggy. To make matters worse, the descent is followed by an equally tiresome bogtrot down marshy Coire Earb. There's a path here too but it is more of a hindrance than an aid. You'll be glad to reach the Land Rover track on which you began the day.

E Top   BEINN A' CHROIN   AN CAISTEAL

Coire Earb

Needlepoint: Distinct paths ease route-finding in cloud. The main problem in poor visibility is the complex summit ridge of Beinn a' Chroin. Follow the stated directions carefully to make sure you know when you're at the summit.

Chilly Willy: Twistin Hill may give some minor winter sport in the vicinity of The Castle, while the route from An Caisteal to Beinn a' Chroin may require more refined winter climbing skills.

On the ascent of Beinn a' Chroin especially, expect to encounter steep snow in the gully leading up to the rock step, which will itself be substantially more difficult to negotiate when iced.

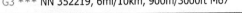

Route 11b An Caisteal alone
from Derrydaroch (Glen Falloch)

G3 *** NN 352219, 6ml/10km, 900m/3000ft M67

Map note: The whole route is on OS 50 and (only just) on OS 56.

If tackling An Caisteal alone, an attractive round trip can be made by going up Twistin Hill (the north ridge) and down the north-west ridge, making a skyline circuit of the mountain's north-west corrie (Coire Andoran, *Corran Doe-ran*, Otter Corrie). The shortest approach, to minimise moor work at the base of the ridges, begins not at the car park used by Route 11a, but a further 2ml/3km down the A82 from Crianlarich at Derrydaroch cottage.

Park in the lay-by opposite the access track and take the track down to the River Falloch. On the far side of the bridge, when the track turns right to the cottage, take a small path that goes straight on to reach open hillside. The grassy slopes that rise ahead to the north-west ridge will form the descent route, but your first goal is Twistin Hill further left.

Make a rising traverse across the hillside to climb Sron Gharbh at the start of Twistin Hill. The approach is from a different angle than Route 11a, but the ascent is of a similarly uninspiring nature. Continue up Twistin Hill to the ▲summit of An Caisteal (as described in Route 11a), then bear right around the head of Coire Andoran to descend the north-west ridge.

This ridge is more complex than Twistin Hill and has more in common with the north-west ridge of Beinn Chabhair (Route 11d Alternative Descent). It drops steeply at first, then becomes a switchback of rocky knolls and hollows. A small path weaves a way down and around, threading an entertaining route out to Stob Glas (*Stop Glass*, Grey Peak) at the ridge end. Below here, the grassy hillside fans out above Derrydaroch.

AN CAISTEAL

Sron Gharbh

NW Ridge

Stob Glas

Viewed from Glen Falloch

Needlepoint: Despite the complexity of the north-west ridge, this is the easiest route in the Glen Falloch Group in cloud.

Chilly Willy: Expect to encounter steep snow both in the vicinity of the castle and on the upper part of the north-west ridge.

ute 11c Beinn a' Chroin alone
from the Balquhidder road

G3 ** NN 445184, 9½ml/15km, 870m/2850ft

Map note: The approach route is not on OS 50, so use OS 56. The start point is just off OS 56 on OS 57.

If you can handle steep, pathless grassy hillsides, Beinn a' Chroin as an individual objective is best tackled from the Balquhidder road to the south. The crescent-shaped summit ridge curves around a high southern corrie (Coire a' Chroin) that cradles a small lochan (Lochan a' Chroin), such that a round of the corrie skyline makes an obvious circular route from the road-end.

NB An up-and-down route from Glen Falloch to the north, via Coire Earb, is less steep but also less aesthetically appealing and infinitely more tedious (incl. East Top: G1 * 10ml/16km, 820m/2700ft, described as Route 11a descent route).

BEINN A' CHROIN

BEINN CHABHAIR

Carn Liath

Summit

E Top

Ishag Burn

Inverlochlarig →

From the road-end car park near Inverlochlarig farm, follow the continuing Land Rover track along the north side of the River Larig as far as the Ishag Burn, then climb steep grass slopes among outcrops to Beinn a' Chroin's East Top. You can either make a direct ascent up grassy rakes among the outcrops or, more easily,

take an ascending diagonal line left around the foot of the rocks. Over the skyline there's a short dip before even steeper slopes make the final rise to the ΔEast Top. Outcrops that bar a direct ascent can be outflanked to left or right, but you'll probably find hands useful whichever line you take.

Beyond the East Top, cross the gap

to the ▲summit (see Route 11a for details). Beyond the summit, instead of continuing down the main path to the An Caisteal bealach, bear left around the rim of Coire a' Chroin to its western point, called Carn Liath (*Carn Lee-a*, Grey Cairn). From here, descend south-east down crag-free slopes to regain the Land Rover track back to the road.

Needlepoint: In cloud, the featureless southern flanks of Beinn a' Chroin do *not* make for ideal hillwalking. On ascent, crags loom out of the mist to complicate routefinding, while on descent you'll have to trust the compass/GPS.

Chilly Willy: In winter be prepared to encounter very steep, very tiring snow slopes with varying degrees of exposure. The best line should cause no major problems for those competent on such terrain, but you may not find the best line.

Baffies recommends a heatwave diversion: Just above the Land Rover track, the Ishag Burn forms some picturesque pools and waterslides that, on a hot summer's day, it would be criminal not to sample.

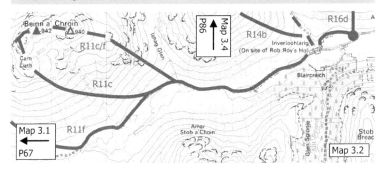

Route 11d Beinn Chabhair alone
from Beinglas Farm (Glen Falloch)

G2 *** NN 321187, 7ml/11km, 940m/3100ft M67

Map note: The whole route is on both OS 50 and OS 56.

As Beinn Chabhair is separated from its two neighbours by an awkward bealach, it is usually climbed on its own from Beinglas farm, 6ml/10km south of Crianlarich on the A82. This approach doesn't show the mountain to advantage, as it forsakes picturesqueness of scenery for ease of ascent, but those in search of more adventurous fare will find a variation that compensates for this deficiency (see Alternative Descent). Parking is permitted at Beinglas farm but, if the car park is full, you can park at

 Inverarnan (NN 319188), an old drovers' inn on the A82 300m south of the farm access track.

If starting at Inverarnan, follow the farm access track over the bridge across the River Falloch, then turn immediately right on a signposted path that leads to the West Highland Way, right of the farm buildings. The farm car park is in front of the buildings. Behind the wooden 'wigwams' to the right of the buildings, follow the Way over a stile in a wall, then take the obvious path that zigzags up the hillside through sparse woodland left of the Ben Glas Burn.

A steep climb brings you to Ben Glas Falls, a series of cascades where the burn tumbles 36m/120ft down the '**Devil's Staircase**'. The path tends to channel water after rain, but of course that's the best time to visit the spot. Above the falls, the path emerges into a wide-open upper glen and continues along the streambank to

Lochan Beinn Chabhair at the foot of its namesake peak. The path is a quagmire in places, but overall it gives a pleasant enough streamside ramble through 'undemanding' scenery to the reedy lochan.

The nondescript summit of Beinn Chabhair now rises ahead, sporting an infinite variety of ascent routes on grassy slopes among crags. For the most straightforward way up, look to the left, where a boulder slope rises to a notch on the north-west ridge, between Meall nan Tarmachan (no, not the Meall nan Tarmachan of Section 6) and Beinn Chabhair.

A developing path starts up the line of the stream that descends from the notch, then grassy slopes climb right to gain the ridge itself. Once on the ridge, the path becomes well-defined and easy to follow as it twists its way upwards around outcrops. After reaching a subsidiary top, the ▲summit is only a short stroll away.

notch

BEINN CHABHAIR

Lochan Beinn Chabhair

Lochan a' Chaisteal

Beinn Chabhair NW Ridge

Needlepoint: The development of a Munro baggers' path has made a once problematic route now easy to follow in cloud, but the Alternative Descent down the complex north-west ridge remains a navigational nightmare.

Chilly Willy: There are no especial difficulties in winter, although you are likely to encounter steep snow in several places on the ascent from Lochan Beinn Chabhair to the summit.

If snow is low on the hill, or the ground is icy, the steep drops above Ben Glas Falls can become exposed and dangerous. In such conditions, it is safer to use the Alternative Start.

Route 11d Alternative (Gentle) Start NN 326202 M67

About 1½ml/2km north of Beinglas farm, the A82 briefly crosses the River Falloch and a farm track leaves the roadside to give an alternative access point to the western slopes of Beinn Chabhair. Keep left at a fork and, at a prominent tree only a couple of hundred metres from the roadside, fork left again on an ATV track (marked as a path on the OS map). The track climbs the hillside and joins the path from Beinglas farm at the 300m contour (NN 329182), well above Ben Glas Falls, at the entrance to the upper glen.

The disadvantages of the Alternative Start are the addition of 1ml/1½km to the round trip and the bypassing of the waterfall. The advantages are a much less steep, much less exposed and much less boggy approach path.

Route 11d Alternative Descent:
Beinn Chabhair North-west Ridge

G2 **** Extra mileage: negligible; Extra ascent: negligible;
Extra effort: considerable M67

L eft of the skyline notch above
Lochan Beinn Chabhair, the north
-west ridge is a confusing **maze of
knolls and unexpected drops**. For
anyone still suffering from a surfeit of
energy at the summit of Beinn
Chabhair, the descent of the ridge

makes an adventurous return route
past the **secret beauty spot** of
Lochan a' Chaisteal. This handsome
lochan is encircled by castle-like crags
(hence its name), which give it a rare
air of seclusion high above the
surrounding glens.

Stob Creag
an Fhithich

AN CAISTEAL

BEINN A'
CHROIN

BEINN
CHABHAIR

Lochan a'
Chaisteal

Needlepoint: To be
avoided in mist.

Baffies: To be avoided,
full stop.

On descent from the summit of
Beinn Chabhair, leave the path on
approach to the notch and stay on
the ridge. Go over Meall nan
Tarmachan, descend steeper slopes to
a dip on its far side and cross another
rise. Ahead now is craggy Stob Creag
an Fhithich (*Stop Craik an Ee-ich*, Peak
of the Raven's Crag), which can be
bypassed on the left to reach Lochan
a' Chaisteal.

The lochan marks the end of the
ridge but not the end of the
adventure, as the hillside beyond,
which separates you from the ascent

path, is beset with yet more knolls
and crags. With judicious routefinding
you should be able to find a way down
(let's hope so, anyway).

To avoid very steep ground above
the Bein Glas Burn on the left (south)
side of the ridge, keep heading west
until you can see a way down. To this
end, although it may seem
counter-productive at first, begin by
keeping the highpoint of Meall Mor
nan Eag (*Myowl Moar nan Aik*, Big Hill
of the Notch) to your left. It would be
a good idea to recce the terrain on the
outward trip.

Route 11e An Caisteal, Beinn a' Chroin and Beinn Chabhair from Derrydaroch (Glen Falloch)

G3 **** NN 352219, 10ml/16km, 1250m/4100ft M67

Map note: The whole route is on both OS 50 and OS 56.

From Glen Falloch the round of all three Munros amounts to **an adventurous skyline circuit** of Coire a' Chuilinn, which lies between An Caisteal's north-west ridge and Beinn Chabhair's north-west ridge. NB The corrie on the south side of the mountains is also called Coire a' Chuilinn. Don't get confused.

Beginning at Derrydaroch farm (as per Route 11b), your first objective is An Caisteal. You can climb either the north-west ridge directly above the farm, (reversing Route 11b) or cross the foot of Coire Andoran and climb the north ridge (Twistin Hill: Route 11a).The north-west ridge is nearer but Twistin Hill is more interesting.

From ▲An Caisteal cross the Bealach Buidhe to ▲Beinn a' Chroin, as per Route 11a, then return to the bealach. The connection to Beinn Chabhair is pathless and more awkward. Descend the grassy gully on the south side of the bealach for c50m/150ft, until you can traverse right across easy slopes beneath An Caisteal's south-west crags to the

BEINN CHABHAIR

AN CAISTEAL

Needlepoint: The route is best tackled in good weather, otherwise the pathless traverse to and ascent of Beinn Chabhair may land you on difficult ground.

Chilly Willy: When grassy rakes become snow gullies, the ascent/descent of Beinn a' Chroin and the ascent of Beinn Chabhair become steep winter climbs.

619m/2030ft bealach at the foot of Beinn Chabhair. To outwit the crags of Chabhair's north-east face, which now loom overhead and bar a direct ascent, climb towards the left-hand skyline on steep grass. The ▲summit rewards with a distant view along Loch Lomond, and you'll certainly welcome a breather to savour it after the killer 314m/1030ft ascent.

The three summits may now be underfoot but the fun continues on the descent of Beinn Chabhair's complex north-west ridge, which is followed down to Lochan a' Chaisteal (Route 11d Alternative Descent). Beyond the lochan, a direct descent north-eastwards down the hillside to Derrydaroch would encounter steep, craggy, wooded terrain. Instead, follow the lochan's outlet stream down to lower ground, then join the West Highland Way for a short stroll back to Derrydaroch.

Route 11f An Caisteal, Beinn a' Chroin and Beinn Chabhair from the Balquhidder road

G3 ** NN 445184, 13ml/21km, 1350m/4450ft M67/71

Map note: The approach route is not on OS 50, so use OS 56. The start point is just off OS 56 on OS 57.

The southern hillsides of the Glen Falloch Group are steep and pathless, making a triple bagging trip from this side even more of a challenge than Route 11e. From the end of the Balquhidder road, first climb ▲Beinn a' Chroin as per Route 11c, then cross the Bealach Buidhe to ▲An Caisteal, reversing Route 11a. To reach the bealach below Beinn Chabhair, return to the Bealach Buidhe and traverse from there (as per Route 11e). Alternatively, take a short cut.

Descend An Caisteal's south-east ridge only as far as a levelling about a quarter of the way down, then descend a broad grassy gully, trending left lower down, to reach the Beinn Chabhair bealach. Climb to the ▲summit as per Route 11e.

To regain the track to Inverlochlarig, re-descend to the Beinn Chabhair bealach and go south down Coire a' Chuilinn on wet ground that will test your powers of equanimity at the end of a tough day.

Needlepoint: The routefinding problems noted for the western approach from Glen Falloch (Route 11a) are exacerbated by the steep, craggy hillsides encountered on the southern approach from the Balquhidder road.

Chilly Willy: In winter, expect to encounter steep snow everywhere! As on Route 11a, the descent from Beinn a' Chroin and the ascent of Beinn Chabhair are the most difficult propositions in the whole Glen Falloch Group.

▲**14 Cruach Ardrain** 87 1046m/3432ft (OS 51 or 56, NN 409212) *Croo-ach Aardran*, High Mound
△Stob Garbh 959m/3146ft (OS 51 or 56, NN 411221)
Stop Garrav, Rough Peak
▲**15 Beinn Tulaichean** 220 946m/3104ft (OS 56, NN 416196) *Ben Toolichan*, Knolly Mountain

Stob Garbh   CRUACH ARDRAIN   Meall Dhamh   Coire Ardrain

Peak Fitness: Attempts to pinpoint the exact summit of Cruach Ardrain have an intriguing history. In the original 1891 Tables, Sir Hugh made the north-east top (NN 409212) the Munro (as it is now) and the south-west top (NN 408211), situated only a short distance away across an insignificant dip of c10m/30ft, a Top. However, his decision was based on a map height of 3429ft for the south-west top and 3477ft for the north-east top. The '3477' was an erroneous guess on his part, as the first two digits were obliterated on his map, and it soon became obvious that the unreadable height was in fact '3377'.

In 1921, therefore, the position was reversed, with the south-west top becoming the Munro and the north-east top being deleted from the Tables altogether. Unfortunately, this merely compounded the problem, because the '3377' was plainly also incorrect. In 1981, therefore, the position was reversed again and the north-east top reinstated as the Munro, having been remeasured as 1m higher than the south-west top.

Stob Garbh has always been listed as a Top of Cruach Ardrain, but from 1891 to 1921 a minor bump on the ridge to Stob Garbh at NN 413217 also revelled in Top status.

When viewed from Crianlarich, Cruach Ardrain is the most **eye-catching mountain** in the whole Crianlarich Group, with a wedge-shaped summit that towers over the forests of Coire Ardrain (unnamed on OS map). By contrast, Beinn Tulaichean is a sneaky little peak that achieves Munro status by hanging on to Cruach Ardrain's coat tails. In truth it is no more than the highpoint at the end of its big sibling's south-east ridge, but you have to admire its audacity – the ascent from the intervening bealach is only 121m/397ft. What was Sir Hugh thinking of? Perhaps, as with the problem of pinpointing Cruach Ardrain's true summit, his dodgy map was to blame.

Both Munros are usually bagged together, either from Crianlarich to the north (Route 14a) or from the Balquhidder road to the south (Route 14b). The former involves more ascent but is deservedly more popular.

Route 14a Cruach Ardrain and Beinn Tulaichean from Crianlarich

G2 **** NN 389251
Cruach Ardrain alone: 8ml/13km, 940m/3100ft
Add-on return trip to Beinn Tulaichean: 2½ml/4km, 350m/1150ft

Map note: Cruach Ardrain is awkwardly situated on the corners of no less than three maps. Both OS 50 and OS 51 are needed for its ascent, plus OS 56 if Beinn Tulaichean is to be included.

The northern approach begins at the Community Woodland car park, situated at the east entrance to Crianlarich, and climbs the west rim of Coire Ardrain. Forest blankets the lower slopes to a height of nearly 500m/1650ft, but forest roads that climb to the upper boundary make access straightforward as long as you follow our detailed directions.

Take the forest road into the woods, go right at the first junction after c1000m (NN 386243) and left at the second after a further 400m (NN 384240). Just over 100m beyond the second junction, you'll cross the former approach path from the A82

CRUACH ARDRAIN

SW Top   Summit

Stob
Garbh

NE Face
Bypass

BEINN TULAICHEAN

(see below), now horribly boggy and
used only by people who have
purchased the wrong guidebook.

Around 700m beyond the second
junction, branch right at a third (NN
389237) and keep to this forest road
even when it seems to be heading too
far west. From its end at NN 383232,
a boggy path makes a short climb to
a horizontal forest ride. Open hillside
now lies less than a couple of hundred
metres to the right. Once outside the
forest fence, follow it up to its highest
point, where the old path comes in
from the left over a stile.

Another route to this point begins in
Glen Falloch at the foot of Coire Earb,
as for Route 11a. After following the
track into the corrie, it is necessary to
ford the River Falloch and climb the
boggy hillside beside the forest fence
to join the forest roads route. It is a
slightly shorter approach but that is its
only advantage.

Note also that the lowest section of
the old path has been renovated,
giving an alternative starting point at
NN 382245, just south of Crianlarich
on the A82 Loch Lomond road, where
there's a bridge over the West
Highland Railway line. The new path
joins the forest roads route between
the first two junctions.

There may be other ways up
through the forest using rides and
felled areas, but all are subject to
re-afforestation and all have enormous
quagmire potential. The forest roads
give by far the least fraught approach.

Once above the forest, a distinct
path climbs a more well-defined,
grassy ridge to the Grey Height and
continues across a broad saddle to the
rocky top of Meall Dhamh (*Myowl
Ghav*, Deer Hill). The ridge then
becomes **entertainingly intricate**,
forcing the path to negotiate a number
of rocky knolls on a 50m/150ft descent

to the foot of Cruach Ardrain's short sharp north-west ridge.

To find the least problematical way up this final obstacle, the path takes a diagonal line up the steep grass slopes to the right of the ridge crest, passing beneath the summit to reach the skyline still further right, on the easy south-east ridge, just below the roof-like summit dome. To reach the true (north-east) ▲summit, cross a short dip beyond the first twin-cairned (south-west) top reached.

Before you re-descend to Crianlarich, the return jaunt to ▲Beinn Tulaichean will give you another tick on the list for minimal effort. The **well -trodden highway** along Cruach Ardrain's south-east ridge descends steeply to the intervening bealach before making the short ascent to Tulaichean's knobbly summit.

Needlepoint: Thanks to the path, the only real cause for confusion in cloud is Cruach Ardrain's summit dome. Remember that to reach the true summit, you must cross the short dip beyond the first twin-cairned top reached.

Chilly Willy: An entertaining winter route, but not one for beginners. The ascent remains straightforward as far as the foot of Cruach Ardrain's north-west ridge but, under snow, the steep slopes leading up to the summit require care.

CRUACH ARDRAIN

GiGi: Anyone who approaches Beinn Tulaichean from Cruach Ardrain, and who has not had the foresight to purchase this guidebook, will miss the most interesting feature of the mountain. Just over (south of) the summit, a landslip has created a **warren of shafts and caves** in a jumble of fissures and boulders. Worth a look.

Route 14a Alternative Descent: Round of Coire Ardrain

G2 *** Extra mileage: none; Extra ascent: negligible
Possible extra angst: not inconsiderable M78

It is possible to make a complete round of Coire Ardrain by returning along the east rim over the craggy summit of Stob Garbh, although routefinding is by no means as straightforward as on the ascent route. If misfortune is your lot in life, you may find yourself faced at the end of the day with a frustrating bushwhack down through the encroaching forest.

A direct continuation around the corrie rim from Cruach Ardrain's summit involves an intimidatingly steep initial descent of the north-east face to gain the bealach below Stob Garbh. The time-worn path down is now so eroded and loose that, in technical terms, it's not very nice at all. A slip could deposit you on the bealach a tad *too* quickly.

To avoid this initial problem, begin the return along the east rim at the Ardrain-Tulaichean bealach and cross easy grass slopes beneath Ardrain's eastern crags to reach the bealach below Stob Garbh. This solution has the additional merit of avoiding the climb back up Cruach Ardrain on return from Tulaichean.

Once you've reached the bealach below Stob Garbh, a path weaves its way up among rocky bluffs to the knobbly Δsummit before heading glenwards along Coire Ardrain's east rim. A couple of minor rises punctuate a gentle grassy descent to the viewpoint of Creag na h-Iolaire (*Craig na Hyillera*, Eagle's Crag).

Now for some more fun, courtesy of the forest that blankets the Creag's lower slopes. If you're feeling adventurous, you may be able to pick a route through the forest rides below. A direct descent is initially barred by the crags that give the eyrie its name. To avoid them, descend right then back left on steep grass. Once into the arboreal maze, good luck with keeping to your chosen line.

If the prospect of a possible bushwhack back to the car park fails to enthuse you, you can opt for a more straightforward descent route. The easiest route down leaves the ridge at the gate in the upper forest perimeter fence, which is encountered at NN 404239, just beyond the last rise before Creag na h-Iolaire. From here, head north-west down the steepening hillside, eventually beside a deep-cut stream, to reach a forest road near NN 396247.

To reach this line from Creag na h-Iolaire, traverse right (north-east) across the hillside until you reach the stream. Once on the forest road, go left to rejoin the approach route at the first junction described previously.

Terminator: On the ascent along the west rim of Coire Ardrain, note the conspicuous Y Gully, named for its shape, that scores Cruach Ardrain's north face. It has little rock climbing potential but provides a good snow climb in winter.

Route 14b Cruach Ardrain and Beinn Tulaichean from the Balquhidder road

G2 ** NN 445184 M86

Beinn Tulaichean alone: 5ml/8km, 810m/2650ft

Add-on return trip to Cruach Ardrain: 2½ ml/4km, 350m/1150ft

Map note: OS 56 covers both mountains, but OS 50 doesn't. The start is just off OS 56 on OS 57.

The southern slopes of Beinn Tulaichean, which rise above Inverlochlarig farm beyond the end of the Balquhidder road, provide a route to the summit that doesn't involve going over Cruach Ardrain first. Moreover, if you're bagging both Munros, an ascent from this side involves less mileage and ascent. But you'll find Route 14a more appealing.

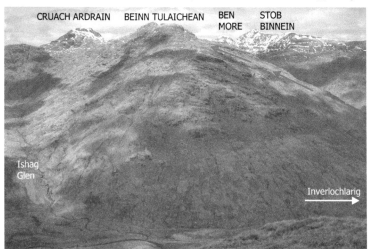

CRUACH ARDRAIN   BEINN TULAICHEAN   BEN MORE   STOB BINNEIN

Ishag Glen

Inverlochlarig

From the car park at the road-end, take the track to the farm, then follow the signposted path to Beinn Tulaichean up the left-hand side of the Inverlochlarig Burn to join a Land Rover track up the glen. Once past the farm fence, leave the track and head skywards. The ascent is straightforward enough, up a grassy hillside among rock outcrops, but it is steep in places and there is no path until various lines of ascent converge higher up. Near the ▲summit you'll pass the landslip noted on Page 80. Continue to ▲Cruach Ardrain as described under Route 14a.

Route 14b Return Variations M86

*O*n the map, two alternative return routes look attractive – one to each side of the Cruach Ardrain–Beinn Tulaichean bealach. Inverlochlarig Glen to the east carries the Land Rover track you briefly sampled on ascent, while Ishag Glen to the west boasts the fine section of streamway mentioned on Page 71. *On the ground*, think twice before attempting either return route.

A direct descent to Ishag Glen from Cruach Ardrain via the short south-west ridge over Stob Glas (a different 'Grey Peak' to its nearby namesake on An Caisteal in Route 11b) is definitely inadvisable. Apart from the initial very steep descent, the ridge ends at a huge rocky bluff overlooking the bealach below Beinn a' Chroin.

The hillsides on each side of the Ardrain–Tulaichean bealach, leading down to Ishag Glen and Inverlochlarig Glen, offer easier descents, but that doesn't necessarily mean that either is a worthwhile option as both are steep and beset with hidden outcrops. On the west side, a return through Ishag Glen, despite the prospect of waterfalls to come, involves a marshy tramp that you would not appreciate us recommending. On the east side, the Land Rover track through Inverlochlarig Glen provides an easy end to the day, but the descent to the glen is rough and often sodden.

▲**16 Ben More** 16 1174m/3852ft (OS 51, NN 432244)
Ben Moar, Big Mountain
▲**17 Stob Binnein** 18 1165m/3822ft (OS 51, NN 434227)
Stop Beenyan (usually pronounced *Stobinian*), Conical Peak
△Stob Coire an Lochain 1068m/3504ft (OS 51, NN 438220)
Stop Corra an Lochin, Peak of the Corrie of the Lochan
△Meall na Dige 966m/3170ft (OS 51, NN 450225)
Myowl na Jeeka, Hill of the Dyke

STOB BINNEIN   BEN MORE

Loch Tay

Peak Fitness: No change to existing Munros and Tops since original 1891 Tables. Creag a' Bhragit, a barely perceptible rise on the south-west ridge of Meall na Dige, around 400m from the summit at NN 447224, was an additional Top until it was deleted in 1921.

As Cruach Ardrain is the highpoint of one great afforested corrie, so the **King and Queen of Crianlarich** are the crowning peaks of another to the immediate east – Coire Chaorach (*Corra Cheurach*, Corrie of Rowan Berries, unnamed on OS map).

Their fine conical summits, towering above dense tree cover, are **commanding sentinels** visible from miles around. Ben More especially rears up in an unbroken line from roadside in shapely summit, looking well worthy of its Gaelic name (which it shares with two other Munros and several other Scottish mountains).

BEN MORE

NE Ridge

NW Spur

Sloc Curraidh

Benmore Glen

Glen Dochart

Despite the height, the steepness, the forest and the 300m/1000ft-deep bealach that separates the pair, the best terrain in the whole Crianlarich Group makes a joint bagging trip eminently practicable. As with the Glen Falloch Group, there are several route options to consider from the comfort of an armchair.

The northern approaches (Routes 16a, 16b and 16c from Crianlarich, climbing Ben More first) and the southern approach (Route 16d from the Balquhidder road, climbing Stob Binnein first) all have merit, so even if you do bag both summits in a oner, it's worth going back some day for another look.

F-Stop: As befits the highest mountain in the UK south of Glen Dochart, Ben More's **seemingly limitless summit view** is reputed to include half of Scotland.

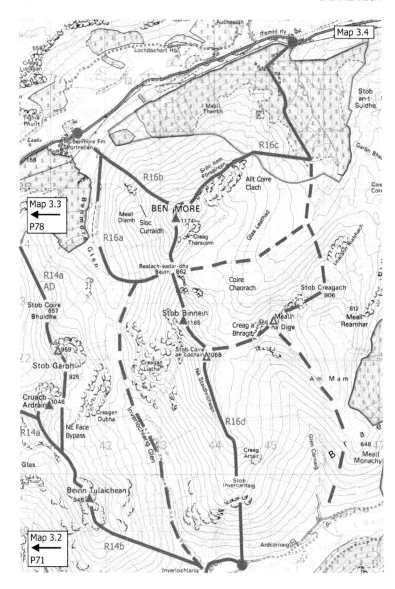

Route 16a Ben More and Stob Binnein from Benmore Farm: Benmore Glen

G2 **** NN 414258
Ben More alone: 6ml/10km, 1000m/3300ft
Add-on Stob Binnein: 1ml/1½km, 300m/1000ft

Two routes up Ben More begin at Benmore farm, on the A85 2ml/3km east of Crianlarich. Route 16b is shorter but relentlessly steep. Route 16a described here takes a more roundabout but considerably less arduous approach, making it the easiest route on the mountain.

From roadside parking just east of Benmore farm, a signposted path joins a Land Rover track up Benmore Glen beneath Ben More's grassy western slopes. When the track ends, a somewhat boggy path continues up beside the Benmore Burn.

Your first goal is the 862m/2828ft Bealach-eadar-dha Beinn, the aptly named bealach between Ben More and Stob Binnein (*Byalach-aitar-gha Ben*, literally the Bealach-between-two-mountains).

It is tempting to take a diagonal short cut up the grassy hillside to reach the bealach but, if you yield to temptation, you'll find yourself on increasingly steep, pathless terrain. The best line holds to the glen as far as the stream prior to the one that comes down from the bealach. There's a large boulder just before this stream

BEN MORE   STOB BINNEIN

S Ridge

Benmore Glen   Bealach-eadar-
                      dha Beinn

Stob Garbh

Inverlochlarig Glen

joins the Benmore Burn at NN 421235. A developing path goes up the stream's right-hand side, crosses to the bealach stream and climbs the right-hand side of that past numerous small waterfalls and pools that tempt on a hot day.

Once on the bealach, Ben More's broad south ridge rears overhead, giving a steep but easy 312m/1024ft climb to the ▲summit. A few rock obstacles on the gentle summit slopes are easily bypassed, but you may have more fun going over them.

After returning to the bealach, the 303m/994ft return trip up and down Stob Binnein's stony north ridge, rimming broken crags at the head of Coire Chaorach, is less steep. The zigzagging path soon deposits you on the **appealingly castellated** ▲summit.

STOB BINNEIN

BEN MORE

Needlepoint: Use the streams that flow down from the Bealach-eadar-dha Beinn as a guide and you shouldn't go far wrong on ascent in cloud.

Chilly Willy: Owing to their height and central location between the east and west coasts of Scotland, Ben More and Stob Binnein attract more snow than most other Southern Highland peaks. The slopes that rise to the two summits on either side of the Bealach-eadar-dha Beinn can become appreciably steep swathes of snow and ice in winter. Stob Binnein's north ridge especially becomes **a beautifully corniced 300m sweep of snow** that is a joy to crampon. It was a winter visit here in the 1870s that made Bill Naismith (of Naismith Rule fame) realise that the Scottish mountains deserved as much respect as the Swiss Alps.

Route 16b Ben More and Stob Binnein from Benmore Farm: Ben More North-west Spur

G3 **** NN 414258 M86
Ben More alone: 4ml/6km, 1000m/3300ft
Return via Benmore Glen: add-on 1ml/1½km
Add-on Stob Binnein: 1ml/1½km, 300m/1000ft

Ben More's north-west spur is the mountain's traditional ascent route, but it is nowhere near as carefree a jaunt as might be expected of such an accolade. It takes **a directissima line** up the steep grass slopes above Benmore farm, left of a shallow corrie, rising 1000m/3300ft in only 2ml/3km. Sure, it's the shortest way up, and it's certainly less boggy than the Benmore Glen route (Route 16a), but increasing exposure with height may daunt the nervous, while you can be assured that **the word relentless was coined to describe the ascent**. Fortunately the extensive northern view, expanding panoramically with height, can be regularly invoked as an excuse for rest stops.

Beginning as for Route 16a, follow the Benmore Glen Land Rover track as far as a gate in a fence near the foot of the spur. Twenty-five metres beyond the gate, the climb begins on an indistinct path that heads

up the hillside. Don't worry if you lose it, as the lower slopes can be climbed anywhere. Higher up, aim right to gain the rim of the shallow corrie, where the now well-worn path becomes increasingly welcome as the ground steepens even more. Given such terrain, the corrie's Gaelic name

BEN MORE

NW
Spur

seems entirely apposite: Sloc Curraidh (*Slochk Coory*, Difficult Pit).

At the head of the corrie the path climbs beside an old dyke through very steep rocky ground. It is barely necessary to put hand to rock, but anyone who is nervous of heights will *not* be enamoured either of the gritty path or the steep drops into the corrie, which is why we grade the route G3. Above the rocks, gentler slopes continue to the ▲summit. Whether you continue to ▲Stob Binnein or not, the Benmore Glen route via the Bealach-eadar-dha Beinn (Route 16a) gives a more pleasant return journey.

STOB BINNEIN

BEN MORE

Needlepoint: The steep ground beside and above the Sloc Curraidh demands care in cloud. On ascent make sure you find the path up the left-hand rim to avoid straying onto difficult terrain.

If descending this way, it is even more imperative to come off Ben More's featureless summit slopes in the right direction and find the path. Take note on the way up or return via the much easier Benmore Glen route.

Chilly Willy: Avoid this route in winter. A slip above the Sloc Curraidh could prove fatal and has done so in the past. The very steep slopes of the upper NW Spur are in any case prone to avalanche.

For a safer (though still steep) approach to the summits in winter, with ice axe and crampons of course, ascend via Benmore Glen (Route 16a) or Stob Binnein's South Ridge (Route 16d).

Baffies: Enjoy! I'll wait for you in the Benmore Restaurant on the outskirts of Crianlarich.

Route 16c Ben More and Stob Binnein from
Coire Chaorach: Ben More North-east Ridge

G2 (optional G3) ***** NN 455276 M86
Ben More alone: 7ml/11km, 1010m/3300ft
Add-on Stob Binnein:
    return via Ben More:
        2ml/3km, 620m/2050ft
    return via Bealach-eadar-dha Beinn and Coire Chaorach:
        2ml/3km, 300m/1000ft
    return via Stob Coire an Lochain and Coire Chaorach:
        2ml/3km, 450m/1500ft

An ascent of Ben More's north-east ridge is the most **exciting and aesthetically satisfying** route to the summit of the mountain, although it makes reaching Stob Binnein a lengthier endeavour. Two steepenings, neither of which need be difficult, add zest to proceedings. More aggravating is the problem of reaching the ridge in the first place, courtesy of afforestation around its foot, but the directions given here should enable you to surmount the forest without undue hassle.

Just west of the bridge over the Allt Coire Chaorach, 5ml/8km east of Crianlarich, a forest road leaves the A85 to run up Coire Chaorach on the east side of Ben More. It is proposed to build a car park near the start of the road, but at the time of writing the route begins at a lay-by 100m west of the bridge, from where a path leads to the road.

Follow the road to a junction at a hairpin bend, stay left on the main road and follow it up Coire Chaorach for around another 1500m. Twenty-

BEN MORE

NE Ridge

First Steepening

Second Steepening

Glen Dochart

BEN MORE

Bypass
Path

Second
Steepening

Top of First Steepening   NE Ridge

five metres beyond a vehicle turning point, a cairn marks the start of a rougher track that climbs to the upper forest boundary.

Note that this cairn can also be reached by a second, grassier track. This leaves the forest road at NN 451272, just around the first left-hand bend after leaving the car park, and takes a lower-level route through the forest. Some may find its woodland meanderings more pleasant than the forest road, and it should certainly be used to avoid vehicle traffic during forestry operations.

After quitting the forest road at the cairn just beyond the vehicle turning point, the rougher track crosses the stream coming down from Coire Clach (*Corra Clach*, Stony Corrie – the shallow corrie on the south-east side of the north-east ridge) and exits the forest at NN 458255. About 100m

after crossing the stream, at a small clearing on a left-hand bend, you can take an easy short-cut up through the remaining trees. Once out onto open ground, bear right to climb the grassy hillside to the crest of the north-east ridge. NB At the time of writing it is proposed to construct a path through the forest beside the Allt Coire Clach to shorten the approach route.

You arrive at the foot of the good stuff, known as Sron nan Forsairean (*Strawn nan Forseran*, Nose of the Foresters), when the ridge narrows and rears up more steeply and rockily. A path picks an easy but entertaining route up the crest of the first steepening, then an agreeable stroll across a short level section brings you to the foot of the second, rockier steepening. Scramble up or take the easy bypass path on the right to reach broken ground that rises more gently to the ▲summit.

If you continue across the Bealach-eadar-dha Beinn to ▲Stob Binnein, as per Route 16a, there are two return options that avoid the re-ascent of Ben More. (1) Re-descend to the bealach and continue down into Coire Chaorach to rejoin the approach track at the upper forest boundary. (2) Bag two more Tops by continuing around the corrie rim from Stob Binnein over ∆Stob Coire an Lochain, the former Top of Creag a Bhragit, ∆Meall na Dige and Stob Creagach (*Stop Craikach*, Craggy Peak), before descending into the corrie.

F-Stop: Whichever way you choose to climb Ben More, there's a perfectly good reason to *descend* the north-east ridge, as an evening descent is enhanced by the sight of the mountain's arrowhead shadow stealing across Glen Dochart below.

Looking down the NE Ridge
from above the second steepening

Needlepoint: Ben More's north-east ridge gives a fairly foolproof foul-weather ascent, as does the continuation to Stob Binnein. If descending the same way, make sure you come off Ben More's featureless summit slopes in the right direction. If continuing around the skyline of Coire Chaorach from Stob Binnein, the twists and turns of the corrie rim will require more determined navigation.

Chilly Willy: The two steepenings on the north-east ridge, so easily negotiated in summer, can prove surprisingly awkward to overcome in winter. The second steepening is particularly exposed and tricky when the bypass path is iced or obliterated by snow, and it is definitely no place to find yourself without ice axe and crampons. As always, do not venture any further than you can retreat. In Gaelic, the hillside crossed by the bypass path is menacingly called Cuidhe Chrom (*Coo-ya Chrome*, Crooked or Sloping Wreath of Snow). Accidents have happened here.

Route 16d Ben More and Stob Binnein from the Balquhidder road: Stob Binnein South Ridge

G3 ***** NN 445184 M86

Stob Binnein alone:
  6ml/10km, 1090m/3600ft
Add-on return via Meall na Dige (omitting Ben More):
  2ml/3klm, 90m/300ft
Add-on Ben More, return via Inverlochlarig Glen:
  3ml/5km, 310m/1000ft

Map note: Both OS 51 and OS 57 are required, plus OS 56 if you return via Inverlochlarig Glen.

Although an approach from the Balquhidder road gives a more roundabout ascent route if both Munros are to be climbed together, the long south ridge of Stob Binnein narrows above deep glens to offer **a**

very attractive ridge walk indeed.
All the hard work comes at the start. From Inverlochlarig car park at Balquhidder road-end, a signposted baggers' path goes straight up the relentlessly steep, grassy hillside to the

Na Staidhrichean   Stob Coire an Lochain

STOB BINNEIN

BEN MORE

Meall na Dige →

Stob Coire
an Lochain

north. All we wish to say about it is that it is a relief to top out at a height of 700m/2300ft on Stob Invercarnaig, where the angle eases before a rise to another, unnamed 790m/2600ft top.

Now, at last, the ridge proper begins. It is broad and grassy at first but then it narrows nicely along a section known as Na Staidhrichean (*Na Stair-ichen*, The Stairway) as it approaches ∆Stob Coire an Lochain. Beyond the Stob's dome-like top, the path crosses a shallow dip for a final zigzagging climb to Stob Binnein's knobbly ▲summit.

The last few metres are steep and rocky, calling for minor handwork. Those of a nervous disposition may not appreciate the brief exposure (hence the G3 rating), but the path

makes light of any difficulty. Some place to put a granny stopper!

If you decide to make the add-on trip across the Bealach-eadar-dha Beinn to ▲Ben More (described in Route 16a), it is not necessary to return over Stob Binnein, although there's nothing wrong in doing so in order to prolong an altitude fix.

For a shorter return route from the bealach, descend the grassy hillside on the west into the upper reaches of Benmore Glen and head south across the bealach at the head of the glen, thereby skirting Stob Binnein. The crossing is somewhat boggy but leads without difficulty into Inverlochlarig Glen, where the Land Rover track described in Route 14b descends effortlessly to your starting point.

Torpedo: To stay higher for longer on a return trip from Stob Binnein's summit, and bag another Top in the process, head eastwards from ∆Stob Coire an Lochain around the head of Glen Carnaig. An 80m/250ft climb from the intervening saddle, passing the insignificant former Top of Creag a' Bhragit, puts you atop ∆Meall na Dige, from where you can descend the broad grassy ridge of Am Mam (The Round Hill) to the roadside.

F-Stop: If you need an excuse for a break on the ascent of Stob Invercarnaig, there are **unbeatable views** of Ben Vorlich and Stuc a' Chroin, seen along the length of Loch Voil (see pic opposite).

Needlepoint: The well-defined crest of Stob Binnein's south ridge, together with the path along it, make routefinding straightforward in cloud.

Chilly Willy: Stob Binnein's south ridge, like its north ridge, carries a beautiful winter cornice when at its best. Writing in the very first edition of the Scottish Mountaineering Club Journal in 1890, Sir Hugh described its winter ascent as 'one of the most interesting and enjoyable walks I have ever taken.'

The route is straightforward as far as the dip beyond Stob Coire an Lochain, but the steep final few metres up Stob Binnein require care. The rock is often iced and exposed, and may be awkward to descend, even in crampons. If in doubt, descend the easier north ridge and return via Inverlochlarig Glen.

4 LOCH EARN

East of the Crianlarich Group described in Section 3, the high country around Loch Earn contains several Corbetts but only three Munros. The area is situated on the edge of the Highland Boundary Fault and is characterised by mainly featureless hills, but neighbouring Munros Ben Vorlich and Stuc a' Chroin are fortunately exciting exceptions.

As befits the nearest Munros to Edinburgh, they are popular mountains whose many and varied ascent routes provide a worthy introduction to Southern Highland hillwalking (Routes 18a – 18d). As for the isolated and much maligned third Munro, Ben Chonzie, we'll leave you to make up your own mind about it (Routes 20a and 20b).

BEN VORLICH   STUC A' CHROIN

Loch Voil

F-Stop: Situated on the edge of the Southern Highlands, these summits afford extensive but impressionistic views of their distant fellow Munros.

The great Prow of Stuc a' Chroin, seen to advantage only on approach from Ben Vorlich, is at its most photogenic late in the day when lit by the westering sun.

▲ 18 Ben Vorlich 165 985m/3232ft (OS 57, NN 629189)
For meaning, see namesake ▲5 on Page 29
▲ 19 Stuc a' Chroin 182 975m/3199ft (OS 57, NN 617174)
Stoochk a Chroa-in, probably Peak of the Sheepfold
(see also ▲12 Beinn a' Chroin)

BEN VORLICH

Ardvorlich

Loch Earn

Peak Fitness: No change since 1891 Tables.

When viewed from across Loch Earn, Ben Vorlich's convex upper slopes give it the appearance of a great pudding, but in reality it is an X-shaped mountain whose sky-high twin tops throw out two northern and two southern ridges. The topography permits several ascent options, especially in combination with an ascent of neighbouring Stuc a' Chroin, whose great Prow is one of the Southern Highlands' most outstanding mountain features.

The normal route up both mountains begins at Ardvorlich House on Lochearnside to the north (Route 18a). A circular route that begins a short distance east along the road at the foot of Glen Ample is equally worthy of consideration (Route 18b). The summits can also be approached from the south-east, from Callander or Glen Artney (Route 18c), while the shortest route up Stuc a' Chroin begins on the shores of Loch Lubnaig to the south-west (Route 18d).

Route 18a, with its refurbished path, is an obvious first place to start, although there's little to choose between it and Route 18b. Both routes approach Stuc a' Chroin via the steep environs of the Prow. If you'd prefer an easier or off-the-beaten-path approach to the Stuc, you might wish to consider Route 18c, while Route 18d up the Stuc is a short sharp shock to the system for the suitably stirred (you know who you are).

Route 18a Ben Vorlich and Stuc a' Chroin from Ardvorlich: Ben Vorlich North-east Ridge

Ben Vorlich + Stuc a' Chroin: G3 (with G4/G5 options) *****
   NN 633233, 9ml/15km, 1140m/3750ft M102
Ben Vorlich alone: G1 **** 6ml/10km, 890m/2900ft

Map note: In addition to OS 57 for the summits, OS 51 is required for the start of the route.

This time-honoured ascent route was, until recently, beginning to show its age, becoming literally bogged down, but path renovation has revitalised it and reinstated it as the premier route up Ben Vorlich.

Loch Earn

Coire Buidhe

NE Corrie

BEN VORLICH

F-Stop: At Ben Vorlich's summit, the whole ascent route is laid out below you to the north, leading the eye over Loch Earn to the Lawers Range. The view to the south is considerably more extensive but, apart from the Prow of Stuc a' Chroin in the foreground, it lacks one important ingredient – mountains.

From Ardvorlich House east gate on the South Lochearnside road, follow the driveway up to the buildings, cross a bridge and take the Land Rover track that runs up Glen Vorlich on the right-hand side of the river. About ¾ml/1km beyond the house, just beyond a small stream at NN 630218, a grassy track forks left to continue up the glen (see Page 101). Ignore this track and keep to the main track, which makes a beeline for the summit of Ben Vorlich ahead.

When the main track ends at the

stream coming down from the great scallop of Coire Buidhe (*Corra Boo-ya*, Yellow Corrie) on the right, **an excellently renovated baggers' path** makes a rising traverse up the left-hand side of the corrie to top out on Vorlich's north-east ridge at around the 650m/2150ft mark. Just before the path turns left for its final climb onto the ridge, note the branch path that continues straight on up the corrie (this will be the return route). At the time of writing, renovation ends at the path junction, leaving a short rough section up to the ridge as evidence of the main path's former state.

A stony path continues up the ridge between Coire Buidhe to the right and a smaller north-east corrie to the left. The angle is steep for a while, then it eases before steepening again to the summit. The two tops at each end of the short summit ridge are connected by 100m of path so well-beaten that it amounts to the Highlands' first aerial motorway. The west top and ▲summit, reached first, is 1m/3ft higher than the east top.

Continuing to Stuc a' Chroin, a stony path descends Vorlich's curving south-west ridge, weaving steeply down among outcrops to the intervening Bealach an Dubh Choirein (*Byalach an Doo Chorrin*, Pass of the Black Corries). The descent gives you plenty of time (more than enough for some) to contemplate the Prow of the Stuc, which towers intimidatingly over the far side of the bealach. On the left (east) side of the bealach is Gleann an Dubh Choirein (see Route 18d), while on the right (west) side is Coire Fuadarach (see Route 18c). On the near side of the bealach, make a note of the initially indistinct path that is the beginning of the return route to Ardvorlich via upper Coire Fuadarach and Coire Buidhe.

Adrenaline junkies will find exhilarating scrambling of all grades on the crest of the Prow, while others may prefer to stick to the stony path that climbs below the crest on the right. Be advised, however, that the upper section of this path is now so worn, gritty, steep and exposed that it may fill you with feelings other than exhilaration. If in doubt, settle for a bypass path that climbs the steep little corrie right of the Prow.

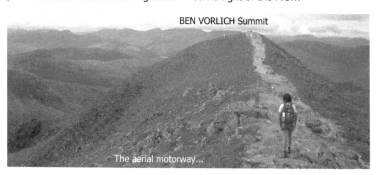

BEN VORLICH Summit

The aerial motorway...

To find the bypass path from the bealach, contour around the foot of the rocks into the little corrie. The path is easy to follow for a while but becomes increasingly indistinct until, in the bowl of the corrie, it becomes lost in rock debris from storms of 2004. You'll find it again as it climbs out of the head of the corrie to the low point on the skyline of the north-west ridge. The ascent is problem-free, but steep and rough enough in places for those who eschew the use of trekking poles to use hands for balance.

The path tops out at a large cairn on the corrie rim, where it joins another path up the Prow's easy north-west ridge. At the foot of the final boulder slope, a smaller cairn marks the spot where a path goes diagonally right to Stuc a' Chroin's summit, some 500m metres to the south across gently rising ground. Alternatively, continue to the top of the Prow for a view of Ben Vorlich over the crags, then cross the broad connecting ridge to the Stuc's ▲ summit.

To re-descend to Ardvorlich, first return to the Bealach an Dubh Choirein, taking as much care on descent as on ascent. On the left (west) side of the bealach you'll find a

---

Torpedo: If omitting Stuc a' Chroin, the simplest way back to Ardvorlich from Ben Vorlich's summit is to reverse the ascent route. For variety, you could return via the Bealach an Dubh Choirein and Coire Buidhe, as described in the main text, but there's another tempting alternative if you fancy a longer day out, although it involves rougher going.

Descend Vorlich's grassy south-east ridge to the wilds of Dubh Choirein (see Route 18d for description), then return northwards to Glen Vorlich through an inviting rocky defile on the east side of the mountain. The path through the defile, although still marked on most maps, has succumbed to the ravages of time and now gives boggy going for much of the way.

Choose to enjoy the experience thus: if you have generosity of spirit to spare, embrace the ecological development as an example of nature reclaiming its own, otherwise welcome it as a crowd deterrent. Not until it reaches the 500m/1650ft mark in Glen Vorlich does the 'path' develop into the grassy track that rejoins the outward Land Rover track at NN 630218, as noted on Page 99.

BEN VORLICH E top

... in winter

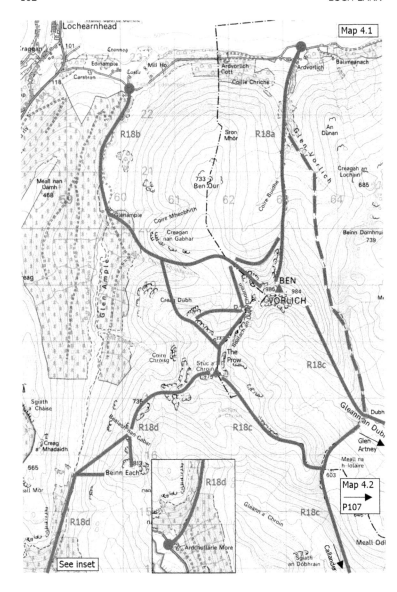

path that contours around the upper reaches of Coire Fuadarach to a saddle on Ben Vorlich's north-west ridge, at the head of Coire Buidhe. The path is indistinct and boggy for a while but improves as it approaches the ridge. From the saddle, it contours around the right-hand side of Coire Buidhe to rejoin the ascent route at the start of the renovated path (as noted above).

STUC A' CHROIN

The Prow

SE Ridge

NW Ridge

Bypass path

Bealach an Dubh Choirein

BEN VORLICH SW Ridge

Needlepoint: The renovated path up Ben Vorlich rivals the Ben Lomond Tourist Path as the easiest foul-weather ascent in the Southern Highlands. Finding your way up and down Stuc a' Chroin in cloud is a different creel of herring.

When approached from Vorlich via the Bealach an Dubh Choirein, with rock looming out of the mist everywhere, the variety of route options can be confusing. On ascent, take care not to be led onto difficult ground. This is true even on the Prow bypass path, which is difficult to follow in places owing to rock debris.

The Stuc's summit cairn is perched at the cliff edge overlooking Gleann an Dubh Choirein. Don't confuse it with a larger cairn set back c.70m from the cliff edge (see Route 18d).

On descent, if using the Prow bypass path, take care to descend from the right spot, from the large cairn on the north-west ridge, not the smaller one higher up. For an easier route in cloud, use Route 18c.

Chilly Willy: Ben Vorlich is a popular winter goal from Lochearnside but its convex upper slopes are deceptively dangerous when iced. Near the summit, on the rim of the north-east corrie, a slip would be difficult to arrest, even with an ice axe, and that makes the standard ascent route from Ardvorlich a more awkward proposition than many expect. Accidents have happened here.

When approached from Ben Vorlich, *all* routes up Stuc a' Chroin, including the Prow bypass path, become snow and ice climbs in winter.

Route 18b Ben Vorlich and Stuc a' Chroin
from Glen Ample

Ben Vorlich + Stuc a' Chroin: NN 602224 M102
    G3 (with G4/G5 options) **** 9½m/15km, 1110m/3650ft
Ben Vorlich alone via its NW Ridge: G2 *** 7ml/11km, 890m/2900ft
Stuc a' Chroin alone via its NW Ridge: G2 ** 8ml/13km, 880m/2850ft

Map note: As for Route 18a, OS 51 is required in addition to OS 57.

This route vies with Route 18a as the easiest approach to a round of the two Munros, courtesy of an ATV track that climbs to a height of c.600m/2000ft on the flanks of Ben Vorlich's north-west ridge, in the upper reaches of Coire Fuadarach. The Bealach an Dubh Choirein is at the head of the corrie, with Stuc a' Chroin's Prow in view all the way up.

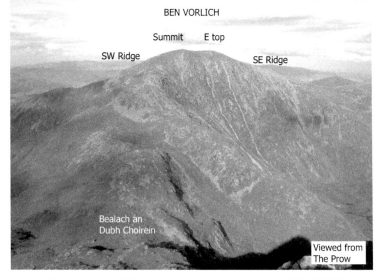

BEN VORLICH
Summit   E top
SW Ridge   SE Ridge
Bealach an
Dubh Choirein
Viewed from
The Prow

From the picturesque Falls of Edinample on the South Lochearnside road, take the Land Rover track up Glen Ample to Glenample farm. The footbridge over the Burn of Ample at NN 596203, opposite the farm, was washed away by a flash flood in August 2004, so follow these directions carefully:

After the track bridges the river at

NN 596208, leave it for a path that runs along the riverbank around the farm perimeter fence. This leads to another track beyond the farm buildings. Go right along this track to a stream less than 100m away. On the stream's far (right-hand) bank, a short path climbs to another track. Cross this second track (ignore any signposts that direct you along it) and continue up beside a fence for less than 100m to a reach a third track.

This is the track you want. Improving with height, it climbs through forestry plantations onto open hillside, eventually becoming a grassy ATV track that climbs high into Coire Fuadarach. It gives a painless approach walk, easily the equal of that from Ardvorlich, and it has the additional benefit of providing ever more imposing views of the looming Prow of Stuc a' Chroin.

When the track ends, gentle grass slopes climb to a saddle on Vorlich's north-west ridge, where you'll cross Route 18a return path from the Bealach an Dubh Choirein to Coire Buidhe. If you're lucky, you'll find an occasional path to ease the ascent. The ridge steepens near the skyline, where it joins the upper south-west ridge for the last short stretch to Ben Vorlich's ▲ summit.

Continue to ▲ Stuc a' Chroin as per Route 18a, then return to the Bealach an Dubh Choirein and descend across upper Coire Fuadarach to rejoin the approach track. If you'd prefer to avoid the environs of the Prow on descent, descend the Stuc's north-west ridge until you have outflanked all crags (including the rock buttress at NN 613186), then descend easier slopes into Coire Fuadarach. Note that, summer or winter, this line offers the easiest route up and down Stuc a' Chroin from Lochearnside.

Needlepoint: Although the approach track doesn't go all the way to Ben Vorlich's summit, keep heading upwards from its end and you should get there even in cloud. Foul-weather considerations for Stuc a' Chroin are as for Route 18a.

Chilly Willy: For a winter ascent of Ben Vorlich, the Coire Fuadarach approach avoids the problem of Route 18a's deceptively steep finish. Depending on the precise line taken up the north-west ridge, however, you may still encounter pockets of steep snow. Winter considerations for the connection to Stuc a' Chroin are as for Route 18a.

Route 18c Ben Vorlich and/or Stuc a' Chroin from the South-east: Callander

Ben Vorlich + Stuc a' Chroin: NN 636107 M102/107
    G3 (with G4/G5 options) *** 13ml/21km, 1250m/4100ft
Ben Vorlich alone via its SE Ridge: G1 *** 13ml/21km, 1170m/3850ft
Stuc a' Chroin alone via its SE Ridge: G1 *** 12ml/19km, 810m/2650ft

On their south-east sides, far from the Lochearnside trade routes to the north, both Ben Vorlich and Stuc a' Chroin throw out long, gentle, grassy ridges that would receive more attention were they easier to reach. If you're looking for an individual ascent of either mountain that avoids the steep sections of Routes 18a and 18b, both ridges give excellent walking.

However, unless you're perverse by nature, the approach to the foot of the ridges may seem less than excellent, which is why we can't bring ourselves to award these south-east routes more than three stars. Long miles of remote, screamingly featureless back-country terrain are not everyone's cup of cranachan.

We suspect few will be tempted this way for a first ascent of the two peaks, but for a second ascent... or if you wish to avoid summer weekend crowds... or if you hanker after a walk on the wild side...

The shorter of two possible approaches begins at the end of the minor road past Bracklinn Falls north of Callander. There are parking spaces at the end of the public road, where a

STUC A' CHROIN   SE Ridge

From Callander

branch forks left to Drumardoch farm. A second approach begins at the end of the public road in Glen Artney

further east, although this one really is for masochists only (Route 18c Alternative Approach).

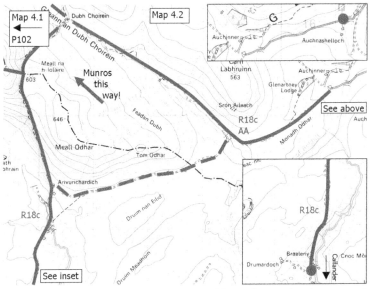

From the road-end near Drumardoch on the Callander approach, follow the continuing Land Rover track past Braeleny farm to the boarded-up buildings at Arivurichardich (try saying that fast). This is unashamedly dismal country, with undulating terrain dented by glens so broad and shallow they barely merit the name.

Just below Arivurichardich the track crosses the Keltie Water, whose bridge was washed away by storms in 2004. On a good day you can use stepping stones to cross both the river and a tributary just upstream of the former bridge. At other times you may need

to paddle. And remember there are yet other times when the water is high enough to wash away a bridge.

From the left-hand side of the upper building at Arivurichardich, the route continues on a former stalkers' path that has seen better days but still gives reasonably good going (except after rain). After a couple of hundred metres, at a fence, it forks. Take the right branch to climb diagonally up the hillside onto the south-east ridge of Stuc a' Chroin, eventually reaching the skyline near the small hump of Meall na h-Iolaire (*Myowl na Hillyera*, Hill of the Eagle).

If heading for Stuc a' Chroin, follow

the continuing path up the inviting ridge (see description below). For Ben Vorlich, cross to the far side of the ridge and descend a frustrating 150m/500ft to the ruined shieling of Dubh Choirein at the foot of Vorlich's south-east ridge. The path marked on most maps has been much reclaimed by the moor, making for somewhat boggy going, but it's not far down.

Dubh Choirein is perhaps the most forlorn and lonely spot in the Southern Highlands. It so well deserves its Gaelic name (meaning Black Corries) that on a dreich day it is a relief to leave it behind before you succumb to existential despair about the inequities of life.

BEN VORLICH

Bealach an Dubh Choirein

SE Ridge

Gleann an Dubh Choirein

Viewed from Stuc a' Chroin SE Ridge

Heading skywards once more, clingy moor and peat hags are soon happily left behind for the grassy south-east ridge and a nice wee path that makes for a surprisingly diverting ascent. Approaching Vorlich's east top, a rocky steepening looks like it might quicken the pulse, but the path weaves its way up easily onto gentle slopes above. The east top is soon reached, followed by the ▲summit. If continuing to Stuc a' Chroin, see Route 18a.

From the ▲summit of Stuc a'

Chroin, descend that mountain's south-east ridge to rejoin the outward route near Meall na h-Iolaire. The broad ridge, which revels in the quixotic name of Aonach Gaineamhach (*Ernach Ganavach*, Ridge of Fine Sand), gives a perfect evening stravaig down a couple of miles of beguiling greensward. Approaching Meall na h-Iolaire, you may be concerned that the path is descending further right than expected. Don't worry – it won't let you down.

Route 18c Alternative Approach from the South-east: Glen Artney

Ben Vorlich and Stuc a' Chroin: NN 711161 M102/107
   G3 with G4/G5 options ** 14ml/22km, 1080m/3550ft
Ben Vorlich alone via its SE Ridge: G1 ** 12ml/19km, 830m/2750ft
Stuc a' Chroin alone via its SE ridge: G1 ** 14ml/22km, 820m/2700ft

All routes: + 2ml/3km road walk (1ml/1½km each way)
All routes: ** (more if you have a need to be alone)

Only those who revel in contrariness need bother to read this. The Glen Artney alternative approach to Route 18c involves more road walking, worse going and even duller scenery. The glen's one claim to fame is that it lies on the Highland Boundary Fault, which separates two distinct geological periods.

The sandstone hills to the south are in the Lowlands, while the mica schist hills to the north (including the two Munros) are in the Highlands. Not that knowledge of these facts is likely to ameliorate one's verdict on the dreariness of the scenery.

Beginning at the car park 1ml/1½km from the road-end, walk to the road-end then bear left on a Land Rover track that crosses a low moor to a junction in Gleann an Dubh Choirein. The track is good as far as here, but it deteriorates to a tiresomely boggy path as it continues along the riverbank up the view-free glen to the ruins at Dubh Choirein.

Climb Ben Vorlich and/or Stuc a' Chroin as described opposite. If climbing the Stuc and descending its south-east ridge to Meall na h-Iolaire, you can avoid the boggy re-descent to Dubh Choirein. Instead, take the stalkers' path down to Arivurichardich and the rutted Land Rover track that runs from there back to the track junction in Gleann an Dubh Choirein.

STUC A' CHROIN

The Prow

SE Ridge

Needlepoint: In cloud, the south-east ridges of both Ben Vorlich and Stuc a' Chroin remain pretty straightforward, but the dismal countryside is even more depressing than in fine weather. Considerations for the crossing of the Bealach an Dubh Choirein to link the mountains are as for Route 18a.

Chilly Willy: Under normal winter conditions, both south-east ridges remain straightforward, although the rocky steepening on Vorlich's south-east ridge may give sport if the path is obliterated by snow. Considerations for the crossing of the Bealach an Dubh Choirein to link the mountains are as for Route 18a.

Route 18d Stuc a' Chroin alone from Loch Lubnaig: South-west Ridge

G2 ** (more if you're an awkward bagger) Route Rage Alert
NN 583136, 7ml/11km, 980m/3200ft M102

This is the shortest way up Stuc a' Chroin, but it's a pernickety little route whose quirky character will keep you on your toes all the way. For non-scramblers who don't wish to bag Vorlich as well, it offers a way up that completely avoids the Prow, but it is nowhere near as easy an ascent route as Route 18c.

Although its 'enigma variations' can prove diverting if you're in the mood, it is definitely not an option for someone simply seeking a straightforward saunter to the summit.

Point 735

STUC A' CHROIN

Viewed from
Beinn Each

The ascent begins well enough, on the signposted 'public footpath to Loch Earn via Glen Ample,' which leaves the A84 at Ardchullarie More on the shores of Loch Lubnaig (car parking in lay-by). A couple of hundred feet up, ignore a minor right branch and follow the main path left over a small stream to climb steadily through deep forest and join a forest track.

The angle eases as the track exits the forest and traverses the hillside to the long, flat saddle leading over to Glen Ample. The track itself becomes very boggy, but a path to its right finds drier going.

The hill on the right is Beinn Each (*Ben Yech*, Horse Mountain). Your first objective is the Bealach nan Cabar (*Byalach nan Cabbar*, Antler Pass), which separates Beinn Each from Stuc a' Chroin further along.

The Bealach nan Cabar is only 310m/1000ft above the high point of the track but the steep and laborious ascent from there to the skyline makes it seem further. The expletive count will vary according to your ability to spot sheep trails that burrow through clinging heather from one grassy oasis to another.

The largest heather-free zone will be found by descending into Glen Ample until directly below the bealach, and climbing straight up from there, but few will wish to make such a detour. Instead, begin just beyond the high point of the track, opposite a wall that climbs the hillside on the left, and make a rising traverse to the right.

Top marks and a pat on the back if you can take a *directissima* line to the bealach, because you won't know exactly where you are until you reach the skyline. Many who pass this way take too steep a line and gain the

skyline too soon, leaving one or two knolls to surmount to reach the bealach itself. Patience, patience.

Hampering progress to Stuc a' Chroin beyond the bealach is Point 735, a frustrating obstacle of a rocky hillock whose negotiation requires a convoluted 70m/230ft ascent and 60m/200ft descent. A small path takes the best line, although it may not appear to do so until you attempt your own variation.

At last you arrive at the foot of Stuc a' Chroin's south-west ridge for a final 310m/1000ft pull to the summit. The path climbs broad grassy slopes to a small dip, floored by wet flats, then continues up a rockier steepening to the summit plateau. If in doubt, you'll find easier ground left of the rocks. After reaching a large cairn, you'll find the ▲ summit cairn a further 70m away at the edge of east-facing cliffs overlooking Gleann an Dubh Choirein.

Beinn Each

STUC A' CHROIN

Baffies: Summer or winter, expect Route 18d to take longer than you'd expect.

Route 18d Alternative Descent: Beinn Each
G2 ** Add-on: ½ml/1km, 170m/550ft M102

After returning over Point 735 to the Bealach nan Cabar, you may find that the heather slopes leading back down to the forest track seem even less appealing than on ascent. A return over craggy Beinn Each seems scarcely preferable but, because you have had the foresight to purchase this guidebook, we can advise you of a path that runs over the top and down the far side, which tips the balance in favour of returning this way.

The extra effort required to climb over Beinn Each makes it a soul-destroying outward route, but on the way back it is surprising how much the prospect of a hassle-free return route, with Loch Lubnaig below as a homing beacon, gains in desirability. Unless the very idea of cavorting down the knee-deep heather of the ascent route brings a glow to your cheeks, you'll find that a return over Beinn Each is worth the extra 170m/550ft climb.

From the Bealach nan Cabar, a few more minor ups and downs require negotiation before you reach the foot of Beinn Each's craggy north face, which is nowhere near as difficult nor as high as it appears on approach. It is nevertheless important to stick to the path, which threads an easy way around the crags. Even when, at one point, the path traverses further left than seems warranted, stick with it.

At the summit, bear right to follow the continuing path down the grassy south-west ridge and try not to lose it. At one point, for instance, in the middle of a steep descent that goes straight down the hillside, the main path suddenly shoots left to stay on the ridge. It eventually wends its way down a shoulder on the near (north) side of a deep-cut stream, to rejoin the approach track.

Hint: The deep-cut stream is an obvious landmark when viewed from the approach track on the outward journey. Recce the inconspicuous start of the path on the north side of the stream, beside a wall (NN 590151).

Needlepoint: If you attempt the south-west side of the Stuc in foul weather, good luck to you. Just finding the Bealach nan Cabar, and recognising it once you get there, will prove… not easy. Once on the skyline, if you stray from the sometimes indistinct path, navigation over or around the various rocky knolls will prove… not easy. Hint for the determined: occasional rusty fence posts along the line of the south-west ridge make useful markers; the path is never far from them for long.

Chilly Willy: While not as easy a winter approach to Stuc a' Chroin as the south-east ridge (Route 18c), the south-west ridge is more awkward than difficult. The steep ascent to the skyline is not made any easier by snow-encrusted heather. The rocky knolls on the ridge will not prove an obstacle technically but, if the path has disappeared beneath snow, the route is even less obvious than it is in summer.

▲ 20 Ben Chonzie 250 931m/3054ft (OS 51 or 52, NN 773308)

Ben Honzie, probably Mossy Mountain (from Gaelic *choinnich*), also known as Ben-y-Hone

BEN CHONZIE

notch

Loch Turret

Peak Fitness: No change since 1891 Tables.

There's no getting away from the fact that this is a dull mountain in dull country, situated on the edge of the Highlands north-east of Loch Earn. With its phenomenally phlat summit, physically pheatureless phlanks and equally phorm-phree surrounding hills, it wouldn't merit a second glance had it not managed to heave itself up over the 3000ft mark. Nevertheless, recent access improvements prompt us to suggest (in a whisper, and please don't tell anyone we said so) that perhaps the time has come to take a phresh look at it and re-assess its poor reputation.

We're not suggesting that the hill has suddenly acquired hitherto unnoticed pulchritude, merely that access tracks on either side, from Glen Lednock in the south-west and Loch Turret in the south-east, now make the summit an amiable objective for some exercise on a phine day.

The Glen Lednock approach (Route 20b) requires 150m/500ft more ascent, but it is nonetheless still the quickest way to the summit. It is 1ml/2km shorter than the Loch Turret approach and its Land Rover track climbs much higher up the mountain. There's not much in it, though, so for a first visit (as if you'll ever go back?), we'd opt for the Loch Turret approach (Route 20a), which is more scenic and allows for return trip variations.

Map note: Both ascent routes are on OS 52. If using OS 51, the start of Route 20a is just off it.

Terminator: Don't believe this re-assessment phooey. Another possible meaning of Ben Chonzie is Mountain of Weeping (from Gaelic *chaoineidh*), aptly referring to the effect it has on those who climb it. Cheerless Chonzie is the kind of over-sized compost heap that makes philately seem an attractive sport.

Needlepoint: In phog, you do not want to lose the phence mentioned in the pholloring route descriptions. Trust me.

Chilly Willy: Whether you agree with Terminator or not, snow on the hill certainly adds to its aesthetic appeal. It's a good place for a first winter outing.

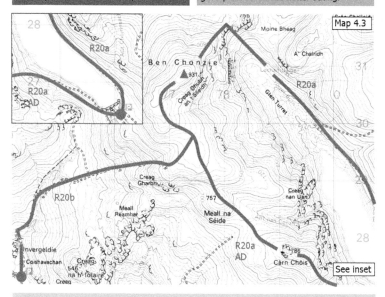

Baffies: After a phun-philled phootslog, make sure you're down in time for afternoon tea at Glenturret Distillery, passed on the road to Loch Turret.

Route 20a Ben Chonzie from Loch Turret

G1 *** NN 822266, 10ml/16km, 570m/1850ft M114

The south-eastern approach to Chonzie is given some initial interest by a glacial trench that contains two bodies of water: a large reservoir (Loch Turret) and a small lochan (Lochan Uaine, *Lochan Oo-anya*, Green Lochan). Note that the road to Loch Turret dam north of Crieff is open to the public despite any notices you may see to the contrary.

From the dam car park, a vehicle track along the east side of the loch runs all the way to Lochan Uaine at the foot of the mountain. The lochside stroll takes you through the ice-scoured trench and past an attractive clutch of heather-clad drumlins at Loch Turret's head. Beyond here, the track is less well-surfaced but continues to give good going all the way to its end at Lochan Uaine.

Beyond here, keep going in the same direction to follow traces of path up the marshy hillside, aiming for a rough rake of grass and boulders that tops out at an obvious notch on the skyline. The rake is quite steep in parts, but it's only 210m/700ft to the skyline. Once up, turn left to follow an old fence up easy convex slopes to Chonzie's grassy ▲ summit dome, only another 240/800ft above.

Route 20a Alternative Descent: High-level Return Route

G1 *** Extra mileage: none; Extra ascent: 90m/300ft M114

Make a round trip by returning along the high ground on the west side of Loch Turret. This gives a high-level walk on mostly good terrain and paths, ending with a less steep (though pathless) descent.

From Chonzie's summit, follow the fence SW then SE along the broad ridge to Meall na Seide (*Myowl na Say-ja*, Hill of the Bed of Hay) and Carn Chois (*Carn Choas*, Cairn of the Cave or Crevice). A short distance further, descend grassy slopes into the corrie on the left then descend diagonally down the hillside to reach the vehicle track along Loch Turret's west shore.

Loch Turret from the notch

GiGi: Gaelic dictionaries give *Seide* in Meall na Seide an alternative meaning: 'a swelling in a person from luxurious living and deep potations.' Of course, an upstanding reader such as your good self will never suffer from such an affliction.

Route 20b Ben Chonzie from Glen Lednock
G1 ** NN 743273, 9ml/14km, 720m/2350ft M114

We award this plodmeister's delight two stars because it gives perhaps the easiest ascent of any Southern Highland Munro, courtesy of a Land Rover track that climbs featureless hillsides above Coishavachan house onto the plateau south of Ben Chonzie's summit.

From the car park beside the white house at the foot of the track, walk up the drive to Coishavachan to find a vehicle track that continues around the buildings and up the glen of the Invergeldie Burn. At a height of 310m/1000ft the track crosses the burn at a dammed pool and climbs beside a tributary onto the shoulder of Ben Chonzie. Ignore a right fork after 70m and, further up at a height of 470m/1550ft, ignore a left branch that goes to Glen Almond on the north side of the mountain.

The track becomes rougher as it climbs but still provides good value all the way up to a height of 800m/2600ft. From near the end of the track, several paths continue across the grass to reach the fence that links Ben Chonzie to Carn Chois, and from there it's only a short stroll to the ▲summit.

With little of interest to provide distraction on the way up, the ascent is little more than an eyes-down work-out. On a sunny summer's day (or sunny winter's day), there's nothing wrong with that, but imagine how dismal the climb was before the track was built and you'll better appreciate Chonzie's poor reputation.

BEN CHONZIE

Baffies: Don't leave Glen Lednock before driving further up the road to view Sput Rolla, a plunging waterfall below Loch Lednock reservoir. Lower down the glen, the Nature Trail at the De'il's Cauldron gorge is also worth a whistle stop.

5 GLEN LOCHAY

At the west end of Loch Tay, Glen Lochay curves deep into the hills north of the Tyndrum/Crianlarich/Killin road through Strath Fillan and Glen Dochart to give access to six flanking Munros. Unfortunately, although the glen itself is picturesque enough, in a green, serene and undemanding kind of way, the featureless hillsides that rise to the heights are rather less inspiring, especially when cloud hangs low on the hill.

When viewed from the glen, only Ben Challum at its head is shapely enough to catch the eye, but it stands

so far beyond the end of the public road that it is usually climbed via its less attractive south side above Tyndrum (Routes 21a and 21b). Creag Mhor, on the other hand, turns out to be more interesting than its lower slopes suggest (Routes 24a and 24b).

The remaining four Munros are, to be kind, **unrepentant heaps**. Meall Ghaordaidh's south-east ridge at least gives a straight up and down route (Route 26a), but Meall Ghlas and Sgiath Chuil (Routes 22a, 22b and 22c) and Beinn Heasgarnich (Route 24c) could sprawl for Scotland.

CREAG MHOR

BEINN HEASGARNICH

Glen Lochay

▲21 Ben Challum 106 1025m/3363ft (OS 50, NN 386322)
Calum's Mountain, possibly named for St. Columba
△South Top 998m/3275ft (OS 50, NN 342420)

BEN CHALLUM   S Top

NW Ridge

Dalrigh

Auchtertyre

Peak Fitness: No change since 1891 Tables.

At the head of Glen Lochay, Ben Challum's domed summit tops a craggy north face whose bounding north-west ridge beckons ascent. Another high-level ridge, slung between summit and South Top, promises more good times.

You just knew there'd be a catch, didn't you? Here it comes: from the end of the public road in Glen Lochay there's a 6ml/10km walk-in, eventually pathless, to the Bealach Ghlas

Leathaid (*Byalach Glass Lyeh-at*, Pass of the Green Slope) at the foot of the north-west ridge. You'd have to be made of stern stuff to opt for that over the much shorter approach from the A82 Tyndrum road on the south side of the mountain.

Challum itself is well aware of such modern hillwalking sensibilities and, in a fit of pique at those who shun the northern profile it would prefer to present to the world, hides its summit from the Tyndrum road behind a terminally dreary southern hillside.

The **tiresome trade route** up the mountain wends its weary way up this hillside, morphing bright-eyed baggers into crestfallen footsloggers (Route 21a). Those who have never felt the lure of hillwalking wonder what we more enlightened souls see in it. The view of Challum's lower slopes from near Tyndrum may well make you wonder yourself.

But there's good news for those who prefer something a tad less soporific. For the sake of an extra couple of miles, and to get yourself into Challum's good books, you can approach the north-west ridge from the Tyndrum side. We wouldn't recommend this route to anyone seeking an easy life but, if you can handle a spot of steep, off-path terrain, never was a bit more effort so richly rewarded (Route 21b).

BEN CHALLUM   S Top

NW Ridge

Gleann a' Chlachain

F-Stop: The summit panorama goes some way to compensate for the dull ascent by the normal route. The mountain's isolation gives it good all-round vistas of Southern Highland Munros, especially the near-at-hand Crianlarich and Tyndrum groups.

GiGi: St. Fillan, one of the prime movers in Scotland's uptake of Christianity, came to Strath Fillan from Iona around 664 and established a monastery at what is now Kirkton farm. For centuries the sanctuary was a haven of peace and learning in troubled times. In the fourteenth century Robert Bruce upgraded it to a priory, which it remained until falling into disrepair after the seventeenth century Reformation.

Route 21a Ben Challum from Kirkton Farm (near Tyndrum): Southern Slopes

G1 ** Route Rage Alert NN 355282, 7ml/11km, 900m/2950ft

Challum's summit environs deserve more than two stars, but the traditional ascent route probably deserves less. From the lay-by on the A82 opposite Kirkton farm, 2ml/3km east of Tyndrum, take the farm access road across the River Fillan (bridge) to join the West Highland Way.

Follow the Way to the farm buildings and the ruins of St. Fillan's priory (see Page 119). Immediately beyond the ruins, when the Way turns left, keep straight on along a farm track that leads up to and across the West Highland Railway line.

About 50m beyond the railway crossing, quit the track to climb diagonally right to a deer fence that can be seen above. Beside the fence you'll find a path that goes all the way to the summit. The fence veers much further right than seems warrantable, but the path hasn't developed here for no reason. Stick with it.

The main interest on ascent lies in avoiding the numerous sections of marshy ground. About half-way up, when the path temporarily levels off

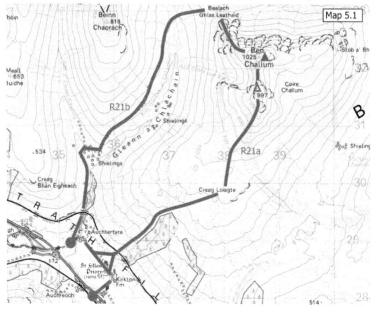

atop Creag Loisgte (*Craik Loshka*, possibly Burning Crag, from Gaelic *Loisg*), there's one stretch of bog that is particularly amusing.

Beyond here, with the unremarkable skyline of the South Top in view at last, the path continues its ascent on the right of the now broken fence. The angle steepens, but improved going more than compensates, courtesy of a stony path that climbs slopes of short grass and boulders.

Matters become more interesting at the △South Top, and about time too, where a curious little defile separates the cairned highpoint from the continuing ridge to Ben Challum's main summit. The ridge is quite narrow and rocky at first, though of zero difficulty. It soon becomes grassy again, giving **an agreeable high-level stroll** as it broadens across a shallow bealach to reach steeper, rockier slopes that climb to the ▲summit.

Needlepoint: The complex topography of the South Top makes it a very confusing place in cloud. On descent, after leaving the cairn on the highest point (and make sure you *are* on the highest point), it is important to find and keep to the path beside the fence. The fence doesn't reach all the way to the top but cairns lead down to it. If you can't see these, aim due south until you do.

The north-west ridge provides a more well-defined route to the summit in cloud, but an optimal line through the rock outcrops will be less easy to find.

Chilly Willy: Under snow, the ridge connecting South Top to summit gives the kind of **silly-grin-making ridge walk** for which the Scottish mountains were designed. In some conditions, though more rarely than in former years, a narrow snow arête forms. There is normally no undue difficulty for anyone properly equipped, but take care at the summit, which is perched close to cornices that form on both north and east sides.

The north-west ridge gives a more difficult winter ascent on steep snow slopes beside the rock outcrops.

Route 21b Ben Challum from Auchtertyre Farm
(near Tyndrum): North-west Ridge
G2 (with G3/G4 options) **** NN 354290, 9ml/14km, 900m/2950ft M120

A southern approach to Ben Challum's **entertaining north-west ridge** is made practicable by a Land Rover track that climbs Gleann a' Chlachain (Glen of the Village) on the mountain's west side. There are many places where the presence of such tracks detracts from the hillwalking experience. This isn't one of them.

The route begins at Auchtertyre farm at the foot of the glen. A Land Rover track, part of the West Highland Way, connects the farm to Kirkton farm about ½ml/1km away. You could begin on the Kirkton farm access road, as per Route 21a, but at the time of

writing you can drive up to Auchtertyre farm and begin there.

Park in the car park just before the bridge that leads to the farm and take the continuing Land Rover track that runs up the left-hand side of Gleann a' Chlachain. Keep right at a first fork then left at a second to follow the track high up the glen between Beinn Chaorach (*Ben Cheurach*, Sheep Mountain) and Ben Challum.

When the gravelly surface turns to grass, contour across tussocky ground at the head of the glen to reach the Bealach Ghlas Leathaid at the foot of Challum's north-west ridge.

The Castle

BEN CHALLUM

NW Ridge

Above the bealach, the ridge rises 450m/1475ft to the summit. The lower half consists of steep grass among outcrops, which include some **notable slabs**. The rocks culminate in a conspicuous **rock 'castle'**, up which a little path threads an intricate and unexpectedly easy way. There are numerous opportunities for scrambling, while those who wish to avoid rock altogether can outflank all obstacles on steep grass slopes further right. The upper half of the ridge rises more gently over broken ground to Challum's ▲summit.

To descend, cross to the △South Top and jog down the trade route (Route 21a). When you reach Kirkton farm, go right along the connecting Land Rover track to Auchtertyre farm.

GiGi: At the time of writing, the route from the Gleann a' Chlachain track to the foot of the north-west ridge is given added frisson by an electric fence that crosses the hillside. Fortunately, there are many places where it can be negotiated, either by **limbo dancing** or the employment of less dignified squirming techniques.

Baffies: Thanks to the many thousands who walk the West Highland Way each year, Auchtertyre farm boasts all kinds of accommodation (rooms, wigwams, camping) plus an all-year-round shop/café that makes a great little whistle-stop at the end of the day. If it's okay with you, and even if it isn't, I'll sit on a bench in the sun and sip tea while you nip up Challum. Address: Auchtertyre Farm, Tyndrum, Perthshire FK20 8RU. Tel: 01838-400251. See also Beinglas farm (Page 63).

NW Ridge in winter

▲**22 Meall Glas** 199 959m/3146ft (OS 51, NN 431321)
Myowl Glass, Green-grey Hill
△Beinn Cheathaich 937m/3074ft (OS 51, NN 444326)
Ben Chay-ich, Misty Mountain
▲**23 Sgiath Chuil** 270 921m/3022ft (OS 51, NN 462317)
Skee-a Choo-il, Back Wing (i.e. Sheltered Spot)
△Meall a' Churain, 918m/3012ft (OS 51, NN 463325)
Myowl a Choorin, Carrot Hill

Meall a'   SGIATH
Churain   CHUIL

Lairig a' Churain

Beinn Cheathaich

Peak Fitness: In the original 1891 Tables, the two Munros were Tops and the two Tops were Munros. This unlikely state of affairs came about because only Beinn Cheathaich and Meall a' Churain were named on Munro's map. The position was reversed in 1921.

This **well-matched but ill-starred couple** will never feature highly in *Magnificent Mountains of the Highlands*, no matter how many volumes that series runs to. Whether they are approached from Glen Dochart to the south or Glen Lochay to the north, their summits recede above sprawling moor and barely rate a second glance. When travelling along the A85 through Glen Dochart, you'd probably drive past them in blissful ignorance were it not pointed out to you that, hey, those two highpoints up there are, gee whiz, Munros.

So why 'ill-starred'? Because, in a good tramping range such as the Glen Lyon hills, the two multi-topped summit ridges wouldn't look amiss. Stick them in the middle of the rough, boggy, strength-sapping, spirit-numbing moor that it is their lot to inhabit and they suddenly become less appealing. Additionally separate them by a deep, peaty pass (the 609m/1998ft-high Lairig a' Churain, *Lahrik a Chooran*, Carrot Pass) and you have the makings of **the mother of all route rages**.

Other Glen Lochay hills have redeeming features. This pair can't even muster interesting Gaelic names that flatter to deceive. That task is delegated to their two subsidiary Tops: Carrot and Misty. It is normal to bag the two summits together and then not return until amnesia sets in.

There are two issues to be resolved before tackling them: which to climb first and whether to approach from the north (Glen Lochay) or the south (Glen Dochart). Both mountains present intimidatingly steep slopes to the intervening Lairig a' Churain. Those of Sgiath Chuil are more easily tackled on

ascent, so we suggest climbing Meall Glas first.

Most older guidebooks describe the Glen Dochart approach only (Route 22b), as it is the shorter of the two and the more easily reached (from the A85 east of Crianlarich). However, we suggest you drive and walk those extra few miles in Glen Lochay, to find the only terrain hereabouts that has pretensions to forming approach ridges, and where access to Meall Glas has been revolutionised in recent years by a Land Rover track that climbs to within 300m/1000ft of the summit (Route 22a).

It is normal GoTH Club policy to disapprove of upland vehicle tracks, but this one we're happy to get down on our knees and kiss. Although we still can't bring ourselves to award the combined ascent of both Munros any more than a single star, an ascent of Meall Glas alone, up and down this track, gives **an easy and scenic training trip** that we're happy to award three stars.

If you do tackle Meall Glas alone, you may prefer to tackle Sgiath Chuil alone using a longer but easier approach by another Land Rover track that begins further east along Glen Dochart (Route 22c).

Baffies: Meall Glas + Sgiath Chuil versus a Killin tea room + a plate of muffins. Difficult decision? I think not.

F-Stop: Permit a dissenting voice. Meall Glas does have one redeeming feature: the summit view. Thanks to its central and solitary position between Glens Dochart and Lochay, it affords **excellent all-round** **close-up views** of the surrounding mountains: Ben Challum to the west, Sgiath Chuil to the east, Ben More to the south and Creag Mhor and the other Lochay Munros to the north.

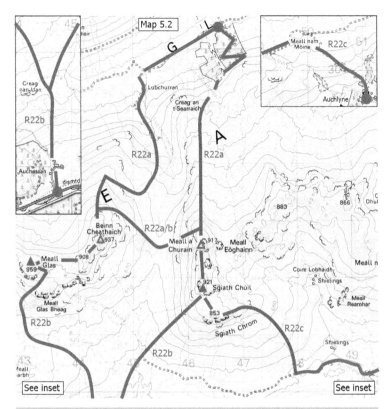

Needlepoint: You do *not* want to attempt to navigate the Lairig a' Churain in cloud or when the steep grass is wet. Ditto the moorland approaches from Glen Dochart to the south (Routes 22b and 22c). Be told. As individual goals, however, each Munro can be reached relatively easily in cloud from Glen Lochay to the north (Route 22a).

Chilly Willy: In winter the smooth grass hillsides that flank each side of the Lairig a' Churain become extremely steep, avalanche-prone snow slopes. Only experienced, properly equipped winter parties should attempt the crossing.

If tackling each Munro individually, the northern approaches (Route 22a) are less steep than the southern approaches (Routes 22b and 22c) and even more preferable than in summer. The Land Rover track makes Meall Glas in particular (say it quietly) **a surprisingly rewarding and scenic winter objective**. As a bonus, the fording of the River Lochay will bring colour to your cheeks.

Route 22a Meall Glas and Sgiath Chuil
from Kenknock (Glen Lochay)

G2 * NN 466364, 11ml/18km, 1190m/3900ft

Meall Glas alone (up and down the Land Rover track and Beinn Cheathaich's
    north ridge): G1 *** 10ml/16km, 890m/2900ft

Sgiath Chuil alone (up and down the forest track and Meall a' Churain's
    north ridge): G2 ** 7ml/11km, 770m/2550ft

From the car park at the end of the public road just beyond Kenknock farm, take the continuing Land Rover track beside the River Lochay and fork left at a junction after c.1ml/1½km. The left branch fords the river and so must you, as the bridge marked on older maps at NN 453356 no longer exists. The crossing is normally an easy paddle.

Beinn Cheathaich

MEALL GLAS

Glen Lochay

Across the river, the track passes the old boarded-up building at Lubchurran and climbs the glen behind it towards the Lairig a' Churain between the two Munros. Before reaching the lairig, the track abandons the glen to curve right onto the broad north ridge of Beinn Cheathaich, the Top at the north end of Meall Glas's mile-long summit plateau. The track ends on boggy flats at a height of 670m/2200ft, from where easy slopes of grass then heath continue to Beinn Cheathaich's Δsummit.

NB At the point where the track bears right towards the north ridge, it is tempting to abandon it for a more direct route to the summit, but you'll

Meall a' Churain   SGIATH
                        CHUIL

find much gentler and easier going on the ridge itself. As you ascend, recce the best route up Sgiath Chuil, which rises steeply across the boggy Lairig a' Churain to the left.

From Beinn Cheathaich, a broad, grassy ridge-cum-plateau curves over the rounded rise of Meall Glas Beag (*Bake*, Little; Point 908 on OS map) to the dome-like ▲summit of Meall Glas. A good path takes the line of least resistance by skirting Meall Glas Beag. After taking in the summit view from Meall Glas, retrace your steps to Beinn Cheathaich and prepare to cross the Lairig a' Churain to Sgiath Chuil.

Intimidatingly steep hillsides rise over 300m/1000ft on each side of the lairig. A direct descent from Beinn Cheathaich leads onto difficult broken ground and should be avoided. It is possible to descend from the dip between Meall Glas and Meall Glas Beag, or from the dip between Meall Glas Beag and Beinn Cheathaich, but the easiest option is a dog-leg descent north of the latter. Re-descend the north ridge a short distance until you can see a way back across easy grass slopes below all difficulties (you can recce the route on the way up).

After negotiating peat hags and tangled heather on the tedious lairig,

you next have to decide which way to climb the even steeper (if mostly grassy) slopes that now rise before you. The skyline is the ridge that connects Meall a' Churain (left) to Sgiath Chuil (right). The shortest route up, for the likes of mountain goats, goes diagonally right to the dip just before Sgiath Chuil's summit, but it is an extremely steep clamber.

For those whose hooves feel insufficiently cloven, the easiest way up is to make another dog-leg by first climbing left onto the north ridge of Meall a' Churain. It is still a steep ascent, but it remains straightforward as long as the grass is dry. Once on the ridge, still steepish slopes, but now with short heath underfoot, continue more easily to ∆Meall a' Churain.

From here, an intermittent path continues along a broad ridge of grass and rocks to the ▲summit of Sgiath Chuil. With all the hard work over, this final stroll, over a minor hump (Carrot Top?), seems very pleasant indeed. The summit cairn is perched atop a rock band that is the most prominent feature of the mountain when viewed from Glen Dochart.

The return route to Glen Lochay begins with a retracing of steps to Meall a' Churain and continues down its north ridge. Unfortunately, the good terrain doesn't last forever. If you're lucky, you'll find a path that eases the going as the ridge flares out onto complex moorland. It's not a great way to end the day, but help is at hand…

Trend right (east), aiming for the upper end of a forestry plantation on the far side of the shallow glen of the Allt Innisdaimh (*Owlt Innish-dev*, Stream of the Deer Pasture). From

here, at a height of 380m/1250ft, a welcome forest track zigzags the final 170m/550ft down to Kenknock.

Meall Glas Beag

MEALL GLAS

Beinn Cheathaich

Route 22b Meall Glas and Sgiath Chuil
from Auchessan (Glen Dochart)

G2 * Route Rage Alert NN 447275, 9ml/15km, 1200m/3950ft M126
Meall Glas alone return trip: G2 * Route Rage Alert 7ml/11km, 800m/2650ft
Sgiath Chuil alone return trip: G2 * Route Rage Alert 7ml/11km, 760m/2500ft

Begin on the A85 at the access road to Auchessan farm (parking on roadside verge or at Ben More car park a short distance east). Follow the road to the last house and take the continuing farm track around its right-hand side. When the track ends at a sheep fank, a good path continues up slopes of grass and bracken between a stream and a deer fence.

From the stile at the upper end of the fence, a boggier path continues

beside the stream, heading more or less northwards onto the moor above. The path comes and goes on wet ground, but stay on the right-hand side of the main stream and you shouldn't go far wrong. The summit of Meall Glas can occasionally be seen ahead over the rising moor and makes a good homing beacon.

Eventually you'll reach the shallow peaty bowl of the aptly named Coire nam Moine (*Corra nam Moa-inya*,

Mossy Corrie), situated at the foot of the south-east face of Meall Glas (only its main stream is named on the OS 1:50,000 map). One way up, described as a matter of course in older guide-books, crosses the Allt Glas (*Owlt Glass*, Green Stream) and climbs beside the Allt Coire nam Moine to the dip between Meall Glas and Meall Glas Beag.

The only path of note, however, takes a more direct route further left. If you find yourself pathless in the bowl of the corrie, wander up the banks of the Allt Glas until you reach the point where this path crosses the stream. Staying left of the crags on the hillside left of the Allt Coire nam Moine, the path heads directly for the summit of Meall Glas, becoming intermittent again as it climbs. Above the crags, veer right to avoid higher crags, then left again to gain the ▲summit. All ways up from corrie to summit climb steep grass, but there's no difficulty if the grass is dry.

Continue to ▲Sgiath Chuil as described in Route 22a, via ΔBeinn Cheathaich, the Lairig a' Churain and ΔMeall a' Churain. At Sgiath Chuil's summit, crags bar an initial descent southwards towards Glen Dochart. To outflank them, retrace your steps c.25m and bypass the rocks on the west. Steep grass slopes (you guessed it) descend to the tangle of boggy moor (ditto) in Coire nam Moine. To ease the remainder of the descent, aim for a dam seen below on the Allt Coire nam Moine (NN 451306).

Follow the stream below the dam for a few hundred metres to reach an old wooden bridge. On the far side of the bridge, traces of vehicle track and then path bear right, descend across the moor to the upper end of a forestry plantation and follow the perimeter deer fence down to the stile you crossed on the outward journey.

GiGi: Upper Coire nam Moine is known as Saobhaidh Madaidh-Allaidh (*Seuvy Matty-Ally*, Wolf's Den), although Scotland's last wolf is said to have been killed in 1743.

Route 22c Sgiath Chuil alone
from Auchlyne (Glen Dochart)

G2 ** NN 510295, 9ml/14km, 780m/2550 M126

This Glen Dochart approach can't avoid the rough going of Route 22b altogether but, as a way of climbing Sgiath Chuil alone, it provides an easier ascent route than that from Auchessan. Admittedly it is 2ml/3km further, but 5ml/8km of it is on a Land Rover hydro track.

Sgiath Chrom   SGIATH CHUIL   Meall a' Churain

Glen Dochart

The track begins on the east side of the West Burn at Auchlyne, reached by a minor road from the A85. Park at or near the start of the track with care and consideration. The track zigzags up to a fork, branches left and undulates across the hillside towards Sgiath Chuil, seen ahead. To avoid rough ground, stay on the track as far as a small dam on a side stream at NN 480303 (the track continues to the larger dam on the Allt Coire nam Moine, noted opposite).

From the small dam, climb straight up the hillside of thick grass above, staying right of the craggy southern slopes of Sgiath Chrom (*Skee-a Chrome*, Curved Wing). On improved going, bear left along the top of the crags, following the ridge line over or around Sgiath Chrom's highpoint, to the broad saddle below the summit of Sgiath Chuil. The ▲summit crags are easily breached by the gap to their left (south-west).

SGIATH CHUIL

▲**24 Creag Mhor** 84 1047m/3434ft (OS 50, NN 391361)
Craik Voar, Big Crag
△Stob nan Clach 956m/3137ft (OS 50, NN 387351)
Stop nan Clach, Stony Peak
▲**25 Beinn Heasgarnich** 62 1078m/3536ft (OS 51, NN 413383)
Ben Heskarnich, Sheltering Mountain (from Gaelic *Seasgairneach*)

Stob nan Clach

Sron nan Eun

CREAG MHOR

Glen Lochay

Peak Fitness: No change to Munros/Top since original 1891 Tables. Stob an Fhir-Bhoghe (*Stop an Heer Voa-ha*, Archers' Peak) was also a Top until 1981.

As is often the case in Glen Lochay, these Munros are characterised by **long, grassy slopes that climb endlessly skywards**. Unusually, rock outcrops dot the hillsides, which you'd think might make for a more interesting ascent than usual hereabouts. In truth, alas, the lasting memory you'll have of these mountains is of slogging up steep grass slopes *around* the crags. Never will you have been more grateful for a high starting point.

Now for some good news. Like Ben Challum, which it faces across upper Glen Lochay, Creag Mhor is a good-looking mountain when viewed from the upper glen beyond the road-end,

BEINN HEASGARNICH

Stob an
Fhir Bhoghe

Kenknock

Sron
Tairbh

Bealach na
Baintighearna

Viewed from
Creag Mhor

even if its aspiring name flatters to deceive. Its **attractively pointy summit** stands at the head of the deep hole of Coire-cheathaich (*Corra Chay-ich*, Misty Corrie), whose skyline gives **a scenic horseshoe ridge walk** that is the best day out in the glen (Route 24b). Ascent to and descent from either end of the horseshoe is steep but, once up, that only adds to the high-level ambience.

Creag Mhor is separated from its neighbour Beinn Heasgarnich by the deep, 650m/2150ft Bealach na Baintighearna (*Byalach na Ben-tyurn-a*, The Lady's Pass). It is a long way down and an even longer way up again to Heasgarnich's summit but, as it adds negligible extra mileage to the return trip from Creag Mhor,

most people grit their teeth and go for it (Route 24a). Unfortunately, Heasgarnich makes a wearisome anticlimax and, even worse, you have to forsake half of Creag Mhor's horseshoe ridge in order to bag it.

So therein lies the rub... Do you climb Creag Mhor as it was designed to be climbed, via the horseshoe, and leave Peskynich for another day (Route 24c), or do you bag the two in a oner? Of course, you could always leave the decision until you reach the summit of Creag Mhor.

Knowing you as we do, we suspect you'll probably return over Peskynich, but just for that we'll subtract one star from the route's rating for failing to complete the otherwise four-star Creag Mhor horseshoe.

Route 24a Creag Mhor and Beinn Heasgarnich
from Glen Lochay

G2 *** NN 461370, 12ml/19km, 1170m/3850ft M136

Map note: As the mountains are on separate maps, the route requires both OS 50 and OS 51.

From the end of the public road along Glen Lochay, just beyond Kenknock farm, a hydro maintenance road climbs north up the hillside to cross into Glen Lyon. Through access to Glen Lyon may or may not be possible for private transport, but you can drive to a hairpin bend less than a mile up. The route begins here, at a high starting point of 350m/1150ft, on a Land Rover track that heads west

into upper Glen Lochay across the lower slopes of Beinn Heasgarnich.

Leave the track at the Allt Batavaim after 3ml/5km to climb the steep, grassy hillside of Sron nan Eun (*Strawn nan Yai-un*, The Bird's Nose) – the end point on Coire-cheathaich's north-east rim. Bands of crags complicate the ascent. You can climb around them to the left or, for more sport, pick a route up grassy rakes

CREAG MHOR

SE Ridge

Sron nan Eun

through them. Alternatively, to avoid them altogether, walk up the glen of the Allt Batavaim and outflank them on the right (see pic on Page 138).

Once up, the route improves mightily as you begin the horseshoe ridge walk around the depths of Coire-cheathaich. With a path underfoot now to speed you on your way, the route crosses a shallow saddle and climbs Creag Mhor's south-east ridge, which narrows invitingly to the sky-touching ▲summit.

As the view to the north opens up, the summit is revealed to be the culminating point of three ridges. In addition to the south-east ridge by which you have arrived, the south-west ridge curves down to Coire-

cheathaich's south-west rim (Route 24b) and the north-west ridge curves out to the subsidiary top of Meall Tionail (*Myowl Tyunnal*, Collection Hill).

Unfortunately, Beinn Heasgarnich lies to the north-east, such that a direct descent to the intervening Bealach na Baintighearna would involve negotiating a very steep spur beset with more of those awkward crags. For a safer descent route, first head west (in completely the wrong direction!) then north on the curving grassy ridge to Meall Tionail. Once the crags have been outflanked, gentle grass slopes spiral down to the peaty bealach. If it seems a long way down, there's a good reason for that.

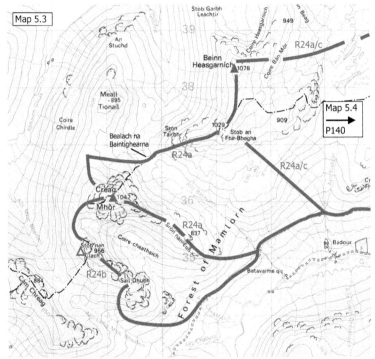

Rearing overhead on the far side of the bealach is the steep, grassy, wonderfully named spur known as Sron Tairbh (*Strawn Terrav*, Bull's Nose). If the climb up it looks like a strenuous slog, there's a good reason for that too. As lines of ascent merge, a path appears in a forlorn attempt to ease the pestiferousness of what seems more than 320m/1050ft of ascent. You top out on a level stretch of ridge that provides only temporary respite before another ascent, this time mercifully short, gains the former Top of Stob an Fhir-Bhoghe. From

here, a whaleback ridge rises northwards to Heasgarnich's flat ▲summit.

There's a choice of two ways back down to the road, both of equal length. The easier option, although it may not seem so at the summit, re-descends the whaleback ridge and maintains a south-east trajectory down easy, crag-free grass slopes to rejoin the outward Land Rover track in the vicinity of the Allt Badour.

The more obvious option at Heasgarnich's summit goes east down Coire Ban Mor (Big White Corrie) to reach the hydro road over to Glen

Lyon at its 500m/1650ft highpoint. This route is tempting not only because it avoids retracing of steps but also because the road is in plain sight from the summit. But there's a catch. On descent into the upper corrie, expect to encounter very steep grass among more of those pesky crags. Lower down, expect end-of-day motivation to falter among frustrating bog and heather.

We have to admit, though, that the lure of the Coire Ban Mor route is difficult to resist, so let's talk it up. Until early summer, you may well come across late-lying snow among the crags, and lower down you'll encounter a fine collection of lochans. To begin the descent, you could do worse than start from the north end of the small summit plateau and aim for the ridge-top lochans seen below. But remember: the Allt Badour route is less aggravating.

F-Stop: Creag Mhor boasts extensive views of the upper end of Glen Lyon, which, since cut off by the construction of Loch Lyon reservoir in the 1950s, has become perhaps **the most remote spot in the Southern Highlands**.

Climbing Sron nan Eun in winter

Needlepoint: In cloud, provided you can find a way through or around Sron nan Eun's crags, Creag Mhor's summit should prove fairly easy to find (although the summit cairn itself may be difficult to pinpoint among a selection box of confusing stony knolls). Navigating Heasgarnich's sprawling slopes requires more precision.

Chilly Willy: Climbing both mountains together is a lengthy outing for a short winter's day and not one that is suitable for inexperienced winter walkers. Technically, the main difficulties will be found on the ascents of the two Srons (the Bird's Nose and the Bull's Nose), where steep snow will be difficult to avoid.

Route 24b Creag Mhor alone from Glen Lochay:
The Coire-cheathaich Horseshoe
G2 **** NN 461370, 12ml/19km, 830m/2750ft M136

Map note: The route requires both OS 50 (for the summit) and OS 51 (for the approach).

The route begins by climbing ▲Creag Mhor as per Route 24a, via Sron nan Eun and the north-east rim of Coire-cheathaich. When you view Beinn Heasgarnich from the summit, hulking across the deep Bealach na Baintighearna, you'll be glad you've chosen in your wisdom to leave it for another day. Much more inviting is Coire-cheathaich's south-west rim, which completes **a circuit of satisfying symmetry**.

From Creag Mhor's summit, broad slopes descend west then south-west, curving gently around the head of the corrie to a dip. A more well-defined grassy ridge then continues around the horseshoe, curving south then south-east to make the short 70m/230ft climb to ∆Stob nan Clach, Creag Mhor's subsidiary Top. The summit is the first of three highpoints.

Beyond the summit, the ridge is **a joy to walk** as it undulates over the two lower highpoints and down along the corrie's south-west rim. The only downside is that it is not nearly long enough, so savour the moment as you stroll past several ridge-top lochans at the edge of steep drops that give an impression of great height.

The ridge ends at Sail Dhubh (*Sahl Ghoo*, Black Heel), the counterpart to

Sron nan Eun across the corrie mouth. Immediately beyond, bands of crags make a direct descent difficult, even more so than on Sron nan Eun.

Before you reach Sail Dhubh, therefore, descend easy slopes into the glen on the right (south-south-west, aiming in the direction of Ben Challum), then spiral down around the foot of the crags to regain the Land Rover track back to Kenknock.

GiGi: The deep recesses of Coire-cheathaich were at one time a royal hunting ground, part of the Forest of Mamlorn (a 'deer forest' not a tree forest).

In the eighteenth century the Gaelic bard Duncan Ban MacIntyre (of Beinn Dorain fame – see Route 39a) spent some years here as gamekeeper and rhapsodised about the corrie in his poetry. His admiration remained undimmed even by cloud cover, which he referred to as Creag Mhor's 'lovely coat.'

Needlepoint: Even in foul weather, the rim of Coire-cheathaich is relatively easy to follow, although precise navigation is needed on the broad initial slopes that curve down from Creag Mhor's summit.

The craggy slopes of Sron na Eun and Sail Dhubh, normally such good viewpoints at either end of the horseshoe, are more difficult to navigate in cloud. On descent especially, make sure you quit the corrie rim for the easy south-south-west hillside before going over the end of Sail Dhubh onto difficult ground. You may have to go to Sail Dhubh and retrace your steps to determine your exact position.

Above all, remember that *cheathaich* means *misty* and that mist, according to Duncan (see previous page) is lovely!

Chilly Willy: The complete round of Coire-cheathaich's skyline, taking in Creag Mhor's summit *en route*, gives **a memorable and sporting winter trip**. In places the rim is abrupt enough to support heavy cornices and give **spectacular walking** (as long as you don't get too close!).

More of a problem is reaching the skyline in the first place. This is no place to learn how to use ice axe and crampons. As on Route 24a, expect to encounter steep snow on the ascent of Sron nan Eun. The descent from Sail Dhubh should prove less problematic as long as you leave the rim before its end and take to the easier slopes on the south-south-west.

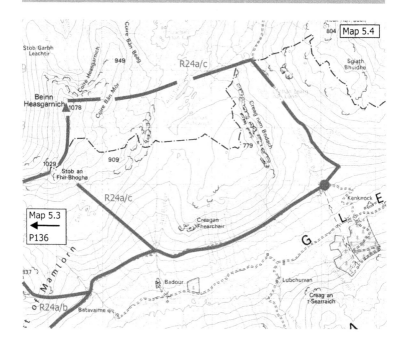

Route 24c Beinn Heasgarnich alone from Glen Lochay

G2 ** NN 461370, 8ml/13km, 700m/2300ft

Map note: Both summit and approach are on OS 51. Unlike Routes 24a & 24b, this route does not require OS 50.

Route 24a describes two possible descent routes from Beinn Heasgarnich: via the Allt Badour and via Coire Ban Mor. As a lone objective, the Munro can be climbed by one route and descended by the other, to give a round trip.

We suggest an ascent by the Allt Badour route. Even though the Coire Ban More route starts 150m/500ft higher up the hydro maintenance road above Kenknock, it makes a tiresome ascent route that goes out of its way to induce Route Rage.

Easily the best way to climb the mountain is via the Land Rover track to the Allt Badour and the grassy hillside that goes straight up from there. To find the best line up, leave the track at its highpoint (NN 427357), at the wee stream a couple of hundred metres beyond the Allt Badour. Climb from there to the skyline, then keep going... and going... Somewhere up there, when we last looked, is the ▲summit.

BEINN HEASGARNICH

Stob an Fhir Bhoghe

Needlepoint: In cloud, do not expect to make directly for the top. If you fail to find the summit at all, you won't be the first.

Chilly Willy: The ascent of Beinn Heasgarnich via the Allt Badour should cause no especial winter problems for the suitably equipped, but expect to encounter pockets of steep snow in Coire Ban Mor.

GiGi: Coire Ban Mor's name may derive from the snow that often lies late into the summer season in its upper recesses, courtesy of the north-south ridge that links Heasgarnich's summit to Stob an Fhir-Bhoghe and shelters the corrie from the prevailing westerly winds. The same phenomenon may also be responsible for Heasgarnich's name.

▲26 Meall Ghaordaidh 93 1039m/3409ft (OS 51, NN 514397)

Myowl Geuh-dy, meaning obscure. Traditionally translated as Hill of the Arm or Shoulder (from Gaelic *Gairdean*, the upper part of the arm), but other derivations are possible. *Gaothar* means Windy, and the isolated summit can certainly be that.

MEALL GHAORDAIDH

SE Ridge

Glen Lochay

Peak Fitness: No change since 1891 Tables.

Meall Ghaordaidh is a big grassy heap to end all big grassy heaps, but compared to some big grassy Glen Lochay heaps it is a geomorphological masterpiece whose southern slopes rise in **an unbroken sweep** from glen to summit. That promises either a monotonous plod or a pleasant afternoon stroll, according to inclination. Whichever you expect, it delivers.

Tip: Unless you enjoy wading through the squelchy stuff, leave the ascent until the ground is fairly dry.

When viewed from below, the north side of the mountain, facing Glen Lyon, seems more interesting, with three ridges that end abruptly at rocky bluffs overlooking the glen, like a poor man's Three Sisters of Glen Coe. However, a long drive into upper Glen Lyon, to trudge up either of the two untracked corries between the bluffs, will in practice prove no more spiritually enlightening than the Glen Lochay approach.

Route 26a Meall Ghaordaidh from Glen Lochay

G1 ** NN 527363, 5ml/8km, 890m/2900ft

This route is **a plodmeister's dream** – straight up and straight back down. You can begin anywhere at the mountain's foot, but the easiest approach begins on the west side of the bridge over the Allt Dhuin Croisg, just beyond Duncroisk house. Above here, an ill-defined south-east ridge gives the best going and the gentlest angle of ascent.

Begin 50m beyond the bridge (parking at a lay-by 100m further along), where a gate gives access to a farm track. Follow the track through grassy fields and up beside the Allt Dhuin Croisg, whose waters are now captured higher up by the area's hydro-electric scheme.

The track becomes indistinct on grass but remains easy enough to follow to a stile over a dry-stone wall. You could bear left here and make a bee-line for Ghaordaidh's summit, but you wouldn't appreciate the acres of bracken you'd have to wade through. Instead, keep to the now distinct track that continues straight on up the hillside, parallel to the stream, heading for the foot of the south-east ridge.

Leave the track at a brief levelling where some wooden sleepers have

been laid over a boggy section, waymarked by a metal pole above left. An ATV track climbs diagonally left to become a path up the ridge. To begin with, it is indistinct and hard to follow in places. If you haven't found it by the time you reach a fence that crosses the hillside from left to right, seek it out beside the fence. The terrain above becomes rougher and more tussocky, such that the path increasingly makes a real difference to the pleasantness of the ascent.

In actuality, the path above the fence divides into two virtually parallel paths. The main path climbs the left side of the broad crest of the ridge and is considerably boggy after rain. The other, smaller path climbs further

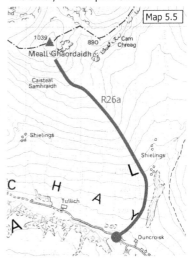

F-Stop: Be fair. Thanks to its isolation, Ghaordaidh's summit has **excellent all-round views**, notably east to the unfamiliar northern flanks of Lawers and Tarmachan, and west along Glen Lochay and Glen Lyon to Ben Challum, Creag Mhor and neighbouring Munros.

right and is less boggy. You probably won't have a choice of route because the fork occurs (and is probably caused by) indistinct ground. Whichever path you end up on, it is probably best to stick to it.

The summit stays resolutely out of sight as you tramp up the convex hillside, with nothing to occupy the mind except to wonder if the summit ever *will* come into view. Couple this with an easy-angled slope and there's a tendency to push too hard. Result: knackeredness. Of course, the ridge *does* eventually level off, but only in order to deposit you in a morass of peat hags at the foot of steeper final slopes. The better of the two paths

now runs left of the peat, on the ridge crest. The path to the right of the peat is better to begin with but soon contours away from the summit and becomes indistinct; if you're on it, cross to the path on the left.

Although it doesn't seem possible, the summit is still c.300m/1000ft above, such that the final slopes go on longer than expected. At least there's some definition to the landscape at last, courtesy of small rock outcrops that break out of the hillside. The path climbs left of the largest outcrops, where a stiff pull brings you to the small table-top ▲summit with its large windbreak. The windbreak is not large for no reason.

MEALL GHAORDAIDH

SE Ridge

Glen Lochay

Summit

Needlepoint: Be fair. The summit remains easy to find even when it is obscured by the thickest cloud. Simply maintain an upward trajectory as long as possible.

Chilly Willy: Be fair. When daylight is limited, Ghaordaidh is **a good winter objective if you enjoy messing around in the white stuff**. Close to the summit, above the frozen peat hags, the scattered outcrops may produce pockets of steep snow. Although not prolonged or exposed or difficult enough to provide much of an obstacle, given that you'll be equipped with ice axe and crampons, they can give good sport if the mood takes you.

6 LOCH TAY

Immediately east of the Glen Lochay hills described in Section 5, a group of eight more prominent Munros lords it over the north shore of Loch Tay. Seven of them form the Lawers Range, named for the highest mountain in the Southern Highlands. The eighth Munro, Meall nan Tarmachan, is an attractive subrange in its own right, with an enjoyably knobbly ridge that links the summit to three lower Tops.

Access to the peaks is facilitated by a minor road that crosses from Loch Tay to Glen Lyon, passing between the Lawers Range and Tarmachan and reaching a high point of 550m/1800ft beside Lochan na Lairige (*Lochan na Lahrike*, Lochan of the Pass). Ease of access is complemented by a Visitor Centre, a nature trail and various renovated paths, making the area **one of the most popular leisure destinations in the Southern Highlands**, and not just with Munro baggers. Nowhere more than here do we hillwalkers have to share our treasured sanctuary with oxygen-starved lowlanders spilling shakily out of their cars to take their first tentative toddlers' steps in the Great Outdoors.

The mountains are characterised by sweeping green hillsides and high-level, mostly grassy ridges, along which you can stravaig to your heart's content between picturesque Glen Lyon and the equally picturesque 14½ml/23km ribbon of Loch Tay.

BEN LAWERS

MEALL GREIGH

Loch Tay

Viewed from Kenmore

Ascents and descents between the peaks are steep in places but, unlike in the Glen Lochay hills, **paths are excellent**. There are only two spots (Lawers' An Stuc and Tarmachan's Beinn Garbh) that will give non-scramblers pause for thought.

The seven Lawers Range Munros can be tackled in various combinations, so there are some logistical decisions to be made. For three easy days, Ben Lawers and Beinn Ghlas (Route 27a), Meall Corranaich and Meall a' Choire Leith (Route 29a) and Meall Garbh and Meall Greigh (Route 31a) can be bagged in pairs. The more problematic An Stuc can be climbed separately (Route 31b or 31c) or appended to Route 27a or Route 31a.

More so than anywhere else in the Southern Highlands, the sheer number of connected Munros tempts with opportunities for more challenging days out. After all, the next Munro is never more than a mile or so away... For those so moved, we suggest route extensions where appropriate.

If even that doesn't slake your thirst for boot-miles, Torpedo recommends two more substantial rounds: the Fab Four circuit of Lawers' eastern corrie (Route 31a + extensions) and the **do-it-once-in-a-lifetime-and-dine-out-on-it-forever** Magnificent Seven (Route 31d).

Meall nan Tarmachan, the eighth Loch Tay Munro, is separated from the Lawers Range by the Lochan na Lairige road. With its lone Munro summit easily bagged above the lochan, you'd think it would suffer by comparison, but nothing could be further from the truth. Its many Tops and intricate main ridge combine to give the most entertaining ridge walk in the whole area and repay repeated visits (Routes 34a and 34b).

GiGi: The Lawers Range was one of the first sites to be purchased by the National Trust for Scotland in 1950, largely to ensure the preservation of its unrivalled alpine flora. Six of the seven Munros can be reached from the Visitor Centre without leaving NTS land, which makes ascents from there the only Munro routes in the Southern Highlands, apart from Route 46a up Schiehallion, that are not subject to stalking considerations.

The range's uniqueness derives from a combination of factors, including climate and altitude, but the main feature that distinguishes it from other Southern Highland upland areas is its geology. Strata of mineral-rich schists break down into soils that are alkaline rather than the more normal acid, enabling plants like alpine saxifrage and alpine lady's mantle to survive here.

For more information, before we betray our embarrassing level of botanical ignorance, check out the Visitor Centre. It goes without saying, but we'll say it anyway: *Do not pick the flowers*.

Baffies: The **Visitor Centre** and **Nature Trail**, situated near the high point of the Lochan na Lairige road, make a tolerable objective for an afternoon tootle from Killin between admiring the **Falls of Dochart** and sampling the village's tea rooms. Small parking fee payable at machine.

N.B. To reduce costs, the NTS closed the Visitor Centre building in 2009 after 36 years of operation. It may re-open in the future. Further details at www.nts.org.uk/Property/94.

▲**27 Ben Lawers** 10 1214m/3983ft (OS 51, NN 636414)
Hoof-shaped Mountain (from Gaelic *Ladhar*, perhaps referring to the
shape of the eastern corrie skyline) or possibly Loud Mountain (from
Gaelic *Labhar*, after the sound of a stream – the Lawers Burn?)
△Creag an Fhithich 1047m/3435ft (OS 51, NN 635422)
Craik an Yee-ich, Raven's Crag
▲**28 Beinn Ghlas** 47 1103m/3619ft (OS 51, NN 625404)
Ben Glass, Green-grey Mountain

Viewed from Meall nan Tarmachan

MEALL   BEN   BEINN
CORRANAICH   LAWERS   GHLAS

Visitor Centre →

Lochan na Lairige

Peak Fitness: No change since original 1891 Tables, even though Creag an
Fhithich is no more than a minor excrescence on Ben Lawers' north ridge.

With a vast hillside dropping uniformly to Loch Tay, Ben Lawers gives an impression of great height and makes **a fitting highest Southern Highland Munro**. It is the highest peak in Britain south of Ben Nevis and, from its summit, F-Stop assures us that, on a good day, you can see both the Atlantic to the west and the North Sea to the east.

The mountain lies in the centre of its eponymous range, with three Munros to either side of it, yet is far from inaccessible. Thanks to a high starting point on the Lochan na Lairige road, it possesses the peculiar distinction of having the shortest way to its summit cross an intervening Munro – Beinn Ghlas (Route 27a).

The gap between the two requires a descent of only 100m/350ft, which makes Beinn Ghlas very lucky to find itself listed in the Tables as a Munro. Yet it has considerable presence, so we don't begrudge it its status. It towers above the Visitor Centre, from where car-caged touros often mistake it for its hidden neighbour.

Owing to the high starting point, the western approach via Beinn Ghlas is understandably the most popular route up Lawers, and a fine route it is too, but it isn't the only one. The summit forms the apex of three ridges: the south-west ridge (from Beinn Ghlas), the north ridge and the east ridge. The two latter ridges enclose a great eastern corrie whose skyline supports the range's three eastern Munros.

You'll probably visit the eastern corrie on your travels in order to bag those three Munros, but it is worth sparing a moment to consider an ascent of Lawers itself from this direction. An eastern approach gives a longer day out but takes you to the heart of the best scenery in the range. Adding an ascent of Lawers to that of the three eastern Munros, by going up the north ridge and down the east ridge, amounts to a skyline round of the eastern corrie (see Routes 31a and 31b for description).

Route 27a Ben Lawers and Beinn Ghlas
from Lawers Visitor Centre
G1 ***** NN 609379, 6ml/10km, 980m/3200ft M148/160

At a starting height of 430m/1400ft, and with Loch Tay sparkling in the glen below (there *have* been unsubstantiated reports of sunshine), you are in the presence of **handsome high mountain scenery** even before you boot up. An excellent renovated path zigzags 670m/2200ft up the south-west ridge of Beinn Ghlas, then a ridge-top path continues to Ben Lawers. It all adds up to a superb leg-stretch.

BEINN GHLAS

From the Visitor Centre car park, the path makes a beeline for Beinn Ghlas, whose domed summit rises ahead atop the gentle south-west ridge. At first the route follows the nature trail on the left of the Burn of Edramucky. When a side path forks left after about 800m, keep to the main path, which crosses the burn.

Ignore a second side path, this time to the right, which takes the nature trail back down to the car park, and continue up to a gate in a fence that gives access to open hillside.

About 150m beyond the fence, the path forks at a conspicuous boulder. The left branch continues up Coire Odhar (*Corra Oa-ar*, Dun-coloured

Corrie) to the Meall Corranaich–Beinn Ghlas bealach and is a possible return route. For now, keep right to follow the zigzagging Beinn Ghlas path up the hillside onto the south-west ridge, then onwards and upwards to the abrupt ▲summit overlooking the long northern glen of the Allt a' Chobhair (see Route 31d).

The summit of Ben Lawers, now in view at last, looks distant from here, but appearances are deceptive. With a height loss of only 100m/350ft, the path down the connecting ridge to the intervening gap gives **a gentle skip-&-saunter** that you'll wish was longer. A re-ascent of only 210m/700ft

leads more steeply but still easily to the rocky ▲summit eyrie, perched at the apex of the three main ridges.

To return, reverse the route. From the bealach between the two Munros, a bypass path contours around the summit of Beinn Ghlas, crosses the bealach to its north-west (below Meall Corranaich) and descends Coire Odhar, eventually to rejoin the ascent path at the conspicuous boulder noted above. This provides variety on the way back, but the path is less well surfaced than the ridge path and views are curtailed. For the small amount of extra effort involved, we'd go back over Beinn Ghlas.

MEALL NAN TARMACHAN

MEALL CORRANAICH

BEINN GHLAS

Coire Odhar

BEN LAWERS

F-Stop: The most compelling reason to return over Beinn Ghlas rather than around it is the **photogenic panorama** laid out before you as you descend to the Visitor

Centre car park above Loch Tay in westering sunlight. Ben Vorlich to the south and the silhouetted Crianlarich Munros to the west provide a glorious horizon.

GiGi: Until the Great Triangulation of the United Kingdom was completed in 1852, Ben Lawers was thought to exceed the 4,000ft mark. In 1878 a local named Malcolm Ferguson was moved to 'restore' it to this more exalted height by paying for a 6m/20ft cairn. It took thirty or so volunteers to build it and cap it with an enormous white quartz cope-stone. Alas, both Malcolm and his cairn are long gone. In 1879 the mountain witnessed another historic first when it became Sir Hugh's first recorded summit, at the age of 23.

F-Stop: Ben Lawers' height and situation (it stands almost in the centre of Scotland) give it **tremendous all-round views** of the Southern Highlands. Geologist John Macculloch, one of the earliest Highland visitors to find the mountains interesting protuberances rather than useless blots on the landscape, wrote in his 1824 book *The Highlands and Islands of Scotland* that the view from the summit was the best in the country (Ben Lomond came second). NB We believe he might have changed his mind had he climbed ▲44 Meall Buidhe.

BEN LAWERS

AN STUC   MEALL GARBH

BEINN GHLAS

Needlepoint: The path makes the ascent virtually foul-weatherproof.

Chilly Willy: The high starting point makes this a popular winter route when daylight is limited, but inexperienced walkers often underestimate the dangers. Ironically, this is especially true when the path is *incompletely* obliterated by snow.

Wind and sun on the south-facing slopes combine to produce freeze/thaw cycles that can result in very icy going. This in turn makes the slopes leading up to the two summits more steep, more exposed and more dangerous than you would imagine from a summer visit.

You may see more foolhardy souls attempting the climb without ice axe and crampons but, if you go under-prepared and under-equipped, you may end up under sedation. Or worse. On the two route extensions, expect to encounter even steeper snow.

Route 27a Extension 1: An Stuc
G3 **** Add-on return: 2½ml/4km, 470m/1550ft M160

An Stuc, the next Munro to the east beyond Ben Lawers, can be an awkward customer to reach from some starting points. We discuss options later in this section, but it is worth noting here that the easiest approach to the summit is along the connecting ridge from Lawers.

If you're still bursting with energy at Lawers' summit, therefore, you might wish to consider bagging An Stuc while you're up there, even though this involves an appreciable return ascent to regain Lawers. The path descends over the barely perceptible Top of ΔCreag an Fhithich to the Bealach Dubh, then climbs more steeply among grass and rocks to An Stuc's ▲summit (see Route 31a Extensions 1 and 2 for further description).

Route 27a Extension 2: Meall Corranaich
G2 **** Add-on: 1ml/1½km, 120m/400ft M148

As noted on Page 150, a path contours from the Beinn Ghlas–Ben Lawers bealach to the Meall Corranaich–Beinn Ghlas bealach, making it possible to bag yet another Munro on the way back from Lawers if you're annoyingly fit. From the 860m/2800ft bealach below Meall Corranaich, a steep path climbs to the ▲summit and another descends the south-west ridge to the Visitor Centre.

No difficulties will be encountered on the latter ridge, but its knolls and sudden drops make for **a playfully convoluted descent**. The minor rise crossed 800m south-west of the summit is a former Top (see opposite). When you come off the end of the ridge, the best going will be found by descending left to gain the path along the right bank of the Burn of Edramucky. See also Route 29b.

Torpedo: While you're on Meall Corranaich, you might as well make the return trip to ▲Meall a' Choire Leith, just to get it out of the way. You know you want to. See Route 29a for description. Return trip add-on: 4ml/7km, 460m/1500ft.

GiGi: Coire Odhar, on the left as you descend from Meall Corranaich, was at one time a major centre of Scottish skiing. Its gentle, grassy, rock-free slopes require only a modest covering of snow to be in condition. In the 1950s early ski tows were erected to aid uplift but, as interest in the sport grew, the crowds moved on to the greater snow-holding corries of Glen Coe and the Cairngorms.

A Scottish Ski Club hut was built in the bowl of the corrie in 1932 but had to be demolished in 1999 after being blown down by a winter storm.

▲29 Meall Corranaich 68 1069m/3507ft (OS 51, NN 615410)

Myowl Corranich, possible meanings include Hill of the Lament (from Gaelic *Corranach*), Hill of the Bracken Corrie (from Gaelic *Coire Raineach*) and Sickle-shaped Hill (from Gaelic *Corran*)

▲30 Meall a' Choire Leith 261 926m/3038ft (OS 51, NN 612439) *Myowl a Chorra Lay*, Hill of the Grey Corrie

MEALL CORRANAICH

Coire Gorm

MEALL A' CHOIRE LEITH

Peak Fitness: No change to Munros since original 1891 Tables. Sron Dha Mhurchaich, an insignificant rise on Meall Corranaich's south-west ridge, 800m from the summit at NN 615410, was an additional Top from 1891 to 1921.

These two rounded summits to the north-west of Beinn Ghlas complete the trio of Munros west of Ben Lawers. Overshadowed in bulk by Lawers to the east and in ruggedness by Meall nan Tarmachan to the west, they are the highpoints on a gentle grassy ridge that runs north-south beside the Lochan na Lairige road.

The most practicable and popular way of bagging the pair begins at the road's highpoint, 3ml/5km north of the Visitor Centre. From here the two summits are equidistant, making a circular trip possible (Route 29a). Unfortunately, boggy approaches make for a 'mixed' hillwalking experience, definitely not one for which the Lawers Range would prefer to be remembered. A more interesting approach to Meall Corranaich begins on its south side at the Visitor Centre, but it makes Meall a' Choire Leith more awkward to reach (Route 29b).

Route 29a Meall Corranaich and Meall a' Choire Leith from Lochan na Lairige road highpoint

G2 * Route Rage Alert NN 593416, 6ml/10km, 730m/2400ft M148

From the cairn at the highpoint of the Lochan na Lairige road, 3ml/5km beyond the Visitor Centre, the ridge that curves south-eastwards to the summit of Meall Corranaich is an obvious approach route. From the parking space below the cairn, walk back along the road, around the right-angled bend, to find the start of the path just before the first passing place. Don't confuse this path with the return path, which leaves the road 20m earlier, at the corner.

The path is boggy in its lower reaches, but the route to the ▲summit is straightforward, with **zero features of interest** to warrant description.

The going improves higher up, when the south-east ridge joins the more well-defined south-west ridge for the final part of the ascent.

Continuing northwards to Meall a' Choire Leith, a good path on short turf gives **an amiable stroll** down a broad, gentle ridge. This is much more like it. After a short rise, the ridge broadens even more and divides around Coire Gorm (*Corra Gorram*, Blue Corrie). The lie of the land tempts you left onto the corrie's left-hand rim (the north-west ridge). Instead, keep right to follow the north ridge around the right-hand rim and up to the flat ▲summit of Meall a' Choire Leith.

MEALL A' CHOIRE LEITH

MEALL CORRANAICH

To return to your starting point, descend Meall a' Choire Leith's steep, grassy south-west slopes into Coire Gorm and tramp up the boggy upper reaches of Gleann Da-Eig. A swampy path takes the best line, crossing the Allt Gleann Da-Eig at a small dam, but in many places it is more of a hindrance than a help.

Cross the low bealach south of the hillock called Meall nan Eun (*Myowl nan Ee-an*, Hill of the Birds) to regain the roadside. As a parting shot by which to remember the two Munros, the peat hags on the bealach will act as a litmus test of your capacity to maintain a humorous disposition in the most dire of circumstances.

Needlepoint: When the ridge from Meall Corranaich to Meall a' Choire Leith divides around Coire Gorm, it is easy to veer left onto the north-west ridge even when skies are clear. In cloud, take extra care to keep right onto the north ridge. In low cloud, the peaty wastelands of upper Gleann Da-Eig can be frustratingly difficult to navigate, such that the bealach south of Meall nan Eun can be ridiculously hard to find. Enjoy.

Chilly Willy: Unremarkable terrain makes for a straightforward winter round if suitably equipped. Avoid the summer bogtrot! Go when the ground is hard!

Route 29b Meall Corranaich and Meall a' Choire Leith from Lawers Visitor Centre NN 609379 G2 ***

Meall Corranaich alone: 5ml/8km, 640m/2100ft M148
Add-on return trip to Meall a' Choire Leith: 4ml/7km, 460m/1500ft

---

The most entertaining route on Corranaich is the descent of its south-west ridge. In combination with an ascent via the path up Coire Odhar to the Meall Corranaich–Beinn Ghlas bealach, and the steeper path from there to the summit, it makes a good round from the Visitor Centre. See Route 27a Extension 2 for description.

For the bagging of *both* Munros, this southern approach carries a catch. If you start from the Visitor Centre, Meall a' Choire Leith lies *behind* Meall Corranaich. This means that on the return trip from it you have to climb back over Meall Corranaich from the intervening 770m/2500ft bealach, or else descend to the road via Coire Gorm (as per Route 29a) and end the day with an hour-long walk on tarmac.

BEN MORE

MEALL NAN TARMACHAN

BEINN GHLAS

MEALL CORRANAICH

BEN LAWERS

▲**31 An Stuc** 34 1118m/3668ft (OS 51, NN 639431)
An Stoochk, The Peak
▲**32 Meall Garbh** 35 1118m/3668ft (OS 51, NN 644436)
Myowl Garrav, Rough Hill (not to be confused with namesake ▲42)
▲**33 Meall Greigh** 136 1001m/3284ft (OS 51, NN 674438)
Myowl Gray, usually translated as Hill of the Herd (of Cattle or
Horses). Another beautiful meaning of the Gaelic word *Greigh*, despite its English pronunciation, is: 'uncommon heat of the sun after
bursting out from under a cloud.' On the other hand, older maps
(including the one that Sir Hugh used) named the mountain Meall
Gruaidh (*Myowl Groo-y*), meaning Hill of the Profile or Cheek.

Peak Fitness: No change to Meall Garbh and Meall Greigh since original 1891 Tables. An Stuc was one of the eight Munros added to the Tables in 1997. Before then it was a Top... but to which Munro did it belong? It could hardly be a Top of Meall Garbh, the nearest Munro, as both summits had the same metric height. It was therefore listed as a more distant if unsatisfactory Top of Ben Lawers. Its candidature as a Munro had long been advocated in SMC circles and its 1997 promotion was probably the neatest solution to a long-standing tricky Tables problem.

Ben Lawers and the three Munros to its east form the skyline of the range's finest feature – the great eastern corrie. Its deepest recesses, hard under the crags of An Stuc, shelter shapely Lochan nan Cat, whose very existence remains unknown to the vast majority of visitors to the Visitor Centre further west.

Tumbling down the corrie into Loch Tay is the Lawers Burn, whose banks carry a path that gives **one of the best approach walks in the Southern Highlands**. Once up, the round of the corrie skyline, beginning on Meall Greigh and crossing Meall Garbh and An Stuc to Ben Lawers, is **the range's most scenic route**.

Meall Greigh and Meall Garbh are the grassiest of all the Lawers Range Munros and can be climbed without difficulty from almost any direction. On the map, long ridges rising from Glen Lyon promise a rewarding round, but in reality they prove disappointing. Flanked by knee-deep heather and clinging moor, and beset by irritating undulations, they offer wearisome approach routes on the mountains'... how can we put this kindly... *less picturesque* sides. Unless you're a masochist seeking a fix of Route Rage, or tackling the Magnificent Seven (Route 31d), don't bother.

An approach from the south, via the Lawers Burn path from Loch Tay, is infinitely superior in terms of terrain, ease of ascent, views and whatever other criteria you can come up with (Route 31a). Having climbed Meall Greigh and Meall Garbh, a continuation around the skyline to An Stuc and Ben Lawers can be regarded as an optional extra (Route 31a Extensions 1 and 2). Note, however, that Ben Lawers adds appreciable ascent at the end of the day, while An Stuc is an appreciable nuisance at any time of the day.

On approach from Meall Garbh, the broken crags of An Stuc's north-east face rear overhead in intimidating fashion, blocking an otherwise easy round of the corrie skyline. The ascent from the intervening gap is only 130m/430ft, of which the hardest section is no more than a short, technically easy scramble, but the ground is becoming increasingly eroded at a worrying rate. The process has been accelerated in recent years following the promotion of An Stuc to Munro status in 1997, and the situation can only worsen.

At the time of writing, scramblers should experience little difficulty reaching the summit but, if you are at all of a sensitive disposition, the north-east face is a place to avoid. We certainly wouldn't want to descend it, even with Kevlar-reinforced underwear, and it should definitely be left alone when the rocks are wet. Fortunately, there's a small bypass path across steep ground on the north side of the bealach, although sensitive souls may find this too somewhat exposed in places.

To avoid all difficulties, approach An Stuc from Ben Lawers (Route 27a Extension 1) or bag it separately, either from Loch Tay (Route 31b) or Glen Lyon (Route 31c).

Route 31a Meall Greigh and Meall Garbh from Lawers Village (Loch Tay)
G1 ** NN 680400, 9½ml/15km, 1100m/3600ft M160

T he route begins at the foot of the Lawers Burn in Lawers village, beside a horn carver's showroom. Parking is restricted. At the time of writing, it is possible to park at the horn carver's car park for a fee, or at the Lawers Hotel, further along the road towards Killin, if you purchase refreshment on return.

Begin on the access track that climbs behind the showroom to Machuim Farm. Follow signs around the farm buildings and you'll soon reach the beautifully constructed path that climbs into the corrie beside the deep-cut Lawers Burn. The path crosses the burn at a bridge (NN 673420) and climbs to a Land Rover track (see below), which continues to

a small dam in the bowl of the corrie (NN 662427).

From here, easy slopes climb to the Meall Greigh–Meall Garbh bealach. However, it is normal procedure to leave the path well before its end to take a more direct line up Meall Greigh's grassy hillside.

The most scenic route up, giving views along the length of Loch Tay, goes straight up the south-east ridge over the unfortunately named Sron Mhor (*Strawn Voar*, Big Nose). For gentler grass slopes, keep to the path as far as the bridge, then continue along the near side of the burn on a good sheep path that will be found a few metres up the slope on the right. When you reach the first appreciable

MEALL GREIGH

Grassy hill No. 1   MEALL GARBH

stream coming down from Meall Greigh, climb its left-hand side. Higher up, trend right onto the skyline to find a path leading to the pudding-shaped ▲summit.

Heading west to Meall Garbh, a gentle knobbly ridge descends to the intervening 834m/2736ft bealach, known as the Lairig Innein (*Lahrik Inyan*, Anvil Pass, unnamed on OS map). Steeper grass slopes then climb to Meall Garbh's north-west shoulder, where the angle of ascent eases as the ridge veers south-west around the head of the eastern corrie.

A couple of hundred metres before the summit, you'll pass a curious transverse ridge, whose cairned high-point can mislead in cloud. At the ▲summit itself, the view west opens up and affords a first opportunity to study in detail the redoubtable north-east face of An Stuc. Unless continuing to it, return to the bealach below Meall Greigh and scamper down to the dam on the Lawers Burn. If you wish to visit nearby Lochan nan Cat, a path of sorts (boggy after rain) follows the south bank of the burn from the dam to the lochan's mouth.

On the map, it may seem tempting to descend from Meall Garbh to the An Stuc bealach and from there to the head of the lochan beside a tumbling stream, but we wouldn't recommend it. The hillside below the bealach consists of very steep, wet grass among sizeable crags. It's *possible* to make a way down left of the stream, but it's not pleasant. Acolytes of

GiGi: The Lawers Burn cuts a curiously deep trench into the hillside, with raised banks that are additionally notable for their innumerable ruined shielings, especially at East Mealour (NN 676415). These are a poignant reminder of the days when Lawers village was the populous centre of a flax spinning industry.

MEALL GARBH

Grassy hill No. 2   MEALL GREIGH

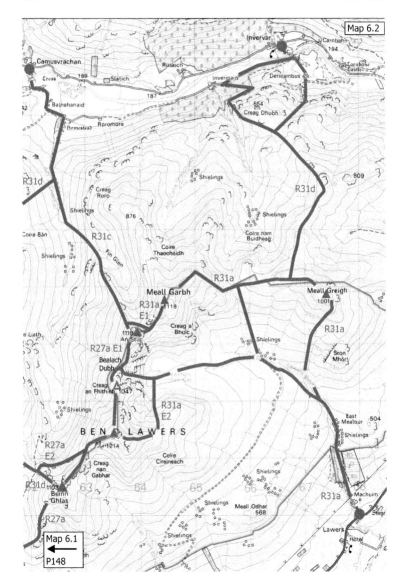

Terminator may appreciate it, others may find it a tad desperate.

From the dam, a Land Rover access track contours around the south-west slopes of Ben Lawers, eventually to descend to the roadside 2½ml/4km from Lawers village. Follow it for about 300m, then branch left on the Lawers Burn path (cairn) for **a glorious walk** down to your starting point. Some 800m down, keep a lookout for a fork where the main path appears to go straight on but in fact zigzags down left to the bridge noted above.

GiGi: Secluded Lochan nan Cat's name is said to derive from the corrie's wild cats (yes, it's the same name in Gaelic) but, when seen from above, the lochan's shape happily (if probably coincidentally) resembles a sitting cat.

Needlepoint: With their featureless slopes and knobbly ridges, Meall Garbh and Meall Greigh can prove awkward to navigate in cloud. On descent from Meall Greigh to the bealach, the path is boggy and indistinct in places. From half-way down, a fence takes a convoluted route to the bealach, well away from the path, but it may nevertheless be worth staying close to it.

On ascent to Meall Garbh, the path stays close to the fence and is more pronounced. Beyond the north-west shoulder, the main path crosses the short transverse ridge noted in the main text, which further complicate routefinding. Again, if in doubt, follow the fence. When it turns sharp right to descend to Glen Lyon, the true summit lies just beyond.

Chilly Willy: The characteristically grassy hillsides of Meall Garbh and Meall Greigh make good training grounds for practice with ice axe and crampons. The summit of Meall Greigh especially is **among the easiest of winter objectives**.

Route 31a Extension 1: An Stuc

G4 **** Add-on from Meall Garbh: 1ml/1½km, 140m/450ft M160

South-west around the skyline from Meall Garbh, the terrain becomes immediately more interesting with lots of exposed rock around. The now unmistakable path weaves its way along a narrow ridge before descending more steeply to the bealach below An Stuc. Convoluted outcrops near the foot of the descent may require a spot of handwork.

An Stuc's intimidating north-east face towers above the bealach, rising to a band of broken crags near the top. A stony path zigzags up to the foot of the rocks then fans out into various lines where tremulous souls have tried to find the least nerve-wracking way up.

Technically, the easiest lines are to the left, but that is also where the earthiest and loosest ground is. More solid rock will be found to the right. We don't wish to over-dramatise what is no more than an easy scramble but, if in doubt, don't turn a drama into a crisis — retreat before getting gripped. The best that can be said

about the ascent is that it is not far up to the short summit ridge and ▲summit.

The north-east face can be avoided by a narrow bypass path, in truth more suitable for sheep than humans, that traverses right from the bealach, across An Stuc's steep northern slopes, to a shoulder on the north ridge. To find the path, walk down the grass on the north side of the bealach, then follow the foot of a jumble of large boulders to below a rock outcrop, where the path will be seen beginning its rising traverse.

It is quite exposed in places above steep, broken ground, so expect to use hands for balance. If you feel uncomfortable on it, you'll have to descend the grassy hillside below it and re-climb steep grass slopes to gain the north ridge. Once on the ridge, straightforward slopes of rock-strewn heath lead to the summit.

The far side of An Stuc is also pretty steep, but a good path among the grass and rocks makes short work of the descent to the Bealach Dubh (*Byalach Doo*, Black Pass) below Ben Lawers. There is one spot where the eroded path negotiates rocks and where you might need to use hands for balance, but there is no difficulty.

Having come this far, you may well wish to complete the round of the corrie by ascending Ben Lawers (Extension 2). However, if the

prospect of a nearly 300m/1000ft ascent fails to fill you with enthusiasm, you can descend directly to Lochan nan Cat from the Bealach Dubh. The route is described on ascent as Route 31b, but here we give a few pointers on finding the easiest way down.

From the low point on the bealach, where the skyline path crosses the streamlet that descends to the lochan, a side path descends south-east into the bowl of a small upper corrie. When the stream exits the corrie on steep ground, descend further right to find easier grass slopes leading down to the head of the lochan.

At the lochanside you'll pick up another path that is becoming increasingly boggy with time. It improves beyond the mouth of the lochan, but you won't leave wet ground behind completely until you reach the dam on the Lawers Burn.

Needlepoint: After the confusing terrain of Meall Greigh and Meall Garbh, the path that continues to An Stuc and Ben Lawers is much more distinctive and easier to navigate in cloud.

Chilly Willy: Meall Greigh and Meall Garbh may give easy winter ascents but, as you might expect, An Stuc is another matter entirely. Both the ascent of the north-east face and the bypass path become winter climbs. After a good winter, the bypass path may remain blocked by snow until early summer.

The 'normal' route up An Stuc NE face

Route 31a Extension 2: (An Stuc +) Ben Lawers – The Fab Four G4 *****

Add-on from Meall Garbh: 2ml/3km, 420m/1400ft M160
Complete round from Lawers village: 11½ml/18km, 1520m/5,000ft

After the excitement of An Stuc, the path up Ben Lawers is so straightforward that it encourages an attempt at speed, which can make the ascent seem steeper than it really is. If you need time to reflect, pause awhile on the insignificant bump that is ΔCreag an Fhithich, lucky still to be in the Tables and now the only Top in the entire Lawers Range, to contemplate the **vertiginous view** down to Lochan nan Cat.

MEALL GARBH

MEALL GREIGH

Lochan nan Cat

BEN LAWERS

From Lawers' ▲summit, the return route completes the round of the eastern corrie by descending the little visited but surprisingly cordial east/north-east ridge. A path runs along the first section, which is quite narrow and passes **a curious rock crater** formed by a landslip.

Lower down, the ridge levels and broadens and is so easy that it tempts you to stay on it for too long before heading glenwards. If you follow the ridge to its end, however, you'll end up descending steep slopes onto tiresome moorland.

It is better to descend left, before the end point, into the upper corrie above Lochan na Cat, and then pick up the lochanside path to the dam. You can recce the options earlier in the day from across the corrie while ascending Meall Greigh.

Route 31b An Stuc alone from Lawers Village (Loch Tay)

G3 *** NN 680400, 9ml/15km, 940m/3100ft M160

Anyone wishing to avoid the adrenaline rush of the north-east face or the long haul from Ben Lawers, can bag An Stuc on a separate expedition using either of two easy approaches. A southern approach from Lawers village (described here) is more scenic but, if you've been up the Lawers Burn path already, to bag Meall Greigh and Meall Garbh, you might wish to consider a northern approach from Glen Lyon, which is both wilder and even easier (Route 31c).

From Lawers village, follow the Lawers Burn path to its end at the dam, then continue along a boggier path left of the stream and around the southern shore of Lochan nan Cat. Above the lochan, the stream that descends from the Bealach Dubh left of An Stuc tumbles down a gully.

Climb the steep grass slopes left of the stream. There is no path at the time of writing, but this may change in time. As lines of attack merge, traces of path are already appearing.

On steeper ground higher up, those who eschew trekking poles may find hands useful for balance. The easiest line veers left, away from the stream, to enter a small upper corrie. At the back left-hand corner of the corrie, a path right of the stream climbs a small defile to gain the skyline at the low point of the bealach.

The climb from there up the south-west side of An Stuc, as previously noted on Page 163, is steep but straightforward. You may use hands for balance at one rocky spot, but there's an unmistakable path all the way to the ▲summit.

Torpedo: A continuation over Ben Lawers, up the north ridge and down the east ridge (described opposite as Route 31a Extension 2), is an attractive option for a longer day. Add-on: 1ml/2km, 280m/900ft.

Needlepoint: In cloud, a crag-free line between Lochan nan Cat and the Bealach Dubh can prove surprisingly difficult to find, especially on descent.

Chilly Willy: Although straightforward in summer, this route can become unexpectedly difficult in winter. Be prepared for very steep snow below the Bealach Dubh and on the south-west ridge of An Stuc, which can seem quite exposed when the path is iced or snow-bound.

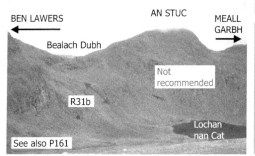

BEN LAWERS

AN STUC

MEALL GARBH

Bealach Dubh

Not recommended

R31b

Lochan nan Cat

See also P161

Route 31c An Stuc alone from Camusvrachan (Glen Lyon): North Ridge

G2 *** NN 620477, 8ml/13km, 940m/3100ft M160

I f you wish to avoid the steep south side of An Stuc above Loch Tay, the north ridge gives a satisfyingly straightforward approach that is both the easiest way up and the least known. It is *so* little known that the ridge carries no path as yet, but the terrain is excellent and the route has an attractive air of wildness on the 'backside' of the Lawers Range.

On the south side of the Glen Lyon road near Camusvrachan house, a side road leads down to a bridge over the River Lyon. There are parking spaces just before the bridge, on whose far side the road is for private use only. Walk up the road to a T-junction, then go left along a Land Rover track for around ½ml/1km to the bridge over the Allt a' Chobhair (*Owlt a Ko-ur,*

Foaming Stream).

On the far side of the bridge, a gate on the right gives access to a grassy track up the glen of the Allt a' Chobhair. It climbs through a defile into the level basin of a hidden upper glen, at whose back the Munros of the Lawers range burst into view one by one. The track runs pleasantly beside the stream, passes some ruined shielings and reaches a ford at the foot of a prominent wall that climbs the hillside on the left.

To avoid crossing and re-crossing the stream, it is better to quit the track at the ford and aim diagonally up the hillside into Fin Glen at the foot of An Stuc's north ridge. A gap in the wall, c.50m up, gives access to the open hill. The ground is rough at first but improves with height.

As you climb, plan the ascent route ahead up the lower slopes of the north ridge, where bands of crags lie across the grassy hillside. Leave the lowest band of crags to the right and climb to the ridge-top between or around the other rockbands.

Once on the skyline, the ridge proper begins. Broad and grassy, it rises to a levelling, beyond which the bold rocky dome of An Stuc forms an attractive objective. Grass gives way to heath as the ridge rises to another levelling beneath the summit slopes. Note the bypass path, described in Route 31a Extension 1, that runs left from here to reach the main ridge at the foot of the north-east face. The final ascent, on rock-littered heath, is surprisingly straightforward for such a problematic ▲summit.

Needlepoint: A foul-weatherproof route up a well-defined ridge.

Chilly Willy: This is an easier winter ascent route than Route 31b, although it is still not a route for the inexperienced.

When the ground is frozen, the steep upper slopes of the north ridge can seem quite exposed in dramatic surroundings.

Route 31d The Magnificent Seven from Invervar (Glen Lyon)
G4 ***** NN 666483, 19ml/30km, 2010m/6600ft M160

The traverse of all seven Munros in the Lawers Range is **a classic hillwalking challenge**. Even more, according to Torpedo, it is an undertaking to relish and an achievement to remember. A round that begins on Loch Tayside to the south will leave a car journey back to the starting point at the end of the day, so it is better to begin in Glen Lyon to the north.

On the Glen Lyon side, the six western Munros form the skyline of the long glen of the Allt a' Chobhair, which cuts deep into the range. Only the presence of Meall Greigh further east necessitates starting east of the foot of this glen, at the hamlet of Invervar (as for Route 40a).

Park in the small car park, just off the main road before the phone box. Above here, Meall Greigh's grassy north ridge climbs to meet its east ridge and give access the summit. It has been noted previously that this is

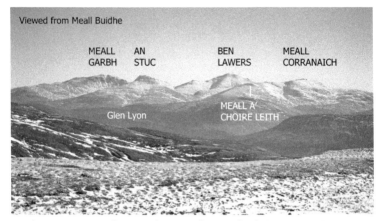

Viewed from Meall Buidhe

MEALL   AN   BEN   MEALL
GARBH   STUC   LAWERS   CORRANAICH

Glen Lyon   MEALL A'
                                CHOIRE LEITH

not the most congenial approach to Meall Greigh, but anyone tackling the Magnificent Seven will naturally rise above such malicious defamation of our glorious countryside.

From the car park, take the continuing road that crosses the River Lyon (bridge) and climbs to meet a Land Rover track at a T-junction. To the left here is Dericambus farm while to the right is Inverinain house. The map shows two paths climbing towards Creag Dubh (*Craik Doo*, Black Crag) at the start of Meall Greigh's north ridge, one from Dericambus and one from near Inverinain.

The former path, beginning at a hairpin bend just beyond Dericambus, is more direct but is grassed-over lower down and heathered-over higher up. The latter, beginning at a gate in the deer fence a couple of hundred metres before Inverinain, is a good Land Rover track. It gives a longer but much easier approach.

Once off-path beyond Creag Dubh,

the moorland gives poor going up to a height of around 800m/2600ft. Matters then improve as the ridge levels out and undulates up to join the east ridge. After bagging ▲Meall Greigh, head west along the main ridge, as described earlier in this section, to ▲Meall Garbh, ▲An Stuc, ▲Ben Lawers and ▲Beinn Ghlas. At Beinn Ghlas, instead of following the trade route down to the Visitor Centre, descend the steeper north-west slopes on a less well-used path that crosses the intervening bealach to ▲Meall Corranaich. Continue to ▲Meall a' Choire Leith as per Route 29a, then keep going down its north ridge.

Once you've passed the craggy headwall of Coire Ban (White Corrie), descend grass slopes into the glen of the Allt a' Chobhair. Here, suffused with a rosy glow from your exertions, you'll pick up the track described in Route 31c, which descends to Glen Lyon and joins the track back past Inverinain to Invervar.

The Tarmachan Ridge:
▲34 Meall nan Tarmachan 89 1044m/3425ft (OS 51, NN 585390)
Myowl nan Tarmachan, Ptarmigan Hill
△South-east Top 923m/3028ft (OS 51, NN 589385)
△Meall Garbh 1026m/3366ft (OS 51, NN 578383)
Myowl Garrav, Rough Hill (not to be confused with namesake ▲32)
△Beinn nan Eachan 1000m/3281ft (OS 51, NN 570383)
Ben nan Yechan, Horse Mountain
△Creag na Caillich 916m/3005ft (OS 51, NN 562377)
Craik na Kyle-yich, Old Woman's Crag

Creag na Caillich — Beinn nan Eachan — Meall Garbh — MEALL NAN TARMACHAN — SE Top

Falls of Dochart, Killin

Peak Fitness: No change to Munro status of Meall nan Tarmachan since original 1891 Tables. The South-east Top did not become a Top until 1997. To further complicate matters, Beinn nan Eachan's east top was a Top from 1921 to 1981, when Creag na Caillich, previously not a Top, was promoted in its place. We trust there were no hard feelings.

MEALL NAN
TARMACHAN

SE Top

The lone Munro of Meall nan Tarmachan on the west side of the Lochan na Lairige road is somewhat outnumbered by the seven Munros of the Lawers Range on the east side. Yet it does more than hold its own. With four times as many Tops as its neighbour, it forms a miniature mountain range whose twisting skyline (the Tarmachan Ridge) provides **a dramatic backdrop** to the Falls of Dochart at Killin.

The ridge snakes and undulates along the skyline for 2ml/3km, giving the most funsome ridge walk not only on Loch Tayside but also arguably in the whole Southern Highlands. Sometimes broad, sometimes narrow, sometimes rocky, sometimes grassy...

one characteristic it never lacks is interest. An added attraction is that, from the high starting point of the Lochan na Lairige road, it doesn't take too long to reach the good bits.

The summit of the Munro itself is easily reached by a renovated path that begins near the Visitor Centre to the south (Route 34a). Even incorrigible baggers, however, will find it worth continuing along the ridge at least as far as the next Top (Meall Garbh – Route 34a Extension 1). Those of a nervous disposition may well decide not to venture further than that. Should you decide the ridge merits a second visit some day, an approach from the north also has its attractions (Route 34b).

Route 34a Meall nan Tarmachan
from near Lawers Visitor Centre

G1 **** NN 605383, 4½ml/ 7km, 650m/2150ft M172

Begin on the Land Rover track that leaves the Lochan na Lairige road 400m north of the Visitor Centre. At the first stream, about 500m from the roadside, just over the first rise, a cairn marks the start of an excellent, renovated path that climbs Tarmachan's grassy south-east shoulder to the △South-east Top. The continuing track leads to a disused quarry and will form the return route for those completing the Tarmachan Ridge (Extension 1).

Over the South-east Top, a short descent leads to the foot of Tarmachan's south-east face and the steepest part of the route. The path climbs a grassy groove on stone steps,

then avoids craggier ground above by veering right up a broad, grassy shelf. This leads beneath the summit to reach the skyline on the north-east ridge, close to the ▲summit.

You can return the same way, but we recommend you first wander along the first section of the Tarmachan Ridge and take a look at Meall Garbh (Page 173). Those who suffer from vertigo will need no encouragement to go no further. To avoid retracing steps, you can descend Meall Garbh's south ridge. Just before the summit, a path leads down onto the ridge, whose gentle grassy slopes fan out to provide an easy if pathless route back down to the approach track.

MEALL NAN TARMACHAN

SE Top

Needlepoint: Even in cloud, the renovated path makes for an easily navigable ascent.

Chilly Willy: It would be a mistake to treat this easy summer route casually in winter, even with ice axe and crampons. When the hillside is snow-covered, the steepness of the ascent from the South-east Top to the summit should not be underestimated. The line of the path is not obvious and, if there are no footprints to follow, it is easy to stray onto difficult ground, especially in deteriorating weather.

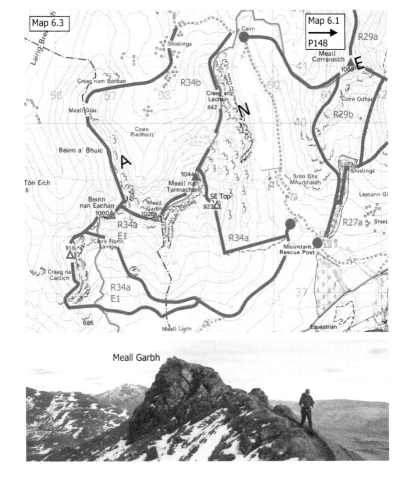

Meall Garbh

Route 34a Extension 1: The Tarmachan Ridge
G4 ***** 7½ml/12km, 820m/2700ft M172
(including ascent of Meall nan Tarmachan)

From the summit of Meall nan Tarmachan, the Tarmachan Ridge snakes invitingly westwards over three lower Tops, with a well-worn ridge-top path all the way. ΔMeall Garbh, the first Top along, is the most interesting of all and can be reached without difficulty from the Munro. The broad ridge leading to it is **entertainingly complex** and harbours two fine lochans, while the castellated summit rears up impressively to form an airy knob of rock.

The descent of the far side of the summit block, involving a couple of easy moves down a rock step, is where the real fun begins. There's a short bypass path for those who don't wish to dirty their fingernails but, if you don't fancy the scramble, it is best not to go any further. Beyond lies an excitingly narrow 50m-long arête that gives excellent tightrope walking practice, then the path descends easier ground before plummeting over an awkward rock band.

Meall Garbh

Beinn nan Eachan

MEALL NAN TARMACHAN

Badly eroded by the passage of boots and backsides, the rock band now forms a **Bad Step** that requires care. Although the scrambling is technically easy, the rock is manky and slopes outward over an appreciable drop. Whoever pioneered this route was having a laugh, because there is easier ground nearby.

If you don't fancy the scramble, look for a developing bypass path that descends the steep grass slope right of the rock band. This path too is becoming more 'interesting' with time. If in doubt, you can always use the excuse of pioneering a new route to retrace your steps and descend easier slopes of grass and boulders from nearer the summit of Meall Garbh.

Once past the Bad Step, the last two Tops of ΔBeinn nan Eachan and ΔCreag na Caillich come underfoot more easily as the ridge rounds the head of Coire Fionn Lairige (*Corra Fyoon Lah-rike*, Corrie of the Fair Pass). The path first weaves its way up through complex terrain to the summit of Beinn nan Eachan, passing the east top (a former Top in the Tables) on the way. The ridge walk then ends on gentler going as the path crosses a long, grassy bealach and climbs Creag na Caillich.

The Caillich's summit is the first of three tops that take you out along the rim of the craggy east face, which is positioned at a right-angle to the main ridge and gives good views back along it.

The return route from the Caillich descends into Coire Fionn Lairige to pick up one of the two branches of the outward approach track that end there. As the east face prevents a direct descent, there is a choice of two ways down.

Meall Garbh

alternative routes

Bad Step

MEALL NAN TARMACHAN

Meall Garbh

Beinn nan Eachan

(1) Southern branch. For better scenery and going, take the continuing path down the Caillich's south ridge. **Caution:** when the path unreasonably shoots left at one point onto very steep ground above the east face, presumably to give sheep a thrill, keep to the ridge until the path rejoins it.

The path then descends diagonally right to avoid all crags, before cutting back left around their foot into the corrie. As it approaches the main stream, it becomes indistinct. If you lose it, follow the stream down to a dam (NN 567367), where the southern branch of the quarry track begins.

(2) Northern branch. For a shorter return route, retrace your steps towards the Beinn nan Eachan bealach until you can descend across upper Coire Fionn Lairige to gain the northern branch of the quarry track at NN 574374.

This branch extends 150m/500ft higher into the corrie than the southern branch and ends at the disused quarry, for access to which the track was originally built. However, the quarry is hidden from above and hard to find, while reaching it involves a boggy tramp that is something of an anticlimax after the ridge walk.

Creag na Caillich

Southern branch

Northern branch

Beinn nan Eachan

Needlepoint: The Tarmachan Ridge sports much more complex terrain than that encountered on the ascent of Meall nan Tarmachan itself, but the well-worn path should still make the route fairly easy to follow in cloud. Most likely spot for misadventure: the descent from Creag na Caillich into Coire Fionn Lairige.

Chilly Willy: The winter traverse of the ridge gives **a famously sporting challenge** with an Alpine ambience. Depending on conditions, major problems are rare for those competent with ice axe and crampons, but the narrow ridge and Bad Step west of Meall Garbh can be daunting to the inexperienced.

Route 34b Meall nan Tarmachan and the Tarmachan Ridge from Lochan na Lairige road highpoint

Meall nan Tarmachan return: G2 * NN 593416, 4ml/ 7km, 570m/1850ft M172
Meall nan Tarmachan + Tarmachan Ridge: G4 **** 7½ml/12km, 770m/2550ft

On the rarely visited Glen Lyon side of the Tarmachan Ridge, the north ridges of Meall nan Tarmachan and Beinn nan Eachan enclose Coire Riadhailt (*Ree-ult*, Law). Meall nan Tarmachan's north ridge gives the shortest ascent route to the summit, but it has nothing further to recommend it over the normal route from near the Visitor Centre.

If you continue around the rim of Coire Riadhailt to Beinn nan Eachan, however, and then descend Beinn nan Eachan's north ridge, the whole amounts to **an attractive skyline circuit** that crosses the best bits of the Tarmachan Ridge far from the madding crowd.

The best starting point, as for Route 29a, is the cairn at the highpoint of the Lochan na Lairige road. From here, cross a short stretch of boggy ground and climb Creag an Lochain, a minor top on Tarmachan's north-east ridge. You'll find a path on the right-hand side of the prominent fence that climbs the ridge.

Higher up, ignore a tempting bypass path that contours around the top of Creag an Lochain; it leads nowhere useful. Over the top of the Creag, bear right, away from the main fence, to descend 40m/130ft beside another, ruined fence to the dip below Meall nan Tarmachan, then climb steeper grass slopes to the ▲summit.

Heading west along the Tarmachan Ridge, climb ∆Meall Garbh and ∆Beinn nan Eachan, as described previously. Continue to ∆Craig na Caillich if you wish, but you'll then have to come back in order to descend Beinn nan Eachan's north ridge, which quits the main ridge a few hundred metres east of the Beinn's summit. The gentle, grassy descent, crossing the almost imperceptible rise of Beinn a' Bhuic (*Ben a Voo-ichk*, Pig Mountain), gives unbeatable views back towards the skyline of the main ridge.

Further down, descend into Coire Riadhailt and cross the stream to reach an old track (not marked on OS map) that runs all the way down to the Lochan na Lairige road. Tarmac is reached at a roadside hut (NN 583417) c.½ml/1km from your starting point.

Winter on Meall Garbh

7 BRIDGE OF ORCHY

The Bridge of Orchy mountains form a compact group of five Munros and three Tops that rise to the east of that hamlet on the A82 north of Tyndrum. As the most north-westerly Munros in the Southern Highlands, they have less in common with their compatriots than with the adjacent Blackmount in the Central Highlands. Both groups are characterised by **bold mountains** that are linked by long ridges and gouged by craggy corries. It is the deep trench between them, which carries the A82 north to Glen Coe, that places them in different regions.

As with the Lawers Range, the alignment of the Bridge of Orchy mountains is such that deciding on the best way to tackle them makes for an interesting logistical exercise. Four of the five Munros **tower imperiously** over the southern edge of Rannoch Moor, giving **great ridge walking** with great views over great corries to a frieze of Central Highland peaks.

They are linked by high bealachs but, because they are strung out in a line, do not readily lend themselves to multi-bagging round trips.

For those who relish such challenges, Torpedo has found a route that gives a round trip over all *five* Bridge of Orchy Munros (The Five Beinns – Route 39c), but the four principals are normally bagged as two pairs: Beinn Dorain + Beinn an Dothaidh (the southern pair: Route 35a), and Beinn Achaladair + Beinn a' Chreachain (the northern pair: Route 37a). We also describe a couple of additional routes for those who prefer to seek out the mountains' most scenic features (Routes 35b and 35c).

Unsung Beinn Mhanach, the fifth, smallest and roundest Bridge of Orchy Munro, lies behind the other four, as if tagged on as an afterthought. It is generally climbed on sufferance but, if approached in the right frame of mind, can provide a diverting day out (Routes 39a and 39b).

BEINN AN DOTHAIDH   BEINN DORAIN

Bridge of Orchy

Loch Tulla

▲35 Beinn Dorain 64 1076m/3530ft (OS 50, NN 325378)
Ben Doe-rin, Mountain of the Otter (from Gaelic *Dobhran*) or
Streamlets (from Gaelic *Dobhar*, perhaps referring to its fluted flanks)

▲36 Beinn an Dothaidh 129 1004m/3294ft (OS 50, NN
331408) *Ben an Daw-y*, Mountain of Scorching

BEINN DORAIN

S Ridge

Auch Gleann

Peak Fitness: No change since 1891 Tables.

These two southern Bridge of Orchy Munros are linked by a 744m/2441ft bealach and are usually climbed together. On approach from the south, along the A82 from Tyndrum to Bridge of Orchy, Dorain appears as a giant cone, making it **one of the most distinctive mountains in Scotland**. The South Ridge Direct is the most relentlessly steep ascent in the Southern Highlands (Route 35b).

On its north side, however, the mountain takes pity on hillwalkers by extending a gentler, more complex ridge towards the Dorain-Dothaidh bealach. Not surprisingly, it is this ridge that provides the normal approach route. A path climbs from Bridge of Orchy to the bealach, and from there each Munro can be bagged in turn (Route 35a).

Beinn an Dothaidh is a less immediately impressive mountain unless you approach it from the north, along the A82 from Glen Coe. From here, its craggy north-east corrie makes it resemble nothing less than **a smaller-scale Ben Nevis**.

Although the summit is most often approached from the Dorain–Dothaidh bealach to the south, the most scenic ascent route is via the rim of that north-east corrie (Route 35c).

BEINN AN DOTHAIDH

NE Corrie

NE Ridge

Achallader

Map note: Beinn an Dothaidh's complex summit plateau is incorrectly represented on OS and other maps prior to 1984.

GiGi: In olden days, when mountains were routinely denigrated for their lack of agricultural potential, Beinn Dorain was the first in Scotland to be appreciated purely for its beauty. The instigator of this whole new way of looking at mountains was the eighteenth century gamekeeper and bard Duncan Ban MacIntyre, who wrote a famous poem *Moladh Beinn Dobhrain* (In Praise of Beinn Dorain). With sensibilities far ahead of his time, he described the Ben as 'the most beautiful mountain I have seen under the sun.' (See also Page 139.)

There is a memorial cairn to the bard at his birthplace (NN 263414) – a ruined hillside township reached by an 800m walk up a Land Rover track from the car park near the end of the A8005 west of Bridge of Orchy (NN 271418). NB There is a larger memorial cairn on Monument Hill (NN 144259), reached by a minor road past Dalmally station off the A85.

Route 35a Beinn Dorain and Beinn an Dothaidh from Bridge of Orchy via Coire an Dothaidh

G1 **** Route Rage Alert NN 300395, 7½ml/12km, 1280m/4200ft M182

On their west sides, above Bridge of Orchy, the two Munros enclose rugged Coire an Dothaidh, whose head forms their intervening bealach. A path climbs to the bealach from Bridge of Orchy railway station. Parking at the station is for train users only, so park at the car park beside Bridge of Orchy Hotel on the A82 and walk up the station road opposite. From the station car park, walk through the underpass, cross the West Highland Way and follow the boot-worn highway up the hill.

Now for the bad news: at the time of writing, the 'path' when wet is an abomination on the face of the earth, which somewhat detracts from the route's four-star rating. Even worse, we baggers have only ourselves to blame for the path's eroded condition. The first section is a stony mess... and that's the *best* bit. The central section

is a series of muddy morasses that are gradually becoming linked into one great Slough of Despond, almost as bad as the one on Beinn Dubhchraig (Route 9a).

But wait... you'll look back fondly on this after the path crosses the stream and impersonates a rocky riverbed as it climbs steeply into the shallow basin of upper Coire an Dothaidh. And here's something else to look forward to: it is even more infernal on descent. If ever a case were needed to justify path restoration programmes, this is it. We recommend you go in a dry spell, after which, if you're lucky, you can tell us we exaggerate.

South of the bealach, a steady 332m/1090ft climb up Beinn Dorain's north ridge leads to its summit, while north of the bealach, a steeper but shorter 260m/853ft climb up Beinn an Dothaidh's south ridge leads to *its* summit. Tackle Dorain first (we'll explain why below).

The well-worn, stony Dorain path climbs steeply at first over slabby ground, then it levels off and turns sharp right across a small plateau with a lochan. Beyond the lochan, the path

Baffies: In the whole of the Southern Highlands, Beinn Dubhchraig included, there is no place that could be more fundamentally improved by the installation of an escalator than Coire an Dothaidh. Copies of my petition are available from the Club secretary.

turns back left to climb an open grass slope that glories under the entirely unwarranted name of Am Fiaclach (*Am Fee-aclach*, The Teeth). At the top of this the path divides.

The right branch is what appears to be a former sheep path whose increasing prominence testifies to the number of walkers who take it by mistake. It is an awkward, vertiginous little path that undulates across steep, rocky ground on Dorain's west face to reach the south ridge just below the summit. It is a variation best left to sheep, guidebook writers and anyone who has not purchased this book.

The main path stays left, climbs through a small outcrop onto the skyline and, on good going, rises gently up a shoulder to a false summit topped by a large cairn. Just below it to the right, atop a rocky bluff, is a second cairn known as Carn Sasunaich (*Carn Sassanich*, Englishman's Cairn), a rare acknowledgement in Scottish Highland mountain nomenclature of

cross-border infiltration.

The true ▲summit, sporting another large cairn, lies a few minutes further away across a dip. Such is the sprawling complexity of Dorain's north ridge that it is really only on this last section, around the rim of craggy Coire Chruitein (*Corra Chrootin*, Corrie of the Hunchback) that there is any sensation of actually being on a ridge.

On descent, recce the route up Beinn an Dothaidh across the Dorain–Dothaidh bealach (this is why it is better– to climb Dorain first). You have two choices. A stony path can be seen climbing diagonally right into a shallow corrie, whose grassy slopes lead up to a broad saddle on the tilted summit plateau between west top and summit.

Alternatively, a less distinct path goes up the broad south ridge to the west top, on slopes of grass and rocks left of the corrie. You'll get better views from the ridge, as well as on the scenic stroll from the west top to the summit along the rim of the north-east corrie. As you'll probably want to

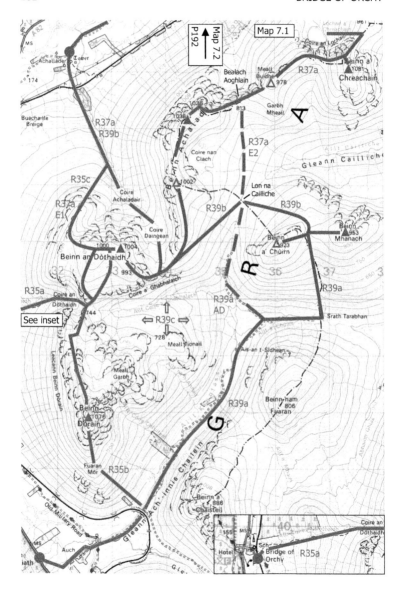

Map 7.1

visit both west top and ▲summit, you could go up one way and down the other. Both are easy.

If only the same could be said for the purgatorial re-descent of the Coire an Dothaidh path, which lurks in wait at the end of the day to enable the swear box to be filled to overflowing.

W top   BEINN AN DOTHAIDH

Summit   SE top

Needlepoint: The well-worn path up Dorain makes the ascent virtually foul-weatherproof, but beware the false summit, which has fooled many a mist-enshrouded walker over the years, especially in days of yore before the path became so distinct. How many Munroists believe they've climbed the mountain but haven't? And did the unknown Sassenach believe he was at the summit when he built his cairn here?

Dothaidh is a bigger foul-weather challenge. The tilted summit plateau of moss and grass is notoriously difficult to navigate in mist. As well as the west top and summit, there is a lower south-east top to add to the confusion.

When trying to find the summit, the rim of the north-east corrie is a useful navigation aid, but don't get too attached to the convex corrie edge or you may end up taking a closer look at the crags than intended. On descent, if you don't find and keep to one of the paths, the Dorain–Dothaidh bealach may be harder to locate than anticipated.

F-Stop: The summits of Dorain and Dothaidh both give wide-ranging views westwards to the Glen Etive hills and the Blackmount. The best viewpoint of all, however, is Dothaidh's west top, which boasts an **immense panorama** over Rannoch Moor to the Nevis Range.

Chilly Willy: In winter, Coire an Dothaidh becomes a snow bowl whose steep flanking hillsides are prone to avalanche. It is no place for beginners but, in good condition, makes an enjoyable winter training playground for those moving on to more difficult winter ascents. Although the route to the bealach has no technical difficulty, steep snow will be encountered on ascent to the upper corrie.

Above the bealach, climbing Dorain and Dothaidh is no more difficult than reaching the bealach in the first place. At Dothaidh's summit, beware cornices overhanging the north-east corrie rim. As a winter bonus, the boggy approach path to Coire an Dothaidh is easier to negotiate when the ground is hard.

Route 35b Beinn Dorain alone from Auch Farm: South Ridge Direct

G3 *** NN 317354, 6ml/10km, 910m/3000ft M182

This route up Dorain isn't readily combined with an ascent of Dothaidh to the north as it goes straight up Dorain's **skyrocketing south ridge**, which rises 850m/2800ft in 1ml/1½km. The very sight of it from the A82 north of Tyndrum is going to make you wish you were fitter.

The route up is fairly problem-free, but to say that it is one long, steep, challenging, relentless, pathless ascent is an understatement. It has a sting in the tail and is no route for those who suffer from vertigo or want an easy life, yet we have a sneaking admiration for its refusal to kowtow to accepted standards of angularity and give it three stars for sheer effrontery.

S Ridge

BEINN DORAIN

Auch Gleann

The bottom section of the ridge forms a craggy nose that is best avoided on the right. To outflank it, begin at Auch farm access road, as per Route 39a, and follow the Auch Gleann Land Rover track to the railway viaduct. Once under the viaduct, ford the Allt Kinglass and climb the steep slope in front of you to a shoulder above the rocks.

Having reached the south ridge proper, the angle of ascent lessens, though not enough to make any appreciable difference to the effort required. At least there are views west now into the Central Highlands. Lying in wait up ahead, meanwhile, to keep your mind occupied, is that sting in the tail...

Just below the summit, a rock band extends across the whole width of the ridge and seems to block the way. It can in fact be outflanked on steep grass slopes to the right (which probably make the best descent route), but there is a fascinating alternative solution to the problem.

If you head straight up the centre of the rock band, on an apron of grass that leads right into the crags, you'll find a hidden grassy gully that curves up left to the top of them. It's a hands-and-feet clamber, but it's not difficult. The ▲summit lies not far above.

No sweat.

Looking down the route through the rock band

The rock band

Needlepoint: In cloud, just keep heading skywards and you should reach the summit, but take careful note of the route through the rock band for the return trip.

Chilly Willy: Very steep, very exposed snow slopes understandably make the south ridge route a rarely attempted winter venture.

Baffies: Food for thought: *Dorainn* (NB with a double 'n') is a Gaelic word meaning Pain or Torment. If the person who named the mountain first climbed it by the south ridge…

Route 35c Beinn an Dothaidh alone
from Achallader farm: North-east Ridge

G2 *** NN 322443, 6½ml/11km, 840m/2750ft M182

This round trip on the north side of Beinn an Dothaidh isn't readily combined with an ascent of Dorain to the south, but it could be combined with ascents of Beinn Achaladair and Beinn Chreachain (see Route 37a Extension 1). As a route to Dothaidh's summit, its advantage over Route 35a is that it ascends and descends around the rim of the north-east corrie (up the north-east ridge and down the south-east ridge), giving **close-up views of impressive rock scenery** from the two shapeliest ridges on the mountain.

The north-east corrie is an off-shoot of Coire Achaladair, which lies between Beinn an Dothaidh and Beinn Achaladair. Beginning at Achallader farm, take the Coire Achaladair path as far as the corrie entrance (see Route 37a for details), then cross rising moor to gain the right-hand rim of the north-east corrie.

The going is rough at first, but ground vegetation soon diminishes to give a less fraught approach than you might anticipate when you first step off the path.

On initial steep slopes that rise to a shoulder, take a curving line to the right to outflank outlying crags and emerge at a levelling overlooking the depths of the corrie. The headwall crags add presence to the **attractive little ridge** ahead, which curves around the corrie lip to Dothaidh's summit plateau.

The ridge is quite narrow at first and is a joy to walk, with short grass and turf underfoot and views down both sides. Too soon it broadens onto the west top for a short stroll across the summit plateau to the ▲summit.

Continuing around the cliff-top, a distinct path leads to the south-east top, then a broad ridge of grass and moss curves down the far rim of the corrie to the Dothaidh-Achaladair bealach. Fairly steep slopes soon ease off to give a problem-free descent. A cairn on the bealach marks the start of the path back down Coire Daingean and Coire Achaladair to Achallader (reversing Route 37a approach).

BEINN AN DOTHAIDH

SE top   NE Corrie

Needlepoint: The main foul-weather routefinding problem is on the descent from the south-east top to the Dothaidh-Achaladair bealach. The featureless, curving ridge is off-route for most Munro baggers and carries no more than traces of path. You wouldn't be the first to miss the bealach and end up in Auch Gleann on the wrong side of the mountain.

Torpedo: To extend a short day, bag the otherwise awkward-to-reach Beinn Mhanach from the Dothaidh-Achaladair bealach (see Route 39b).

Chilly Willy: An exceptional winter route for experienced winter walkers. There are normally no major technical difficulties, although in hard snow conditions care is needed on the steep ascent to the north-east corrie rim.

As in summer, the most entertaining part of the route is the curving ridge to the summit plateau. At its best, the crest becomes a narrow snow arête, with memorable views of iced crags across the snowbound corrie.

As always on Dothaidh in winter, but especially on this route, take care around summit plateau cornices.

▲37 Beinn Achaladair 94 1038m/3405ft (OS 50, NN 344432)

Ben Achallader, Mountain of the Field by the Hard Water
(from Gaelic *Ach-a-ladair*), named after the farm at its foot
△South Top 1002m/3288ft (OS 50, NN 342420)

▲38 Beinn a' Chreachain 61 1081m/3547ft (OS 50, NN 373440)

Ben a Chrechin, Clamshell Mountain, named for the appearance of its
stony summit dome
△Meall Buidhe 978m/3209ft (OS 50, NN 359438)
Myowl Boo-ya, Yellow Hill

Summit   BEINN ACHALADAIR   S Top

Loch Tulla

Peak Fitness: No change to existing Munros and Tops since original 1891 Tables. Point 961 on OS map was an additional Top from 1891 to 1921.

When viewed from the roadside, these two apparently unappealing Munros to the north of Dorain and Dothaidh form an extensive but featureless, scree-encrusted mountain wall. But, as so often in the Southern Highlands, appearances are deceptive, because that uninviting wall buttresses a long and undulating ridge whose traverse reveals some **exceptional hidden mountain landscapes**.

Route 37a Beinn Achaladair and Beinn a' Chreachain from Achallader farm

G3 ***** NN 322443, 11½ml/18km, 1240m/4050ft M182/192

As described in Route 35a, Beinn an Dothaidh and its southern neighbour Beinn Dorain enclose the double corrie of Coire an Dothaidh, which consists of a deep lower basin leading to a shallow upper basin. In the same manner, Beinn an Dothaidh and its northern neighbour Beinn Achaladair enclose a double corrie in which lower Coire Achaladair rises to the upper bowl of Coire Daingean (*Corra Dinyun*, Firm or Strong Corrie).

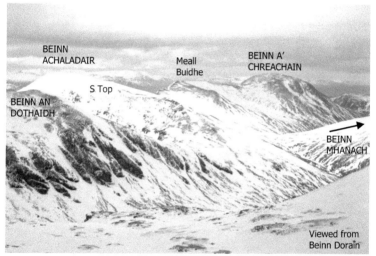

BEINN ACHALADAIR

Meall Buidhe

BEINN A' CHREACHAIN

S Top

BEINN AN DOTHAIDH

BEINN MHANACH

Viewed from Beinn Dorain

There the similarity ends. Compared to its southern counterpart, Coire Achaladair/Coire Daingean is a more open and friendlier place, with a gentler angle of ascent. From Achallader farm a path follows the right-hand side of the stream all the way to the Dothaidh-Achaladair bealach at the corrie head, and you'll be relieved to hear that overall it is in a better state than the one in Coire an Dothaidh. From the bealach, a scenic ridge walk takes you over Achaladair and Chreachain, and off the far end, to make **a rewarding round trip**.

Begin at Achallader car park, reached by a dirt road from the A82 on the shores of Loch Tulla.

GiGi: The ruined tower at Achallader is all that remains of a Campbell castle that was burned down by the MacDonalds in 1689 during one of many clan skirmishes.

Behind the buildings, a farm track leads to a bridge over the West Highland Railway line, then a path follows a fence to the right-hand bank of the Allt Coire Achaladair and climbs gently into the V-shaped corrie. To keep you on your toes, the path showcases a selection of boggy wallows but, compared to the Coire an Dothaidh path, it's a paragon of virtue. (Even so, we wouldn't go after rain.)

Once it enters Coire Achaladair, the path becomes patience-testingly boggy for a while as it crosses the grassy hillside above the stream, but matters are about to improve so stick with it (sometimes literally). At the head of the corrie, the path makes a brief trip across the stream to avoid a crag, then it crosses back and improves immensely as it climbs into the higher Coire Daingean.

Even the stream, which up to now has done nothing of note, decides to show off some admirable tumbling skills. After entering the shallow scoop of Coire Daingean, the path meanders pleasantly among grassy knolls and liberal scatterings of bare rock as it makes its final climb to the bealach.

BEINN
ACHALADAIR

SE Top

NE Spur

NE Corrie

Bealach an
Aoghlain

Meall Buidhe

Terminator: Beinn Achaladair's North-east Spur, which forms the left-hand rim of the north-east corrie when you look down it, looks desperate from above but in fact offers an adventurous ascent route.

Although much of the rock is moss-covered, scrambling of all grades can be found, and it is also possible (surprisingly) to weave a G3 way up from rock step to rock step with barely any scrambling at all.

Above the bealach, broad grass slopes rise to Achaladair's ΔSouth Top. A small path soon disappears on boggy ground but reappears higher up when the ridge becomes more well-defined. Over the South Top, a broad saddle leads to Achaladair's long, flat, rocky, confusing summit ridge. Why confusing? The cairn at the far end, at the edge of

BEINN A' CHREACHAIN

Meall Buidhe

Bealach an Aoghlain

BEINN ACHALADAIR

Achaladair's craggy north-east corrie, seems to be the highest point, but the true ▲summit (2m/6ft higher) is a couple of hundred metres before then. Don't miss it.

The route onwards to Beinn a' Chreachain begins with a descent around the rim of the north-east corrie, a twin for Beinn an Dothaidh's. Rough but easy ground leads down to a steep hillside cluttered with rock outcrops. The path weaves its way down without difficulty, although there are a few places where hands will come in... handy.

On the 813m/2667ft Bealach an Aoghlain at the foot of the steep descent (unnamed on OS map), the terrain improves again, and this time it's for good. An easy climb up grass slopes to the summit of ΔMeall Buidhe is followed by an effortless stroll along a broad, flat, turf ridge, which drops only 6m/20ft in ½ml/1km as it heads for the rim of Coire an Lochain (Beinn a' Chreachain's northern corrie).

Before reaching the rim, the path

quits the ridge to take a diagonal short cut right, down across the grassy hillside, to the rim's low point – the 924m/3032ft bealach below Beinn a' Chreachain. The corrie remains out of sight further left, but don't worry, the best and safest views of it are to be had later.

Across the bealach, the path becomes indistinct as it climbs increasingly rock-strewn slopes to the skyline, which turns out to be the rim of another large corrie, complete with its own sparkling little lochan, on the east side of Beinn a' Chreachain. Whoever named this corrie had a gift for understatement – it is called Coire Dubh Beag (*Corra Doo Bake*, Little Black Corrie, unnamed on OS map).

The ▲summit lies a short distance to the right (south), reached by a good path along the corrie rim. All this, and the most interesting part of the day is still to come!

From Chreachain's summit. return along the skyline, i.e. the rim of Coire Dubh Beag, to the junction with the

rim of Coire an Lochain, then bear right to follow the path down the narrow, grassy north-east ridge between the two great corries. Wonderfully airy stuff.

Soon, in the secluded bowl of Coire an Lochain, Lochan a' Chreachain comes into view beneath towering buttresses that drop 250m/800ft to its shores. In the whole Southern Highlands, only the Prow of Stuc a' Chroin rivals this spot for **imposing mountain architecture**. From the bealach below the former Top of Point

961 ahead, easy grass slopes descend to the lochan, but do *not* attempt to descend before then.

Anyone looking for an excuse to delay the return trip will find **innumerable opportunities for waterside lounging** beside the rock-lined lochan and all the way down the cascading Allt Coire an Lochain below it. A developing path on the left bank of the stream points the way homewards and makes for a quick descent. Just above the West Highland Railway line you'll reach a junction of

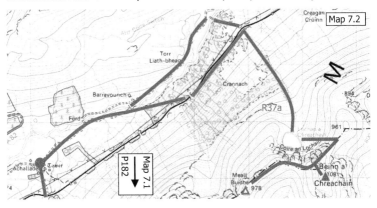

fences with a stile over each, and from here there's a choice of ways back to Achallader.

The stile on the left gives access to a waymarked path that undulates through the Old Caledonian pine forest of Crannach Wood, weaving **an arboreal mystery tour** to the bridge over the line at NN 349454. Beyond here the path descends to the near bank of the Water of Tulla and, at the bridge over the river just beyond the ruins of Barravourich (NN 338453), joins a Land Rover track back to Achallader. The path is mostly excellent but it does occasionally succumb to boggywallowness and can be tiring at the end of a long day.

For an easier but less interesting alternative way back from the fence junction, go right beside the fence (don't cross the second stile) to find an indistinct path that goes through a railway underpass and descends to a footbridge over the Water of Tulla at NN 353468. You wouldn't be the first to give up on this awkward little path and seek stepping stones to cross the river, but matters improve on the far bank, where you join the Land Rover track to Achallader 1½ml/2½km before the Barravourich bridge.

BEINN ACHALADAIR   Meall Buidhe

Lochan a' Chreachain

Coire an Lochain

F-Stop: The lip of Beinn Achaladair's north-east corrie and the summit of Beinn a' Chreachain offer **the most sublime panoramas** in the whole Bridge of Orchy group, with the vast, watery flatness of Rannoch Moor leading the eye to seemingly limitless horizons.

The best views of Coire an Lochain are obtained from its north-east side, from Point 961 and, even better, Point 894. You can descend to the lochan from anywhere on this side of the corrie.

Needlepoint: Route 37a is a relatively straightforward foul-weather route, as long as you don't lose the path. Near the summit of Beinn a' Chreachain, the junction of corrie rims between Coire an Lochain and Coire Dubh Beag offers the greatest opportunity for cloudy confusion. And make sure you don't attempt to descend into Coire an Lochain too soon.

Chilly Willy: Apart from avalanche hazard in Coire Daingean, the route has little winter difficulty as far as Beinn Achaladair. The continuation to Beinn a' Chreachain is more challenging because of the steep descent to the Bealach Aoghlain. Further along, Chreachain's north-east ridge can become **a beautiful, narrow snow arête**. Care is required.

Route 37a Extension 1: Beinn an Dothaidh

G2 *** Add-on: 1½ml/2km, 260m/850ft M182

Above Achallader farm, the path to the Dothaidh-Achaladair bealach passes beneath the cliffs of Beinn an Dothaidh's north-east corrie. You could add a scenic third Munro to the day by ascending around the near rim, crossing Beinn an Dothaidh's ▲summit and descending the far rim to rejoin the main route at the bealach (see Route 35c for description).

Route 37a Extension 2: Beinn Mhanach

G1 * Add-on: 4ml/7km, 480m/1550ft M182

If you arrive at Beinn a' Chreachain with energy to spare, you might wish to consider adding Beinn Mhanach to the trip. This will mean omitting Coire an Lochain and Crannach Wood from the itinerary but, if you're desperate for ticks, it will save you having to bag Mhanach on a separate expedition.

Instead of descending to Coire an Lochain from Beinn a' Chreachain, return to the Bealach an Aoghlain below Achaladair and contour across the grassy eastern hillside to the bealach below Beinn a' Chuirn. The traverse is damp and pathless but perfectly easy. To climb Mhanach, follow directions as per Route 39b: bag the ▲summit, return, traverse to the Dothaidh–Achaladair bealach and descend from there to Achallader (or reverse Route 35c over Dothaidh!).

▲**39 Beinn Mhanach** **211** 953m/3127ft (OS 50, NN 373411)
Ben Vanach, Monk Mountain. Contenders include St. Columba (as
with nearby Ben Challum), St. Fillan (see page 119) and Adamnan
(Columba's biographer).
△Beinn a' Chuirn 923m/3028ft (OS 50, NN 3604090)
Ben a Hoorn, Mountain of the Cairn

Beinn a'
Chuirn

BEINN
MHANACH

Auch Gleann

Peak Fitness: In the 1891 Tables, Beinn a' Chuirn was the Munro and Beinn Mhanach was the Top. This erroneous situation was reversed in 1921.

This **humble, bosomy Munro** (it has rounded twin tops) is overshadowed by the other Bridge of Orchy mountains in terms of both height and form, and is probably only ever climbed because of its status. Sheepishly, it cowers at the head of Auch Gleann behind its four bullying big siblings, but on a hot summer's day you'll find it **a surprisingly pleasant objective** in its own right. The reason for this, not apparent from its position on the edge of OS 50, is its isolated situation at the head of Loch Lyon, on OS 51 further east.

You can add Beinn Mhanach to previous routes by reaching it from the Achaladair–Meall Buidhe bealach (Route 37a Extension 2) or from the Dothaidh–Achaladair bealach (Route 39b), although both of these routes cross marshy ground. The latter approach is the most popular, but the best approach, in terms of both terrain and scenery, is undoubtedly along Auch Gleann (Route 39a).

Route 39a Beinn Mhanach from Auch Farm
G2 *** NN 317354, 12ml/19km, 890m/2900ft M182

The main advantage of this approach is that it follows a 5ml/8km Land Rover track all the way along picturesque Auch Gleann to the foot of the mountain. Moreover, the twin summits are in view all the way, forming **a photogenic composition** at the end of the glen. Beinn Mhanach is on the right and Beinn a' Chuirn (its West Top) is on the left.

BEINN MHANACH

Beinn a' Chuirn

Begin at the access road to Auch farm on the A82 between Tyndrum and Bridge of Orchy. Park on the road verge, take the paved road down to the farm and follow the continuing Land Rover track along the glen, ignoring all side branches. The track crosses the West Highland Way, fords the Allt Coralan (usually passable dryshod on stepping stones) and passes under the curving viaduct of the West Highland Railway line.

As it progresses up the glen, the track fords the Allt Kinglass four times, giving four easy paddles. Between fords 1 and 2, and again between fords 3 and 4, an occasionally muddy but mostly grassy path runs along the near bank, enabling you to avoid crossing the river at all if you so choose.

When the main river bears left beside some **perfectly proportioned drumlins**, just before the buildings at well-named Ais an t-Sithean (*Ash an Tchee-han*, Back of

GiGi: Ais an t-Sithean was the home of Duncan Ban MacIntyre, Beinn Dorain's poetic champion (see Page 179). There's nothing here now except cowsheds and sheep fanks.

the Hillocks), the track goes straight on beside a tributary (the Allt a' Chuirn). There are three more fords to come, but by now the stream is usually shallow enough to be crossed on stepping stones.

The track forks at the foot of Beinn a' Chuirn. Follow the right-hand branch to its end on the bealach leading to Loch Lyon, where weirs and waterslides on the Allt a' Chuirn may prove irresistible on a hot day. As an excuse for a lengthy sojourn, you can use the time to study the unfamiliar

backsides of Beinn Dorain and Beinn an Dothaidh before tackling the toughest part of the day – a 480m/1550ft ascent on steep grass up Coire a' Chuirn (unnamed on OS map) to the Mhanach–Chuirn saddle above.

The Allt a' Chuirn comes down from the saddle and indicates the line to be taken. The hillside can be climbed on either side of it. On the right-hand side, you can veer away to head directly for Mhanach's summit. More congenially, stay on the left-hand side, where a very rough track gives you a

LAWERS RANGE

Loch Lyon

View from Beinn Mhanach

F-Stop: Beinn Mhanach's summit view, in all directions, seems to be **too finely tuned for coincidence**. To the west, the four higher Bridge of Orchy Munros are close at hand, but who would expect Ben Nevis to be *just* visible over the Achaladair–

Chreachain bealach, or Ben Alder to be *just* visible across Rannoch Moor around the flanks of Chreachain? Walk to the east end of the summit plateau and you'll find an even more stunning view, along Loch Lyon to Ben Lawers.

head start, the cooling stream stays close at hand on a hot day, and the angle eases off towards the saddle. Above the saddle, gentle turf slopes climb to the flat, stony ▲summit.

Needlepoint: Navigation should remain straightforward, even in cloud.

Before descending, you may wish to make the short trip across the intervening saddle to bag Δ Beinn a' Chuirn, whose summit requires an ascent of only 74m/243ft.

Chilly Willy: A good, steep snow plod, but a long walk-in on a short winter's day.

Route 39a Alternative Descent from Beinn a' Chuirn
G2 * Add-on: 1ml/1½km M182

Whereas the right-hand branch of the Auch Gleann track ends at a height of 370m/1200ft on the bealach leading to Loch Lyon, the longer left-hand branch ends at a height of 550m/1800ft beneath the craggy western front of Beinn a' Chuirn. The additional height makes this a tempting ascent alternative, but that craggy hillside has to be outflanked further along, in the vicinity of the Achaladair–Chuirn bealach, where marshy going will make you wish you'd gone the other way.

If you nevertheless decide to descend this way from Beinn a' Chuirn to make a round trip, stay well right on leaving the summit, aiming in the direction of Beinn a' Chreachain, until you can see easy grass slopes curving back left to the Achaladair–Chuirn bealach (see also next route).

BEINN MHANACH

Beinn a' Chuirn

BEINN ACHALADAIR

BEINN HEASGARNICH

Loch Lyon

bealach

Coire Daingean

Viewed from Beinn an Dothaidh

Route 39b Beinn Mhanach from Achallader Farm via Dothaidh–Achaladair bealach G1 *

Return trip from bealach: 5ml/8km, 430m/1400ft M182
+ Return trip from Achallader farm to bealach: 10ml/16km, 1010m/3300ft

On the plus side, this route up Mhanach is slightly shorter than Route 39a and involves a less steep final climb. On the minus side, there is more ascent and worse terrain. In practice, as the route goes over the Dothaidh–Achaladair bealach, you'd only use it for an add-on bagging trip to Mhanach while making other ascents in the area – Beinn an Dothaidh (Route 35c) or Beinn Achaladair + Beinn a' Chreachain (Route 37a Extension 2). For strong walkers it is perhaps the most popular route up Mhanach, but we give it one star only for the summit view.

From the Dothaidh–Achaladair bealach, reached from Achallader farm by Route 37a, make a descending traverse of Achaladair's grassy eastern hillside to the 638m/2093ft Achaladair–Chuirn bealach. The key to an effortless traverse is a narrow path that connects the two bealachs. From the cairn on the Dothaidh–Achaladair bealach, at the top of Coire Daingean, look for another cairn, 70m away across the bealach, that marks the start of this traverse path.

It is not a great path, but it improves after a wet start and does the business before disappearing on the marshy Achaladair–Chuirn bealach. This latter bealach is called Lon na Cailliche (*Lon na Kyle-yicha*, The Old Woman's Marsh), and it sure lives up to its name.

Across the bealach, a direct ascent would take you onto the craggy ground of Beinn a' Chuirn's western front. Circumvent the crags on the left. An old fence climbs from the bealach, with traces of a wet path beside it. When the fence turns sharp left, the path continues diagonally up the hillside below the crags but soon disappears. Continue in the same direction to outflank all steep ground and reach drier, less clingy grass slopes that curve up to the Mhanach–Chuirn saddle. Continue to the ▲summit and return the same way.

If bagging ∆Beinn a' Chuirn on the way back, make sure you don't get into difficulty on those crags. To regain the Achaladair–Chuirn bealach from the top, as noted in Route 39a Alternative Descent, head in the direction of Beinn a' Chreachain until you can see a safe way down.

GiGi: When descending to the Achaladair–Chuirn bealach, whether from the Dothaidh–Achaladair bealach on the outward journey or from Beinn Mhanach on the return journey, recce the ensuing ascent route across the bealach. The path up to the Dothaidh–Achaladair bealach can be especially hard to find on the return trip so, on the outward journey, make a note of landmarks to aim for on the way back.

Needlepoint: Route 39b is best left for a clear day. When Beinn a' Chuirn is shrouded in cloud, navigating a curving route up (and especially down) the featureless slopes above the Achaladair–Chuirn bealach, to avoid the west-facing crags, isn't easy. Nor is finding the traverse path back to the Dothaidh–Achaladair bealach.

Chilly Willy: Provided you avoid Beinn a' Chuirn's crags, the route up Beinn Mhanach from the Achaladair–Chuirn bealach should present little winter difficulty. However, the path from the Dothaidh–Achaladair bealach to the Achaladair–Chuirn bealach crosses steep ground. If it is obliterated by snow, the traverse can become surprisingly exposed.

BEINN DORAIN

BEINN AN DOTHAIDH

Beinn a' Chuirn

BEINN ACHALADAIR

S Top   Summit

BEINN MHANACH

Route 39c The Five Beinns: All Five Bridge of Orchy Munros from Auch Farm

G3 ***** NN 317354, 21ml/34km, 2200m/7200ft M182

According to Torpedo, Auch farm is perfectly placed as the starting point for an enterprising round of all five Bridge of Orchy Munros, beginning up the south ridge of Beinn Dorain and returning from Beinn Mhanach along Auch Gleann.

As the four principals stand in a line north of the farm, each one hiding the next, their traverse has **a real sense of adventure** with ever-changing views. Torpedo grants that it's a long way (the longest route in this book!), but he also maintains that you get nothing for nothing.

Climb the south ridge of ▲Beinn Dorain (Route 35b) then continue to ▲Beinn an Dothaidh (Route 35a), ▲Beinn Achaladair and ▲Beinn a' Chreachain (Route 37a). Return to the bealach between ΔMeall Buidhe and Beinn Achaladair, traverse to the bealach below ΔBeinn a' Chuirn (Route 37a Extension 2). Climb ▲Beinn Mhanach (Route 39b) and return along Auch Gleann (Route 39a).

8 GLEN LYON

Glen Lyon is the longest and arguably **the most scenic glen in the Southern Highlands**. Sandwiched between the grassy hillsides of the Lawers Range and the Glen Lyon Horseshoe, it eschews dramatic mountainscapes for **a serene, sylvan, soothing beauty**.

The glen road gives access not only to the 'backside' of the Lawers Range, which separates the glen from Loch Tay to the south, but also to six more Munros on its north side. Four of these form the Glen Lyon Horseshoe, AKA the Carn Mairg Range after the reigning peak. The broad, undulating ridge that links the summits is as green and uneventful as you'd expect hereabouts, yet a trampers' delight for these same reasons (Route 40a).

The two remaining Munros stand in isolation further up the glen.

Easygoing Meall Buidhe would not look out of place on the Horseshoe (Routes 44a and 44b), but Stuchd an Lochain asserts a more rugged individuality with a craggy corrie that is by far the glen's most (only!) imposing mountain feature (Routes 45a and 45b).

North of the Horseshoe, not strictly in Glen Lyon itself, stands another isolated mountain that brings this section's Munro tally to seven. Not that 'isolated' is an adequate description of the celebrated Schiehallion, which positively revels in its solitariness as the most distinctive and aloof mountain in the Southern Highlands (Route 46a).

There is nothing around here for the likes of Terminator, but others will find in Glen Lyon and its environs plenty of easy excursions to keep them cheerfully occupied.

CARN GORM

An Sgorr

Viewed from the path up Meall nan Aighean

The Glen Lyon Horseshoe:

▲40 Carn Mairg 91 1041m/3415ft (OS 51, NN 684512)

Carn Merrak. A direct translation from the Gaelic gives the meaning Cairn of Pity or Regret, which supposedly commemorates a plague that decimated Glen Lyon in the seventh century. A more likely meaning is the less poetic Rusty Cairn, from the Gaelic *Meirg*, perhaps referring to autumn colours.

△Meall Liath 1012m/3320ft (OS 51, NN 693512)
Myowl Lee-a, Grey Hill
△Meall a' Bharr 1004m/3294ft (OS 51, NN 668515)
Myowl a Vaar, Hill of the Top

▲41 Meall nan Aighean 169 981m/3218ft (OS 51, NN 694496)

Myowl nan Yun. *Aigean* means Abyss in Gaelic, but the most likely meaning is Hill of the Fawns or Heifers, from the Gaelic *Agh*.

▲42 Meall Garbh 186 968m/3176ft (OS 51, NN 647517)

Myowl Garrav, Rough Hill
(not to be confused with its namesake ▲32)

▲43 Carn Gorm 103 1029m/3376ft (OS 51, NN 635500)

Carn Gorram, Blue Cairn
△An Sgorr 924m/3032ft (OS 51, NN 640509)
An Skorr, The Peak

Peak Fitness: No change to existing Munros and Tops since original 1891 Tables, although until 1997 Meall nan Aighean was known as Creag Mhor (not to be confused with ▲24 in Glen Lochay). The older name is now accepted as belonging to a crag on the south-east hillside. Meall Luaidhe (*Myowl Looy-a*, Lead Hill, NN 656510), the furthest gentle swelling south-east of Meall Garbh's east top, was an additional Top until 1981.

The four Munros of this **Queenly Quartet** link arms to form a crescent-shaped horseshoe around the hamlet of Invervar at the heart of Glen Lyon. They are rounded, grassy, virtually featureless mountains whose summits are little more than mammary highpoints on a sweeping, plateau-like ridge. That doesn't sound very appetising, we admit, but if the sky is blue and you have a desperate need to head towards it and wander lonely as a cloud to your heart's content, there is no more inviting place in the Southern Highlands.

Paths and terrain are excellent, escape routes are numerous and high bealachs enable the summits to be bagged in a single expedition for

barely more upward effort than an ascent of Ben Nevis.

The Glen Lyon Horseshoe isn't everyone's bowl of porridge, but on a good day there are worse things to do than stravaig this **great rollercoaster in the sky**.

CARN MAIRG

MEALL NAN AIGHEAN

Glen Lyon

Above Inverinain (Route 31d)

GiGi: Recalcitrant local estates have attempted to come to terms with the passing of the Land Reform (Scotland) Act 2003 by regimenting access to the mountains. Chesthill Estate, on whose land the Glen Lyon Horseshoe stands, has a history of restrictive practices towards walkers. The huge iron gate at the start of the walk was padlocked until the Act enforced free access.

The estate now wishes you to walk the horseshoe in a clockwise direction and stay out of all corries and glens! You are not obliged to heed such advice, but do take note of stalking restrictions (main season:

mid Aug to 20 Oct). Further information available on local notices or at:
   website: www.chesthill.com
   tel: 01887-830312

Similar stalking restrictions (main season: 20 Jul to 20 Oct) also apply at Lochs Estate, on whose land Meall Buidhe and Stuchd an Lochain stand. For further information, check local notices or contact the estate manager at Managed Estates:
   email: me@managedestates.co.uk
   tel: 01786-462519

No stalking takes place on a Sunday.

Route 40a The Glen Lyon Horseshoe from Invervar
G1 **** NN 666483, 11ml/17km, 1450m/4750ft M205

This is a tricky route to rate as opinions on it vary widely. We award it four stars for when the sun's out, but ambitious ramblers might well give it more, while rock jocks will certainly give it less. And if you go on a dreich day, you've only got yourself to blame.

If you think four Munros in a day is pushing it, check out the Shorter Options on Page 209. The four-bagger can be tackled in either direction but we prefer an anti-clockwise circuit. In this direction, routefinding is easier, views are improved (the morning sun is behind for views ahead, while the afternoon sun is behind for views back), the initial ascent is less tiring and the day ends beside the tumbling Invervar Burn.

Begin at Invervar, 8ml/13km from Coshieville at the foot of Glen Lyon. There's a hidden car park a short distance down a side road just before the telephone box. From here, cross the glen road, go through the iron gate opposite and follow a Land Rover track up through woods on the right-hand (east) side of the Invervar Burn. Leave the track at the first telegraph pole beyond the woods for an excellent path that climbs Meall nan Aighean's south-west ridge around the rim of Coire a' Chearcaill (*Cyarcle*, Circle).

At a levelling at a height of 530m/1740ft, the path crosses a wider stalkers' path that comes up from the right, crosses the ridge and heads left to a dilapidated hut in the bowl of the corrie. The stalkers' path begins on the approach track 20 metres before the telegraph pole and makes an equally excellent alternative ascent route but, as it stays below the crest

of the ridge, we prefer the ridge path for the views.

The path continues up the broadening ridge almost all the way to Aighean's summit and makes for **a pleasant, well-graded ascent**, despite the disconcerting sight of the Horseshoe skyline stretching away to the west, *behind* you, as you climb north-east. The path becomes indistinct higher up but, thanks to short grass underfoot, it is hardly needed. The rocky ▲summit is the further away of two rounded tops, being 7m/23ft higher than its neighbour and the most easterly point of the day.

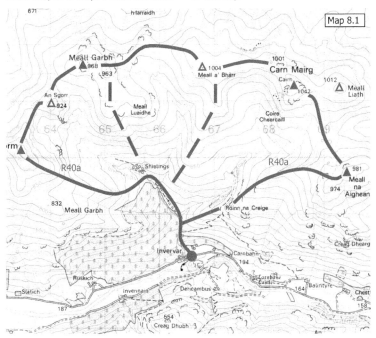

Looking west on
Meall a' Bharr

Now the skyline traverse proper begins as the route heads north across a broad, hummocky saddle to a second pair of rounded tops, the leftmost of which is Carn Mairg, the highest summit in the range. The right-hand rise is ΔMeall Liath, which Top baggers will wish to visit, but the main path gives it a body swerve. On descent to the saddle you'll pass a spring at NN 692497, worth noting on an otherwise waterless ridge walk that, on a hot summer's day, will help sweat off a few kilos as part of a calorie-controlled diet.

Approaching Carn Mairg, the obvious way up would appear to be via the saddle between it and Meall Liath, but the path cuts left below the skyline to ascend a grassy rake and find a more congenial way up through the boulderfield that skirts the ▲summit. As the northern view opens up, Schiehallion looks attractive across a deep intervening glen, but that's for another day.

Heading due west at last from the summit, **the great sweeping spine of the Horseshoe draws you onwards**. A short descent leads to a stony crest and a broken fence that will be with you all the way to the next Munro and beyond.

The path finds good going on grass below the crest, crosses a small rise (Point 1001) and reaches the most effortless part of the walk, along the great flat top of ΔMeall a' Bharr. We don't care what Terminator says about the Glen Lyon hills, this section of the Horseshoe gives **a superb sky-high stravaig**. NB Beware older maps that misplace Meall a' Bharr's name away from the summit.

Coming off the end of Meall a' Bharr, a short descent leads to a long, 864m/2835ft-high bealach, at the far end of which is the only lochan *en route*. An even shorter ascent then takes you up Meall Garbh, the third rounded, twin-topped Munro of the day. Go over or around the east top to reach the 5m/16ft higher ▲summit (west top). The former Top of Meall

Luaidhe lies c.800m off-route south-east of the east top.

One more Munro to go. Halfway down to the next bealach, the fence of which you have now become so fond bears right towards Loch Rannoch and should be left to its own devices. Across the bealach, a direct ascent of the final Munro of Carn Gorm is blocked by the nuisance of a peak that is ∆An Sgorr.

Despite its name, and the presence of a few crags on its far side, this is a tedious little excrescence. This late in the day you'll probably be cursing the extra 80m/250ft of ascent and descent required to surmount it and reach Carn Gorm beyond.

For those who so wish, and we make no moral judgements on the matter, there's a bypass path around the thing. Unless you're a Top bagger, we suspect you'll take that path. For some reason, it is well-worn.

Carn Gorm is the most westerly and shapely Munro of the group. F-Stop has even managed to produce photographic evidence that makes it look pointy from some angles. Even so, and even if you choose not to go over An Sgorr, the 290m/950ft pull from bealach to summit is the stiffest of the day. The true ▲summit lies 100m beyond the trig. pillar and rewards with the best views on the whole Horseshoe.

To descend, take the path that curves down Carn Gorm's south-east ridge and around the upper boundary of a large forestry plantation into the upper glen of the Invervar Burn. After reaching the stream, stay on the near bank and, hidden around a corner, you'll find a bridge (NN 659494) that gives access to the approach track on which you began the day. On a sunny (midge-free) summer's evening, the stream is very inviting.

Meall a' Bharr

CARN MAIRG

MEALL GARBH

GiGi: The curious, beehive -shaped building passed near the start of the walk is a restored eighteenth century lint mill, used to mechanise the production of linen from local flax. Worth a look.

F-Stop: As befitting the last Munro of the day, Carn Gorm is a good place to take a break, and the best views in the range encourage the (in)activity. There are **terrific views** not only up and down Glen Lyon but also across it to the Munros of the Lawers Range and Tarmachan. Above all, though, it is the view back along the Horseshoe, all the way to Meall nan Aighean 5½ml/9km away, that will leave you gasping at what you have just achieved.

Needlepoint: You'd think that good paths, and a broken fence along much of the ridge, would make the route fairly foul -weatherproof, but don't bank on it. The path is sometimes indistinct and sometimes non-existent. Just one wrong turn in the featureless landscape and you'll discover why the Horseshoe has earned its navigational notoriety.

Chilly Willy: The main winter problem on the Horseshoe is not technical difficulty but length. These are benign winter mountains that in normal conditions give a good yomp in the snow, but in less than perfect conditions you can easily run out of light. Bagging the four Munros as two pairs, as described under Shorter Options, will give two less fraught days out.

Route 40a Shorter Options M205

CARN GORM

MEALL NAN AIGHEAN
SW Ridge

If you run out of time or energy after climbing the first two Munros, you can always leave the last two for another day. After bagging ▲Meall nan Aighean and ▲Carn Mairg, there is a choice of at least three ways down, all of approximately equal length.
Round trip: 7ml/11km, 1000m/3300ft.

(1) Return to the saddle between Carn Mairg and Meall nan Aighean and traverse easy ground above Coire a' Chearcaill to regain the approach route on Aighean's south-west ridge.
(2) From the saddle, descend right (west) into Coire a' Chearcaill to reach the old hut noted above and the start of the stalkers' path back to Aighean's south-west ridge.
(3) For a change of scenery, head west along the skyline from Carn Mairg to Meall a' Bharr and descend the latter's pathless but easy south-west ridge to the Invervar Burn path.

To bag the last two Munros as a separate expedition, walk up the Invervar Burn path to an old corrugated tin hut and shielings marked on the map at NN 656498, then head straight up the hillside to the summit of ▲Meall Garbh. From there, continue to ▲Carn Gorm and descend as described previously.
Round trip: 7ml/11km, 1080m/3550ft.

▲44 Meall Buidhe 248 932m/3058ft (OS 51, NN 498499)
Myowl Boo-ya, Yellow Hill (not to be confused with its namesake
▲184 in the Western Highlands or with ▲6 Beinn Bhuidhe)

Peak Fitness: Meall Buidhe has been a Munro since the original 1891 Tables, although until 1921 it was called Garbh Mheall (*Garrav Vyowl*, Rough Hill). That name is now applied only to the lower north top. The south-east top was an additional Top until 1981.

If the rounded summits of the Glen Lyon Horseshoe are unremarkable, the similar but lower summits to their west, punctuating little-visited country on the north side of the upper glen, are even more so. Only Meall Buidhe heaves itself over the magic 3000ft mark to attract humankind to its lonely top. Yet we like Meall Buidhe. While some mountains flatter to deceive, unassuming Meall Buidhe scorns

vulgar ostentation... which only makes its amazing summit even more remarkable. We're talking about **one of the best viewpoints in the whole Scottish Highlands**.

The most effortless ascent route begins at Loch an Daimh (*Loch an Daff*, Stag Loch), near the head of Glen Lyon (Route 44a), but you can also reach the summit from Loch Rannoch to the north (Route 44b).

Route 44a Meall Buidhe from Loch an Daimh

G1 *** NN 512464, 5½ml/9km, 520m/1700ft M212

This is a two-star route that gets a third star for a summit you'll be loath to quit, although the bland hillside on which the ascent begins gives zero indication of this. Just before the end of the side road to Loch an Daimh, beginning at a height of 410m/1350ft, a Land Rover track on the right climbs the hillside in the direction of Meall Buidhe's summit. Follow it to a T-junction a short distance up, then go left to find the start of a continuing path.

One path, hidden among the heather barely 10 metres from the T-junction, climbs straight up the hillside to the level skyline above. We'll call it Path 1. A second path begins a

few hundred metres further along, at the top of the next rise. We'll call it Path 2.

You'll have noted that the road-end information board of Lochs Estate suggests using Path 2 only but, in the generally boggy terrain hereabouts, Path 1 gives a dry and agreeable descent, so we suggest that outside the stalking season you make a round of it by going up Path 2 and down Path 1 (see Page 203).

As it climbs the boggy hillside, Path 2 improves and deteriorates in turns. Not until approaching the skyline, which is revealed to be the lower rim of peaty Coire Beithe (*Corra Bay-a*, Birch Corrie), does it veer left at a

MEALL
BUIDHE

Glas
Choire

SE top

F-Stop: Meall Buidhe's summit is completely encircled by a virtual roll-call of Southern Highland and Central Highland peaks. Morning is the best time for the incomparable view across The Great Flatness (Rannoch Moor) to Glen Coe and the Nevis Range. For the full show, make the short trip over to Garbh Mheall.

Torpedo: Meall Buidhe and Stuchd an Lochain (Route 45a) make such short trips from the high starting point of Loch an Daimh that you can do them both in a single day. Say after me: Yes, I can.

gentler angle and reach firmer ground on the corrie's west-bounding ridge.

On the way to the ridge you'll join Path 1, and on the crest of the ridge you'll join yet another path. Note both of these junctions for the return trip. The number of paths that exist on the mountain are testament to decades of attempts to find the best ground.

As height is gained, the ridge splays out across delightful (not!) peat hags, where the path becomes difficult to follow. Mercifully, this part of the route is short.

Even if you lose the path, it soon becomes obvious again on easy grass slopes that rise from the peat to the next skyline. Here you find yourself on the rim of Glas Choire (*Glass Chorra*, Green Corrie), a vast, featureless north-east corrie that has been hidden from view until now.

Along the rim to the right is the rounded top of Meall a' Phuill (*Myowl a Foo-il*), while to the left is the insignificant swelling (but former Top) that is Meall Buidhe's south-east top. Meall a' Phuill means either Hill of the Hole (referring to the depths of Glas Choire) or Hill of Mud (no prizes for guessing the origin of that derivation).

The path goes left, well away from the corrie rim, to make the short climb to the south-east top. All that remains then is **a languid stroll** around the continuing rim to its highpoint, AKA the ▲summit of Meall Buidhe. With a glorious view across Rannoch Moor in front of you, and a new spring in your step, this final ½ml/1km saunter across the turf is not nearly long enough. You may well spend more time at the summit, testing your mountain-spotting prowess, than you will skipping back down to the road.

On the return trip, you may prefer to follow the corrie rim all the way round to the green-baize top of Meall a' Phuill before descending. Back down among the peat hags, you'll discover, if you haven't already on the way up, that just about every bit of dry ground carries a little path. Aim for Coire Beithe's west-bounding ridge and you'll regain the main path at some point.

After leaving the ridge lower down, keep left at the junction of Path 1 and Path 2 to make a round trip as noted above. If you can't find Path 1, or if you lose it, aim for a reedy lochan on the flat ground at the lower rim of Coire Beithe. The path passes its left side and soon reaches gentle, dry ground that gives an effortless final descent with loch-wide views.

CENTRAL HIGHLANDS

MAMORES   BEN NEVIS   GREY CORRIES

Rannoch Moor

View from
MEALL BUIDHE

Needlepoint: As the view is the thing, it would be silly to climb Meall Buidhe when it's in cloud. In any case, you'd *definitely* lose the path at some point in featureless Coire Beithe and end up milling around boggy shallows that lead nowhere fast.

Chilly Willy: In winter, Meall Buidhe's gentle demeanour and high starting point combine to give an easy ascent to a spectacular view out of all proportion to the effort involved in reaching it. This is **an excellent winter route for beginners** (adorned with ice axe and crampons glinting in the sunlight, of course).

Route 44b Meall Buidhe from Loch Rannoch
G2 ** NN 504565, 9ml/15km, 720m/2350ft

Few hillwalkers choose the Loch Rannoch approach to Meall Buidhe over the Loch an Daimh approach. Apart from the long drive to the start of the route, there's a 3½ml/6km walk-in and the terrain is rough. Nevertheless, if you happen to be passing this way...

Begin at the west end of Loch Rannoch, at the bend on the minor road just outside Bridge of Gaur. There's a car park just west of the bend. A grassed-over Land Rover track heads south beside the Allt a'

Mheanbh-chruidh (*Owlt a Menuv Chroo-y*, Stream of the Little Horseshoe), aiming directly for the great pudding of Garbh Mheall ahead. The track rises gently across heather moorland, so go in autumn to add a splash of colour to proceedings.

After 2½ml/4km the track reaches a fork at the foot of Garbh Mheall. It is possible to leave the track here and climb the steep facing slopes direct, going straight up through broken crags or finding an easier route to the right of them. However, very

Garbh Mheall

MEALL BUIDHE

Loch Rannoch

Loch Eigheach

rough ground and burgeoning afforestation on the lower slopes make this option increasingly less than enticing.

You are more likely to be seduced by the track's right-hand branch, which continues up the glen of the Allt Sloc na Creadha (*Owlt Slochk na Cray-a, Stream of the Claypit*) to the right of Garbh Mheall. It runs for a further 1ml/2km to the foot of Coire nan Cnamh (*Corra nan Crav, Corrie of Chewing, probably of cattle*), between Garbh Mheall and Meall Buidhe.

From the end of the track, the summit of Meall Buidhe can be seen for the first time at the head of the deep-cut corrie. Climb the corrie's less steep left-hand side, seeking patches of grass and game paths to ease the heathery going (Garbh Mheall did not earn its Gaelic name for nothing). Higher up, the terrain improves and the angle eases as you cross the shallow bowl of the upper corrie to gain Meall Buidhe's ▲summit.

Needlepoint: In foul weather, this is a much more straightforward approach to Meall Buidhe than Route 44a. There is no path in Coire nan Cnamh, but by following the stream to the skyline you should stay on target.

Chilly Willy: Routefinding may be easier on the Rannoch side of the mountain than on the Lyon side, but Coire nan Cnamh faces north-west and holds snow longer than the south side of the mountain, making the Bridge of Gaur approach a tougher winter proposition. Be prepared to encounter steep snow slopes.

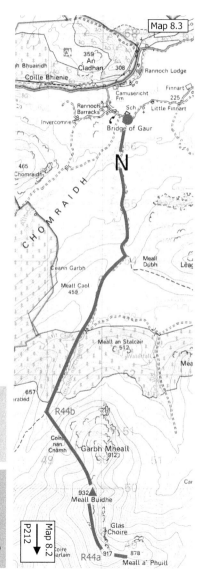

▲45 Stuchd an Lochain 197 960m/3150ft (OS 51, NN 483448) *Stoochk an Lochin*, Peak of the Lochan
△Sron Chona Chorein 927m/3041ft (OS 51, NN 493445) *Strawn Chonna Chorrin*, Nose of the Meeting of the Corries

STUCHD
AN LOCHAIN

N Ridge

Loch an Daimh

Peak Fitness: No change since 1891 Tables.

Stuchd an Lochain stands isolated on the south shore of Loch an Daimh, directly across the water from Meall Buidhe. On approach it looks no more exciting than any other grassy heap hereabouts, but for once those featureless lower slopes conceal not one but two notable mountain features, which is two more than the

other six Munros in Glen Lyon can muster between them.

Screened from roadside rubberneckers around a corner of Loch an Daimh, the Stuchd's northern flank rises in one great sweep from the lochside, so gouged by glaciation that little of it remains except **an enormous craggy corrie** (Coire an

Lochain, *Corra an Lochin*, Corrie of the Lochan). The summit perches on the corrie rim, high above a circular lochan and at the apex of a rousing north ridge that must surely have been sited in Glen Lyon by mistake.

By far the best approach to the mountain, despite an over-worn path, is from the lochside via the corrie rim (Route 45a), perhaps returning down

the north ridge (Route 45a Alternative Descent). If you need a quick tick or an easier way up in winter, an approach from Glen Lyon, via the Stuchd's dreary southern slopes, will save a minimum of effort but forego a maximum of scenery (Route 45b). During the stalking season Lochs Estate wishes you to use Route 45a (see Page 203).

Route 45a Stuchd an Lochain from Loch an Daimh
G2 *** Route Rage Alert NN 500463, 5ml/8km, 650m/2150ft M218

W e award the route three stars in honour of its enthralling summit, although the lower section of the approach path is currently in such a dire condition that you may have difficulty appreciating the mountain's true potential.

Begin at Giorra Dam, at the end of the minor road to Loch an Daimh, at a height of 400m/1300ft on the north-east side of the mountain. Take the hydro road to the left side of the dam and the continuing vehicle track along the south shore of the loch (it goes to a boathouse).

Just around the first right-hand corner (NN 509461), leave the track for a path that climbs the hillside to Point 887. This highpoint on the east rim of the Coire an Lochain is sometimes called Creag an Fheadain (*Craik an Aiten*, Waterpipe Crag), although that name more properly applies to crags overlooking Loch an Daimh lower down.

The hillside up which the path climbs is littered with broken crags that complicate routefinding. The route indicated on the estate's road-end notice board ascends directly from the boathouse. We advise you to keep to the path.

To find the easiest line, it makes a shallow rising traverse into a steep, grassy depression, which it then climbs to the skyline. Unfortunately the path is so infuriatingly boggy that you'll spend more time off it than on it.

It may be only 400m/1300ft to the skyline but it's a stiff pull, alleviated

GiGi: Stuchd an Lochain has a unique claim to fame in that it was the scene of the first ever recorded ascent of a Munro, around 1590. The bagger, more (in)famous for abducting ladies and executing Macdonalds than for his hillwalking exploits, was Colin 'The Mad' Campbell of Glen Lyon. Although some say you have to be mad to climb mountains, Colin's excuse was to stalk game.

only by views back down the green trough of Glen Lyon. Patience, patience. Your reward awaits.

The path reaches the skyline on the east ridge of Point 887, not far below the top. Note this point for the return trip, to ensure that you leave the ridge in the correct place to avoid the crags. A broken fence along the crest of the ridge accompanies you up the last couple of rises to Point 887's domed top, where the view finally opens up over Coire an Lochain to the Stuchd's summit on the far rim. Now the fun can begin.

With good going underfoot at last, the path turns south-west to follow the old fence around the broad, curving corrie rim and across a shallow saddle to the rounded Top of ΔSron Chona Chorein. The actual highpoint of the Top, should you wish to visit it (and why wouldn't you?), lies 30m back from the highest point reached by the fence. There's also a bypass path that contours below the Top to save a modicum of ascent and re-descent (only to be used on the return journey, obviously). A glance at the map will show that the Top is well-named, with corries indenting it on all sides.

Turning west, **a spacious stravaig** leads onwards along the rim of Coire an Lochain, between its abysmal depths and the sharply contrasting southern hillside, which falls away tamely to Glen Lyon (Route 45b). In the dark craggy recesses of the inner corrie nestles Lochan nan Cat, which unlike its namesake on Ben Lawers (Route 31a) forms an almost perfect circle and doesn't look at all like its eponymous beastie. Beyond another shallow saddle, steeper slopes rise to the Stuchd's distinctive half-dome ▲summit.

STUCHD AN LOCHAIN

Sron Chona Chorein

STUCHD AN LOCHAIN

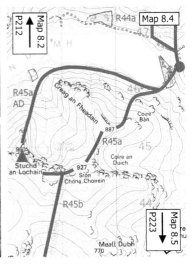

F-Stop: The summit view would be almost as good as that from Meall Buidhe, if Meall Buidhe weren't in the way. The attractive mountain basin seen below, hemmed in by steep hillsides at the head of Loch an Daimh, rivals the head of Loch Lyon as the least trodden country in the Southern Highlands.

STUCHD
AN LOCHAIN

N Ridge

Sron
Chona
Chorein

Lochan
Na Cat

Needlepoint: There are occasions in the Scottish Highlands when you may notice the odd spot of dampness in the air. In such conditions, both the boggy ascent path and the steep Alternative Descent via the north ridge are best avoided. If the mountain is in cloud, the main navigational problem is on the return trip – finding the correct place at which to come off the east ridge of Point 887, to avoid the crags below. Our advice is to wait for better conditions – the path really is purgatorial when wet.

Chilly Willy: When the path is obliterated by snow, the ascent to the east ridge of Point 887 can become surprisingly steep and exposed, especially if you fail to find the easiest line. There are no real obstacles as long as you avoid craggy ground, but this is no place to learn how to use ice axe and crampons.

The steep slopes rising to Stuchd an Lochain's summit dome may also give pause if iced. Although they are no steeper than the slopes of Point 887, the adjacent drop to Lochan nan Cat certainly adds to

the *frisson*. Coire an Lochain is **spectacular in winter**, but you'll obtain only limited views of the lochan itself owing to the generally convex nature of the corrie rim. Don't get over-ambitious in your efforts to peer over the edge or you may end up with a lochside close-up.

The Alternative Descent of the north ridge is naturally a considerably more difficult proposition, but when it's good it's very very good. Who'd have thought you'd find **an exhilarating little test piece** for budding Alpinists in Glen Lyon?

Route 45a Alternative Descent: North Ridge

G3 **** Zero additional mileage, 50m/160ft *less* ascent M218

Vertigo sufferers should return by the route of ascent, but anyone desirous of a tad more excitement should consider descending the north ridge to the lochside and returning along the shoreline to Giorra Dam.

Unique in Glen Lyon, the narrow and **beautifully proportioned upper ridge** is an unexpected treat. At one point it is so narrow that there is room on it for little else but the grassy path. A 'Bad Step' adds zest to proceedings, but it is pretty straightforward, so there is nothing here for followers of Terminator to get excited about.

From Stuchd an Lochain's summit, easy heath slopes descend to the Bad Step, which acts as a gateway to the narrowest section beyond. The Step is no more than a brief rocky drop, easy-angled and with little exposure. It barely even rates as a scramble, but it does require a spot of handwork (and maybe backside work). At the foot you are ushered onto a seductive section of level ridge in a terrific situation above Loch an Daimh. Its only drawback is its shortness.

At the far end, the route seems to disappear over the abyss, but the path finds a way down steep grass slopes among crags to reach wet ground in lower Coire an Lochain below Lochan nan Cat. These tedious final slopes make a disappointing end to the descent, but they are still less aggravating than those encountered on the normal ascent route. Take a diagonal route down to the lochside, then follow the shoreline back beneath the crags of Creag an Fheadain to reach the boathouse and the track to the dam.

Loch an Daimh

Stuchd an Lochain N Ridge

Route 45b Stuchd an Lochain from Cashlie

G1 ** NN 490418, 5ml/8km, 660m/2150ft M223

An ascent of Stuchd an Lochain via its monotonous southern slopes avoids both the northern crags and the northern scenery. Other things being equal, we'd say an approach from this side is for unrepentant tickers only. However, as the normal route up from Loch an Daimh to the north is eroded to distraction, a southern approach has the not inconsiderable merit of being less likely to disrupt the equanimity of the ascent party.

Park at the east entrance to Cashlie house, at a height of 300m/1000ft in upper Glen Lyon, and walk up the drive. Just before the house, a gate on

STUCHD AN LOCHAIN

An Grianan

Cashlie

Glen Lyon

Viewed from MEALL GHAORDAIDH

GiGi: Loch an Daimh was formerly called Loch Giorra. Following its damming for hydro-electric power in the 1950s, its waters backed up to join Loch an Diamh, which was then a smaller loch further up the glen. The combined loch is now named after the upper loch, but the dam is called Giorra Dam in memory of the lower loch. Pipelines carry water from Loch an Daimh (where Route 45a starts) *under* Stuchd an Lochain to Cashlie in upper Glen Lyon (where Route 45b starts).

the right gives access to open hillside on the right-hand side of the Allt Cashlie. Follow this stream all the way up and you'll reach the rim of Coire an Lochain near the summit of the mountain.

The first part of the ascent is steep and pathless but the going is good, on short grass beside a fence. Height is gained fast. Soon you pass the rocky bluffs of An Grianan (*An Gree-anan*, The Sunny Spot), the bold lump of a hill on the left, and enter the wide open spaces of Stuchd an Lochain's broad southern corrie. In contrast to the northern Coire an Lochain, this is so shallow, grassy and featureless that it is easy to lose your bearings in it, even on a clear day.

The going deteriorates somewhat in the bowl of the corrie, but the ground is nowhere near as boggy as might be expected and much drier than on the Loch an Daimh approach. Follow the line of the main stream up and out of the corrie and you'll reach the skyline at the rim of Coire an Lochain, which drops away on the far side of the mountain for a sudden and startling change of scenery.

If you're not sure which is the main stream, just keep heading up the gentle grass slopes and you'll reach the skyline at some point. Until then, there is zero scenic interest. Once on the rim of Coire an Lochain, with the summit dome of Stuchd an Lochain to your left (hopefully!), the Loch an Daimh approach is joined for the last few hundred metres to the ▲summit.

Sron Chona Chorein

Cashlie

STUCHD AN LOCHAIN

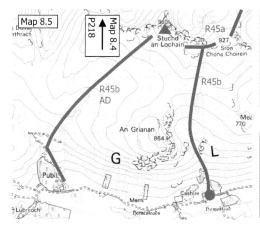

Map 8.5 P218

Needlepoint: In cloud, keep climbing beside the Allt Cashlie, or heading in a northerly direction, and you should reach the rim of Coire an Lochain at some point. But it will be a dismal ascent.

Chilly Willy: No problems should be encountered in the southern corrie in winter, although (as noted previously) the steep slopes of the summit dome may give pause if iced.

Route 45b Alternative Descent

G1 ** Add-on: 2ml/3km road walk

An Grianan separates Stuchd an Lochain's southern corrie from another shallow corrie (the south-west corrie) down which the Allt Camaslaidh flows to Pubil house, 2ml/3km west of Cashlie on the Glen Lyon road. Pubil is at the same height as Cashlie and is the same distance from the summit of Stuchd an Lochain.

You could climb the mountain from here, but we prefer the ascent from Cashlie on account of better going and better views on the rim of Coire an Lochain. However, providing you don't mind an end-of-day road walk back to Cashlie, a descent to Pubil allows a circuit to be made.

From the summit, descend south-

west down easy grass slopes to reach the bowl of the south-west corrie. A smattering of peat bogs has to be negotiated, but aim for the Allt Camaslaidh and you should find reasonable going along its banks. In places, a streamside sheep path even encourages speedy progress over gentle terrain.

As on the Cashlie route, the hillside steepens above the road, but the going remains good. At a height of 500m/1650ft you'll come across a hydro road that makes light work of the final 200m/650ft descent to Pubil. The initial long hairpin can be shortcut. Once down, all that remains is the 2ml/3km road walk back to Cashlie.

▲**46 Schiehallion** 59 1083m/3553ft (OS 42, 51 or 52, NN 714547)

Sheehallion, fancifully translated since Victorian times as Fairy Hill of the Caledonians, from the Gaelic *Sithean* (Pointed Hill or Fairy Hill) and *Chaillean*. With less prudishness and greater fidelity to the mountain's shape, earlier eighteenth century mapmakers translated it as Maiden's Pap, from the Gaelic *Sine* (Breast) and *Chailinn* (Maiden).

SCHIEHALLION

E Ridge

NW Ridge

Loch Tummel

Peak Fitness: No change since 1891 Tables.

We admit it, we don't know what to make of this ultimate mountain in *The Ultimate Guide* to the Munros of the Southern Highlands. It certainly dominates its landscape, showing up as a graceful cone from the west and an equally attractive wedge from the Queen's View along Loch Tummel to the east.

It also has a greater historical importance than most. Even the Ordnance Survey succumbs to the mountain's exalted opinion of itself and features it, uniquely, on *three* separate maps.

Yet when you climb the thing, it turns out to be nothing more than **a great muckle lump**, with a long whaleback ridge of irritating broken quartzite that rises over an irritating succession of irritating false summits. Did we mention it was irritating? But then again, there's that nice new gravel approach path, and that **extensive summit view** over loch and woodland, unhampered by surrounding mountains…

Maybe you'd better just go see for yourself. If ever a mountain needed to be climbed *because it is there*, it is Schiehallion. The normal route uses a new path to climb the gentle but bouldery east ridge (Route 46a), while seekers after solitude may wish to try the steeper but pathless north-west ridge (Route 46b).

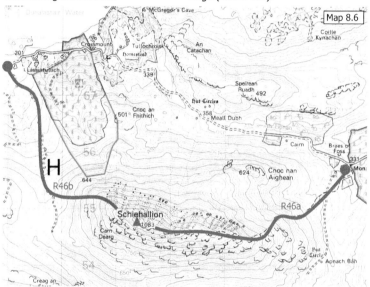

GiGi: In the eighteenth century the Astronomer Royal Nevil Maskelyne made use of Schiehallion's regular shape to seek evidence in support of Newton's gravitational theories. A previous such experiment on the Ecuadoran volcano Chimborazo in 1749 had proved too difficult to manage, but Schiehallion magnanimously rose to the challenge.

Maskelyne spent four months on the mountain in 1774, taking a number of astronomical observations at various locations to see how much they were affected by gravitational pull. From these readings he was able to estimate Schiehallion's mass and extrapolate from that to the mass of the earth and other bodies in the solar system.

In support of the experiment, Charles Hutton was given the task of surveying the mountain. To simplify presentation of his findings he came up with the idea of joining points of equal height on the map, and in so doing he invented contour lines.

Route 46a Schiehallion from Braes of Foss: East Ridge

G1 *** NN 753557, 6ml/10km, 760m/2500ft M225

From Schiehallion's conical summit, the whaleback east ridge tilts down to a shoulder, below which the ascent route begins at a car park near Braes of Foss farm, at a height of 330m/1080ft (small parking fee payable at machine). No route in the Scottish Highlands has two such contrasting halves, with **a brilliant new path** up to the shoulder and execrable going beyond.

The path was built by the John Muir Trust at a cost of £817,000, following purchase of the north-east side of the mountain in 1999. With its surface of compacted gravel, the path is such a vast improvement on the boggy morass of the old path that it rivals the new Cobbler path (Route 2a) for the access improvement it has brought.

The path crosses the moor and wends its way up the shoulder for around 2ml/3½km (3400m to be precise). It ends at a height of 830m/2720ft, at a junction with the old path and the start of the whaleback ridge. A short distance beyond here, at NN 726545, the horseshoe-shaped Maskelyne Cairn commemorates one of the Astronomer Royal's observation points.

The character of the route changes completely when you set foot on the quartzite and begin the prolonged plod up the rockpile of the east ridge, from false summit to false summit. The slope is gentle but the terrain is anything but. A stony line worn among the rocks by generations of hillwalkers attempts to find the least aggravating going but, when the rocks become too jumbled, especially higher up, you'll be left to your own devices.

As distraction, a panoramic view opens up behind over a great tranche of lowland to the Cairngorms. If motivation still falters, spur yourself on with some creative visualisation of the even more expansive view that awaits at the summit.

It is a relief to have interest rekindled at the ▲summit cairn, which is perched atop a short, narrow ridge of tilted quartzite pavement that drops in tiers of small crags to the south. Take care when you go exploring, especially if the slippery rock is wet.

After pausing to take in the view westwards, and to debate the mountain's worth, all you have to do then is descend. Some find the rubble more infuriating to negotiate on the way down than on the way up, which gives Schiehallion another claim to fame. It is a mountain on which, uniquely, you may well find yourself asking someone coming up: 'Is it far to the bottom?'

E Ridge

Braes
of Foss

SCHIEHALLION
Summit

Baffies: Memo to self: Request JMT to extend the new path all the way to the summit.

GiGi: At NN 752553, beside the path on the right, c.200m from the gate at the end of the car park, an isolated cup-marked boulder lies among the bracken. It is thought that the many small hollows or 'cups' were carved into the rock pre-Bronze Age, between 3000BC and 2000BC, but their purpose remains a mystery. Art, cartography, ritual... you decide.

The sheep fanks further along, at the foot of the path's first steepening (NN 748547), date from the beginning of the nineteenth century, when sheep began to replace cattle as the mainstay of Highland life. Several hundred metres south of here at NN 747540, off-route along an old Land Rover track, is the hut circle of Aonach Ban

(*Ernach Bahn*, White Ridge), dating from c.1500BC to early AD. Other archaeological findings dot Schiehallion's mountainsides. For further information, see www.jmt.org/east-schiehallion-estate.asp.

The new path from Braes of Foss

Needlepoint: The quartzite wasteland of the whaleback ridge is ankle-twistingly slippery when wet and ridiculously confusing in mist. Cairns and the stony 'path' make navigation fairly simple much of the time, but in thick cloud there are one or two places where you may lose your bearings, hopefully temporarily.

Chilly Willy: Quartzite? What quartzite? Schiehallion's viewpoint summit makes an even more inviting objective when the awkward rocks are under snow, so give the route **an extra star for a winter ascent**. Beginners note: ice axe and crampons are still required, of course, as is care on icy summit rocks.

Somewhere on SCHIEHALLION

Route 46b Schiehallion from near Kinloch Rannoch: North-west Ridge

G2 ** NN 690575, 5ml/8km, 880m/2900ft M225

The north-west ridge is much steeper than the east ridge and carries only an occasional path of sorts. However, a grassy Land Rover track climbs to the 600m/2000ft contour and there is much less quartzite to contend with above there.

The route as a whole takes more effort than the east ridge route and will never rival it in popularity, especially since the building of the new path, but there is not as much to choose between the two approaches as at first appears.

The track is one of two that leave the road on the south side of Dunalastair Water at East Tempar farm, 4½ml/7km along Schiehallion Road from Braes of Foss car park and 2ml/3km from Kinloch Rannoch. Park on the grassy roadside verge c.150m to the east. Take the right-hand track beside the Tempar Burn; the left-hand track goes to the farmhouse only.

The track climbs open hillside left of the stream. It aims directly for the north-west ridge then continues beyond its foot to end at a height of

SCHIEHALLION

NW Ridge

Loch Rannoch

600m/2000ft on heather slopes above the bealach to Schiehallion's west.

To avoid the heather, leave the track somewhere between the 500m and 550m contour to seek out grassy oases that give easier going. There is no one best way, but at the time of writing a small trackside cairn, if you can find it, is as good a point as any to start the ascent.

Trend back left towards the ridge then stay right of its broad crest to avoid steep heather and quartzite

rubble. Higher up, a path comes and goes and is occasionally useful, but it is easier to find on descent than ascent. Above 900m/2950ft, the average angle lessens as the ridge becomes more rubbly and rises in a series of steps.

Unlike on the east ridge, most of the quartzite is avoidable until the final boulder pile. You'll make liberal use of hands here but only for balance, so we refuse to grade the route any higher than G2.

SCHIEHALLION

NW Ridge

Needlepoint: Without an obvious path to follow, you are unlikely to find the optimal route up the north-west ridge in cloud, and keeping to the correct line on descent will require even more precise navigation. Best left for a fine day.

Chilly Willy: Apart from occasional steep snow, the north-west ridge should give no especial winter problems providing you avoid the broken crags on the left-hand side of the crest. However, the normal route up the less steep east ridge will provide a more enjoyable winter experience.

F-Stop: Schiehallion's isolation makes its summit a commanding viewpoint in all directions, although many Munros are so far away that you may struggle to identify them individually. To the west especially, the mountainside drops away dramatically

to reveal an uninterrupted view along Loch Rannoch, pointing and beckoning to the distant mountains of the Central Highlands. Those mountains eagerly await your foot-fall, armed of course with the next volume of *The Ultimate Guide to the Munros*.

INDEX

Luath Press Limited
committed to publishing well written books worth reading

LUATH PRESS takes its name from Robert Burns, whose little collie Luath (*Ga* swift or nimble) tripped up Jean Armour at a wedding and gave him the chance speak to the woman who was to be his wife and the abiding love of his life. Burns called one of 'The Twa Dogs' Luath after Cuchullin's hunting dog in Ossian's *Fingal*. Luath Press was established in 1981 in the heart of Burns country, and now resides a few steps up the road from Burns' first lodgings on Edinburgh's Royal Mile.

Luath offers you distinctive writing with a hint of unexpected pleasures.

Most bookshops in the UK, the US, Canada, Australia, New Zealand and parts of Europe either carry our books in stock or can order them for you. To order direct from us, please send a £sterling cheque, postal order, international money order or your credit card details (number, address of cardholder and expiry date) to us at the address below. Please add post and packing as follows: UK – £1.00 per delivery address; overseas surface mail – £2.50 per delivery address; overseas airmail – £3.50 for the first book to each delivery address, plus £1.00 for each additional book by airmail to the same address. If your order is a gift, we will happ enclose your card or message at no extra charge.

Luath Press Limited
543/2 Castlehill
The Royal Mile
Edinburgh EH1 2ND
Scotland
Telephone: 0131 225 4326 (24 hours)
Fax: 0131 225 4324
email: sales@luath.co.uk
Website: www.luath.co.uk